# A PENNSYLVANIA IDEA:

# TAX REVISION BY COMMISSION IN PENNSYLVANIA
## 1889-1949

Jared C. Lobdell

# TABLE OF CONTENTS

# PREFACE

In seven chapters, following this preface, this study examines an almost unknown and certainly unregarded area in the history of the United States – the attempts to achieve tax equity (in the Commonwealth of Pennsylvania) through the creation of small self-expert tax revision commissions. In a sense, I suppose it could be said that this is an exercise in economic history, and certainly it has been designed as an exercise in the application of history and social science techniques to a particular policy problem. On the whole, however, it might be most accurately described as an exercise in the history and political science of applied economic analysis.

The first chapter is the Introduction, setting out the problem of state tax revision commissions, some views on the problems of state taxes, and the approaches to be taken here. (Some of the approaches not taken are noted a little later on in this Preface.) The second chapter discusses the "policy problem" of commissions in the United States and particularly of state tax revision commissions – by which I mean, roughly, what are these commissions and how do they work in the policy arena? The next four chapters deal with individual commissions – Chapter III with the 1889 Pennsylvania commission, Chapter IV with the 1897 Wisconsin commission, Chapter V (in two parts) with the 1919 and 1923 Pennsylvania commissions, Chapter VI with the 1947 Pennsylvania commission. The final chapter is, of course, a conclusion.

When I was a small child, the late Richard Ely patted me on the head and predicted a great future for me. Dr. Ely has been dead more than sixty years now, and I suppose I am the youngest economist who can claim such personal contact. This point is important, though it

1

might not seem so at the outset. Richard Ely is one of the major figures in the early history of tax reform, he appears (of course) in the pages following, and I have been unable to write this study as other than a personal document, or at least a document of personal inquiry.

The techniques of analysis used – rather a mixed bag – will be made clear in due course. Let us look now at techniques not used, and then at some general background. This may seem an odd way to begin a study of tax revision commissions in the United States, or indeed of anything else, but it is important to make clear at the outset what roads are not followed in the study. In particular, it is important to make clear that there are some roads the author would like to have followed but could not – either because the data were not available (the general reason), or because the road turned out not to lead anywhere relevant to our quest. (This is, it will be noted, part of the pattern of personal inquiry.)

Two principal questions to which answers would have been welcome, and two principal modes of inquiry for answering these and other questions, all had to be abandoned until such time as data now unavailable become available (if ever), or until such time as modelers of political-economic behavior come up with models more applicable in this context. (I have, of course, used some models, and I hope used them well, but there was one in particular I wanted to use but found no use for.)

Since the tax commissions considered here were small groups of men, sitting (at least putatively) around tables, trying (at least putatively) to come up with some kind of agreed-upon report, it might well seem that techniques of cognitive mapping and small-group behavior analysis would be relevant. Since the commissions were involved in what has been called the process of state tax innovation, it might well seem that a

2

political-science model of state tax innovation would be relevant. Of these possibly relevant techniques, only small-group behavior analysis (in the form used for voting-behavior analysis) could reasonably be employed. We will come to the explanation for this shortly.

The questions we had wanted to answer, but upon which we have been forced to abandon our search, are these: first, was there some kind of measurable chance for agreement on policy in those cases where there was neither substantive nor substantial agreement? – and second, could the commission process reasonably have been expected to produce effective tax revision, without the "Progressive" *Zeitgeist*? Obviously there are other relevant questions: those that came to my mind and the minds of my advisors are, I believe, answered in the study that follows. But these two had to be abandoned, though there are some indications what the answers might be, and these indications are noted in the text of the study.

The technique for determining the answer to the first question was to have been cognitive mapping. A cognitive map is a way of representing a person's belief system by points (concept variables) and arrows (causal assertions about the effect of concept variables on other concept variables). That is, a cognitive map is a particular kind of model of a belief system (or set of belief systems), generally derived in practice from assertions about belief systems. The concept variables may be continuous (as variables of amount), or ordinal (more or less of something), or dichotomous or binary (presence or absence of something). In Robert Axelrod's pioneering study (Axelrod 1976, pp. 59-66), the initial example of a concept variable is "the amount of security in the Persian Gulf" and ours was to have been "the amount of tax equalization" or of tax equity or of tax reform – though we should

3

note that one possible concept variable in a cognitive map is, quite simply, utility.

The causal assertion (the second basic assertion in a cognitive map) is the relationship of the concept variables one to another. It may be positive (augmenting) or negative (inhibiting). The arrows expressing causality may thus be accompanied by plus-signs or minus-signs, for positive or negative effects. In short, a cognitive map is made up of signed directed digraphs (signed digraphs, for short) connecting the concept points. Since the effect variable of one causal belief, or of more than one, may be the cause variable in another belief, or in more than one, the mapping is generally continuous and complex. This would have important implications in our inquiry, if we could have assembled the basic data.

The *point* of a cognitive map is to determine (1) what decision should be made ("Decision-Making Problem"), or (2) what will happen in response to changes in variables ("Forecasting Problem"), or (3) what has led to changes in the variables ("Explanation Problem"), or (4) what would be the consequence of changing the sign of a given causal assertion ("Strategic Problem"). When we mapped the belief systems of Commission members, we would be searching for reasons that variables did not change (what we might call negative explanations) or why no strategic changes took place. Or we might be searching for flaws in the decision-making process, or looking to see if Commission members had a standard cognitive map.

What do we mean by flaws, and why am I going into all of this when I have already designated cognitive mapping as a road not taken? Flaws might come through imbalances or cycles in the cognitive map: by imbalances are meant paths from A to B that have inconsistent indirect effects, plus-on-balance as against minus-on-balance, while

4

cycles are paths that have an arrow from their last point to their first point, thus assuring that causations flows both ways. It is obvious that detecting flaws or cycles in individual cognitive maps would enable us to explain agreements among members we would have expected to disagree, or disagreements among those we would have expected to agree.

This is but one aspect of the use to which the technique might have been put. It might also have been used to determining whether commissions might have "worked" – that is, whether they might have produced agreements on recommendations that would, if passed into law, have produced tax revisions leading to greater tax equity. Unfortunately, only in two or three cases were there sufficient data for the drawing of full cognitive maps, and those that could be drawn did not permit the kind of comparisons between interest-group leaders or among blue-ribbon Commission members that had been hoped for. Because there are no extant minutes of Commission meetings available, the cognitive maps had to be drawn from published statements, and even newspaper files and scrapbooks were insufficient for the task. We were constrained to assume no flaws and no relevant cycles. In this context, I would like to thank Professor George Frost Kennan for his continuing attempts to locate his father's files from the 1897 Wisconsin Commission.

Another part of "working" – the actual passage of recommendations into law – might, it was hoped, be covered from a different approach, the modeling of political innovation. Unfortunately, the model ready to hand (Hansen 1983), though interesting, had weaker explanatory value than had been hoped. Professor Hansen has suggested approaching the history of tax policy changes through a kind of "monopoly theory" of political party control (pp. 38ff). By this theory, the stronger the partisan control of a government, whether national, state, or local, the more likely (all other things being equal) that the government will increase taxes. Also, and more to our point, the stronger the partisan control, the more likely will be any shift in the burden or incidence of taxation (pp. 142ff). And equally to our point, government's lack of strong partisan control might reasonably lead to the appointment of an extra-governmental or quasi-extra-governmental agency such as an ad-hoc tax revision commission.

But we should note here Professor Hansen's rather rueful conclusions that "General propensity to innovate is not much help in explaining broad-based tax adoptions. . . . Examination of state dates of innovation tells us little about the internal politics of a state. . . . A continuous variable (competitiveness) cannot easily account for specific decisions. . . (p. 147). To be sure, from 1914 to 1976 (about half of which period overlaps half of ours), some 83 percent of sales taxes, 76 percent of income taxes, and 73 percent of corporate income taxes were introduced under unified state governments – that is, where the legislature and the governorship were in the hands of the same party. Moreover, in the latter part of that period, there was a statistically significant (albeit not very exciting) correlation between "competitiveness" (lack of one-party control) and slowness to adopt a state income tax (p. 155).

Though this is what we would expect to find (split control does not ordinarily lead to passage and enactment of significant legislation of any kind), in fact the dice are rather loaded against our using Professor Hansen's tentative model of tax revision behavior. The loading comes partly from the fact that the periods of concern are only partly overlapping and partly from the fact that her model looks more to necessary than to sufficient conditions for tax revision. But most of all it

6

comes from the fact that we are considering, as the centerpiece of our endeavors, a phenomenon that does not even appear in Professor Hansen's index, the phenomenon of the commission. She does, of course, note the turn-of-the-century fiscal reforms of Progressives and Mugwump Republicans – quite correctly – but her concern is not with, nor has she controlled for, the peculiarities of the "Progressive" political process (Hansen, pp. 61-102). And that process, we will discover, is central to our concerns in this study.

It would, to be sure, have been possible to devise a general theory of tax innovation that would take the "Progressive" commission process into account. But, perhaps paradoxically, there is (in my view) too much information available – too many raw data – for a single study to do that in a fully rigorous way. That is why this study examines a few instances of the process of tax revision by commission, to suggest a possible program for future study, and to draw tentative conclusions about the five commissions studied. This matter is discussed more fully in Chapter I, but it should be said here that the conclusions seem to me sufficiently strong to suggest they will hold in general for all tax revision commissions, and I would like to see someone follow this lead.

One other road that might have been followed was to take these tax revision commissions as representative of a process common to various efforts in the Progressive Era, or the Era of the Search for Order (Wiebe 1967). Some indications of their exemplary or emblematic nature are, in fact, given in the text. But although a review of current opinion on the nature of this era is relevant, and a brief review is given in the next few paragraphs, the fact remains that tax revision commissions in our period do not fully exemplify the Progressive mode of behavior. We might fairly say, however, that they assume it as background, and that is the reason for this brief review.

7

At the beginning of the period of our concern, Congress (and by extension a state legislature) was considered to provide a forum in which private groups served themselves as best they could. We should not be far wrong, if wrong at all, if we were to take this as the keynote, in combination with the desire for community self-determination and its particular outgrowth, enmity to the railroads. By the 1880s, the railroads "had alienated a remarkable range of Americans: the farmer saw them as the arrogant manipulator of his profit, the small-town entrepreneur as the destroyer of his dreams, the city businessman as the sinister ally of his competitors, the labor leader as the model of the callous distant employer, and the principled gentleman as the source of unscrupulous wealth and political corruption." And this was particularly tied to the agrarian variation of the embryonic Populism of the 1870s and 1880s that rejected the possibility of democracy in any setting beyond the local community. (Wiebe 167, pp. 32, 52-53[quotation], 61.) But Populism was not the creed of the gentlemanly reformers, and it was not destined to be the creed of the successful reformers. The vision of Frederick Jackson Turner, seeing the roots of democracy in the frontier, was not a Populist vision, nor was it fully a Progressive vision – a point of some importance. In a sense, it was in between the two (Weibe 65-66, 88, 97). There was a considerable space in between.

There was not, however, a considerable time: indeed, Populism died in the 1896 election, though it may have been reborn since. Wiebe called that election a remarkably abrupt and clean removal of old causes and old champions that left thousands adrift. But then, virtually at that moment (though with earlier adumbrations), there began the shift toward Progressivism and the rise of the middle-class expert, divided perhaps into two broad categories. The first included those with strong professional aspirations in such fields as medicine, law, economics, administration, social work, and architecture. The second comprised specialists in business, labor, and agriculture. (The possibilities for overlap can be detected here.) The universities, of course, played a crucial role. And almost every group within the new class experienced its formative growth toward self-consciousness in roughly the ten years from 1895 to 1905. (Wiebe 1967, pp. 105-127).

In this shift toward *expertise*, the ideas that filtered through and eventually took the fort were bureaucratic ones and the bureaucratic orientation shifted the focus "from essences to actions" and especially actions in stages. In Wiebe's view, the bureaucratic orientation (arriving around 1900 and gaining momentum after 1910) did not reach its peak of success until the nineteen twenties. And when it did, though the same words were used in political discourse that had been used before, the "good men were no longer moral exemplars but leaders of broad power; minimum waste implied a smoothly functioning bureaucracy, not a handful of honest men on low salaries . . . and the harmonious society, now usually composed of interacting groups instead of isolated individuals, depended on the government's presence, not its absence." Particularly, as all citizens became rational, they would naturally arrive at the same general answers. Experts would, of course, always know more in their particular fields, but national rationality would ensure consensus on major issues. (Wiebe 1967, pp. 148, 149, 161[quotation], 162.) Of course, it did no such thing, but that discovery was still in the future.

If we look at the broad-scale political life of the American nation, Progressivism probably reached flood-tide around 1912, with the "Bull-Moose" Presidential candidacy of Theodore Roosevelt. But it may be argued that the bureaucracy of the Progressives, the outer core of rules and inner core of administrative management, was far more central to

9

the 1920s than concentration on Harding and Normalcy would have us believe. It failed with Hoover between 1929 and 1933, but clearly it did not fail entirely.

I have summarized and quoted Professor Wiebe not to preach his gospel but to remind my readers of current views on the Era of the Search for Order – not, as I have said, because the tax revision commissions we will be considering exemplify the characteristics Wiebe defined, but so that those characteristics may be kept in mind as a kind of counterpoint for what follows. One other "contrapuntal" idea should also be noted here, though in this case there may be more harmony than counterpoint.

In much of the study of these commissions, and particularly (for obvious reasons) in Chapter IV, on the Wisconsin Commission of 1897-98, mention will be made of the Wisconsin Idea. I am struck by the importance of the middle ground between Populism and Progressivism in the Era of the Search for Order, and it may be worthwhile to suggest the possibility that the Wisconsin Idea might fit in this middle ground. Let me begin by quoting from a recent biography of the man who wrote the book entitled *The Wisconsin Idea*, Charles McCarthy. The year is 1911, the year of the Wisconsin income tax.

"It was one of those rare, almost magical times, when everything worked in unison -- the people, their representatives, the entire legislative machine, including the Legislative Reference library." (McCarthy was Librarian of the Legislative Reference Library.) "McCarthy was euphoric after this session, convinced that the whole world could be 'saved' and reformed through the 'right sort' of information." (Casey 1981, p. 76.) And that is the common view of the Wisconsin Idea – which is why this study is not meant to exemplify the Wisconsin Idea, as commonly understood, in action. If, however, we

10

heed the words of John R. Commons, economist and historian, we may well conclude that the Wisconsin Idea, properly understood, defined a situation in which leading and expert representatives of conflicting interests must be involved in drafting legislation or participating in commissions (Thelen 1978, p. 109). It may turn out that having representativeness and *expertise* co-inhering in the same persons is no less magical than the almost magical times of 1911. That indeed is part of our story here, in the chapters that follow.

With this for background, and our unsuccessful attempts at models for our use out of the way, we may begin our comparative study of tax revision by small self-expert commissions in the Commonwealth of Pennsylvania (with one Wisconsin Commission for comparison's sake) from 1889 to 1949. The study is revised from my 1986 Ph. D. dissertation at Carnegie Mellon University, and I thank my Committee, Peter Stearns, Dan Resnick, Joel Tarr, Mark Kamlet, and Pat Larkey, for their help and advice, as well as Chandler Stolp and Pat Crecine, and as the *eminence grise* of my endeavor, the late Herbert Simon. Remaining errors and infelicities are mine: certainly my Committee members tried to argue me out of some of the passages that I have left in.

I wish also to record my gratitude, not only for the pat on the head from Professor Ely, but for the opportunity to know, and to some extent sit at the feet of, such Wisconsin Institutionalists as Elizabeth Brandeis Rauschenbush and Professor Harold Groves. I regret I was not on the University of Wisconsin campus earlier, but at least I was early enough to know them.

Jared C. Lobdell

Elizabethtown, Pennsylvania
December 2006

# CHAPTER I: INTRODUCTION

More than seventy state tax revision commissions were created, met, and made their recommendations between the Civil War and the onset of the Great Depression. The results were at best mixed: indeed, the commissions were so generally unsuccessful in achieving their putative goals – usually expressed as some form of "tax equalization" – that one might wonder if the true goals lay in some other direction altogether.

One reason the exact number of these commissions is difficult to determine is that there are problems in defining what constitutes a commission. For our present purposes, a commission is a body provided for by a legislative enabling act, appointed wholly or in part by the governor of the state, and having at least some "public" members who are not members of the legislature. The Library of Congress contains reports from sixty-two such commissions appointed from the end of the Civil War to 1931. But only sixteen of these, including the successful Wisconsin Commission of 1897 and the Texas Commission of 1899, were appointed before 1901, while that same Wisconsin Commission noted that "upwards of thirty tax commissions" had been appointed between the solitary antebellum Connecticut commission of 1843 and the appointment of the Wisconsin Commission itself (Kennan 1899, p. 169). On the other hand, the author of the Wisconsin report (Kossuth Kent Kennan) considers the meetings of the Tax Conference of Pennsylvania Interests in 1892 and 1895 as separate Commission meetings, even though the Conference was (1) a continuing body and (2)

13

not a public body at all (Tax Conference 1892, p. 1). The estimate of more than seventy is probably the best available at this time.

Of this number, perhaps twenty-five or more (nineteen with reports in the Library of Congress) came before 1905, there are in the Library twenty-seven between that year and the end of 1920, and sixteen in the Library from the next ten years. These are all special commissions, appointed for a term certain, with no provisions for continuation beyond that term: they are thus to be distinguished from bodies of tax commissioners appointed as regular supervisors of state tax assessment or collection in the various states. We are concerned here with one-time tax revision commissions whose purpose is generally to recommend laws for improving tax equity.

We are also concerned only with those commissions of a size sufficiently small to suggest that the members of the Commission did their own work – that is, that they were self-expert in matters of taxation, at least to some degree, and that they in fact were appointed to sift and winnow the data among themselves, so as to recommend the best course of action for the state. The larger commissions that have come into being since the Depression have generally been made up of interest-group representatives meeting to sift and winnow the reports and recommendations of staff economists, a perfectly defensible proposition but more limited. Only twenty-eight post-Depression reports are found in the Library of Congress – all of them post-World War II. Of these, eight are from Pennsylvania.

Given that only three of the seventy pre-Depression commissions were from Pennsylvania, this seems worthy of note. It might, of course, be argued that Pennsylvania's pre-Depression commissions were so successful that the use of commissions to recommend tax revision survived in that state where it declined in others – but Pennsylvania's tax

14

commissions in the pre-Depression years were in fact not significantly more successful than those of any other state, which is to say they were not very successful at all.

It might be argued that Pennsylvania governors in the years after World War II appointed commissions to give legitimacy to what they wanted to do anyway, or to avoid the consequences of being unable to do anything in a state where power was pretty much evenly divided between Republicans and Democrats (see Bell 1966, pp. 4-6). This, if true, would suggest that the success of these commissions would be quite hard to measure, and that the measurement might have nothing whatever to do with tax revision per se.

I suppose it might also be argued that Pennsylvania traditions make the appointment of tax revision commissions a "natural" step to take. I have no clear idea how one would go about attempting to demonstrate this point. In any case, whatever the reason, it is clear that, if the post-World War II experience in Pennsylvania was atypical, the pre-Depression experience was not. Pennsylvania had three tax revision commissions between the adoption of the State Constitution of 1873 (which prohibits a graduated income tax) and the onset of the Depression – in 1889 (reporting in 1890), in 1919 (reporting in 1921), and in 1923 (reporting in 1925 and 1927). While this is marginally more than the average state, the 1919 Commission had a much more limited mandate than most, and the difference may be insignificant. Pennsylvania also had a commission appointed in 1947, with six members and a chairman, which will also be discussed here, even though some institutional problems suggest it may not be as revealing as we would like.

So Pennsylvania, which attracts attention for the number of its commissions after World War II, is in fact representative of states in general between the Civil War and the Great Depression. It would of course be disingenuous if I were to claim I chose the Commonwealth of Pennsylvania at random for the study that follows: I chose it in fact because the 1979 Pennsylvania Tax Revision Commission (Cyert Commission) paid me to choose it. But my findings reported in this study were largely irrelevant to their task, and are largely relevant to a different task – finding why state tax revision commissions of the older sort did not work (depending, of course, on how we define "work").

By "work" I mean here one of three things. A commission can be charged to address a particular problem and can propose laws that, to the best understanding then current, will solve the particular problem. That is one kind of working, or, if one prefers the term, of success. Second, a commission's proposals can in fact be passed into law. Third, if passed into law, the proposals can in fact produce the desired result. The first and second definitions of success or "working" are in some degree independent of each other, though poor proposals enacted are dubious success, and though one would like to believe that "good" recommendations will be passed into law. The third measure of success has the other two as necessary but not sufficient conditions: even if the laws recommended should improve the situation, and even if they are in fact passed, it does not therefore follow that the situation will be improved. Understanding may be faulty, or the whole process may be overtaken by unanticipated events.

Obviously, an exhaustive study of seventy commissions, requiring knowledge of the politics and public opinion of some thirty-five states, would produce a work of stultifying length, and probably stultifying dullness. On the other hand, restricting the study entirely to the Commonwealth of Pennsylvania, where only one commission was even dubiously successful in the first two senses, would leave unanswered the

16

question, What (if anything) makes a successful tax revision commission?

I have therefore set the Pennsylvania experience (and particularly the experience of the 1889 Commission) against that of the 1897 Wisconsin Commission, generally considered to have been exceptionally successful – though, as it turns out, so much so as to be the exception that proves the rule (Kennan 1898, p. 8, and see Chapter IV below). With the comparison established, I have turned to the 1919 and 1923 Pennsylvania commissions, one "successful" and one less so, before turning, for the sake of greater completeness, to the last small self-expert Pennsylvania commission, set up in 1947. Before any of this can be done, however, it is necessary that we establish both our background and our model.

In this introductory chapter, therefore, we will reconstruct beliefs about taxation that were current at the times our commissions were meeting – in particular, ideas about state income taxation, which went through some quite astonishing metamorphoses in the cases of Richard Ely and E. R. A. Seligman, probably the two leading tax theoreticians of the time (see Ely 1888, Ely 1924, Seligman 1892, Seligman 1911). We will also try to summarize the theoretical literature, or as much of it as seems relevant, on the way commissions work (particularly Tutchings 1979). And we will try to get an idea of the general financial problems of the states between the Civil War and the Great Depression (Yearley 1970).

The most notable document in the first part of our period is Professor Richard Ely's Minority Report to the 1888 Maryland Tax Commission (Ely 1888). This dissent – which is longer than the rest of the Report put together – was substantially the same as his textbook published shortly thereafter (Ely 1888b). In it, he divides taxes which

17

are properly imposed statewide, for the purposes of the state as a whole, from taxes properly imposed locally for local purposes – by the first meaning principally income tax, by the second, principally a land tax. This is, as we shall see, quite similar to the argument presented by John Armstrong Wright to the Pennsylvania Revenue Commission (Wright 1889, p. 105) – "The question then is as already stated. How to devise a system of taxation which will treat all persons justly and equably, and harmonize conflicting interests? It must be apparent to everyone that the system which will most nearly secure these results is one based on income." But he notes, withal, that "the authorities of the counties, cities, boroughs, and townships shall be empowered to levy such taxes as may be required for their local necessities, on the real estate and on the horses, wagons, carriages, etc., within their limits" (Wright 1889, p. 107) – thus bringing himself roughly to Ely's point of view in 1888.

But by the time Ely was in Wisconsin in 1897, he was no longer among those who believed that the system which would "treat all persons justly and equably" was indeed "one based on income" (Ely 1896). At the same time, E. R. A. Seligman, moderately enthusiastic about state income taxation in the early 1890s, was veering around to strong disbelief (Seligman 1911) – which position he immediately abandoned when Wisconsin adopted its state income tax (Brownlee 1971, p. 125).

John A. Wright had died shortly after submitting his own Minority Report to the Pennsylvania Revenue Commission (Wright 1890), and in any case, his opinions were not, so far as I know, spread beyond Pennsylvania, though they have been noted by Yearley (Yearley 1970, p. 229). Kossuth Kent Kennan, though his own book on income taxation (Kennan 1910) has much to recommend it (it is, for example, far better on state income taxation than Seligman's), was generally far more interested in rationalizing tax administration in Wisconsin than in seeking any fundamental change in the nature of taxes levied (Kennan 1910, pp. 210-235, and passim). In short, after a brief boom in the 1880s, interest in state income taxes virtually died out until the decade of the First World War, and did not reach its earlier height until the 1920s (Brownlee 1971, pp. 41-44, 122-23, Yearley 1970, pp. 235-50, 321-23).

It was not that the distinction between state and local (or county) expenditures suddenly ceased to operate, or that everyone went madly dashing off in the direction of Henry George's Single (Land) Tax, or that the people in general or tax experts in particular ceased to be interested in tax equalization. Indeed, so far as the last of these is concerned, Governor Emanuel Philipp of Wisconsin was later to claim that, at the turn of the century, tax equalization was the only species of tax reform anyone was interested in (Philipp 1973, pp. 97ff). No, what happened was that the U. S. Congress passed, the President signed, and (in 1895) the Supreme Court overturned a federal income tax – that, at least, is what led Seligman to drop his work on income taxation, and it may have been what led Ely to change his mind (Seligman 1911, pp. 15-18, 421-25, 493-530, Ely 1899-1901). It is not, of course, entirely clear why it should.

Seligman, in his introductory chapter to his book on the income tax (Seligman 1911), after observing that the Court's decision had led him to drop the matter for a decade and a half, goes on to describe the various attempts societies have made to determine ability (his word is "faculty") to pay – from a poll tax, to property as a test of faculty, to expenditure and product, and finally to income, each determined by the appropriate stage in economic and political development, the whole process having a kind of Darwinism or even Marxist inevitability to it (pp. 3-36). But if inevitable, why be put off by a narrow (5-4) Supreme Court decision, with strong dissents by the minority?

Ely, I believe, became fascinated with the possibility that the cumbersome and decentralized nature of property tax administration could be overcome – indeed, he was fascinated by the land tax and land economics generally and founded the still-extant journal *Land Economics*. Land economics was (were?) indeed part and parcel of the Institutionalist approach of the University of Wisconsin economics in the first half of this century. But whereas Ely (apparently) switched his favor from income taxes to wealth taxes because he believed the latter could be properly administered, Seligman switched his because he thought the former could not be. In 1911, he observed, speaking of the Court's decision, that "whatever be our opinions as to the correctness of the decision, it must be declared, on the whole, not entirely unfortunate that the law was overturned. So glaring were its shortcomings of principle, and so defective were some of its administrative provisions, that it is safe to say it would have been to a very large extent unworkable, and would in all probability have produced more lawsuits than revenue" (Seligman 1911, pp. 529-30).

In any case, despite claims to the contrary by some early advocates of state income taxes, Seligman had never been particularly enamored of income taxation on the state level (Seligman 1911, pp. 421-25). Probably we could say that enthusiasm for state income taxes, and the arguments for state income taxes, more or less parallelled the progress of federal income taxation. This is not to say that the validity of the economic arguments depends in any degree on public enthusiasm for the institution -- though, admittedly, public enthusiasm for the institution equally does not depend on the validity of the economic arguments. The people of Connecticut, for example, in 1992, more or less accepted

Governor Lowell Weicker's arguments for the state income tax, but it cannot be said that they were enthusiasts, and this has been fairly typical.

However, the arguments are not likely to be made unless those who make them think someone is listening. Apparently, no state tax revision commissions before the 1888 Maryland and 1889 Pennsylvania commissions seriously considered state income taxation (Yearley 1970, p. 229). This does not mean, pace Professor Seligman, that there were neither significant state income taxes nor arguments for them before the twentieth century: in fact, at this date, it looks a bit as though Seligman's 1911 discussion of state income taxes was not only overly pessimistic from our point of view but overly pessimistic at the time (Brownlee 1971, pp. 47-64, 124-34). "More and more" (Seligman wrote) "it has been realized by state officials and commissions that any hope of a satisfactory state income tax is illusory. As far back as 1889 the Special Tax Commission of Maine reported as follows: 'Many theorists advocate an income tax as the fairest form of taxation. In theory there is much to sustain it. In practice it is almost universally a failure'" (Seligman 1911, p. 419). That is not an entirely fair summary, as Kossuth Kennan's own work makes clear.

What Kennan does admit is that the evidence of those states that made a prolonged effort at state income taxation – including Pennsylvania before the 1873 Constitution – makes clear the degree to which these taxes generally failed owing "to the failure of administration, which, in turn, may be attributed to four causes – the method of self-assessment, the indifference of state officials, the persistent effort of the taxpayers to evade the tax, and the nature of the income. . . . failure will continue to accompany the tax until our industrial system takes on such form as to make possible the use of some method other than self-assessment" (Kennan 1910, p. 236, quoting Delos Kinsman).

In essence, though both the United States as a whole and most of the several Confederate states had an income tax during the Civil War, and though at least ten states had income taxes for more than a quarter of the nineteenth century, those who argued for state income taxes were neither numerous nor persuasive (Yearley 1970, pp. 171-91, 225-35). Indeed, Ely's and Wright's reports were the only significant documents arguing for such a tax. The most frequent tax reform proposed by late-nineteenth- and early-twentieth-century commissions was separation of state and local taxing, with local taxes to be based generally on property, and state taxes (in the current vernacular) on "whatever" (Yearley 1970, pp. 194ff).

Thus, for example, the California Commission on Revenue and Taxation proposed, in 1909, an amendment to the State Constitution "to separate the sources of revenue for state purposes from the source of revenue for county and municipal purposes" (California 1910, p. 13). The Texas Tax Commission of 1899 similarly recommended amending Article VIII of that state's constitution to "allow a separation of the levy and collection of the State revenues from the county taxes" (Texas 1899, p. 4). Nor is this desire restricted to these two states: to take the most obvious example, it is part of John A. Wright's "Memorandum" to the 1889 Pennsylvania Commission, though there it is linked with his general argument that a justly enforced tax on income from all sources is the fairest tax of all (Wright 1889, pp. 105-17, esp. 114-17).

We will see the point, and the problem, recurring as we consider our tax revision commissions in the chapters that follow. And we will see that the "whatever" – the sources for state tax revenues from other than income taxes – while a matter of continuing concern for the

22

legislature, tended to be slighted in the literature, perhaps in line with what is suggested by an observation of the late Professor Harold Groves: "Perhaps taxation is a dull subject; perhaps the property tax is the dullest branch of the tax system; and very likely the intangibles property tax is the dullest member of a dull family" (Groves 1967, p. 117). But it was an important one in the first part of our period (pp. 121-22).

More will become evident on the beliefs current at the times our commissions were operating when we look at the reports of the commissions themselves. But before looking at those reports, we need to look at the ways policy commissions work and the milieu in which these were working. Commissions are a somewhat out-of-the-way part of our democratic system, and not a great deal of theoretical work has been done on them, but a 1979 study, though dealing specifically with presidential rather than gubernatorial commissions, is relevant to our purposes here. This study (Tutchings 1979) is called *Rhetoric and Reality: Presidential Commissions and the Making of Public Policy*. In it, he presents a model for an idealized policy commission process and then suggests that eventual outcomes (our "successes" or "failures") are "linked to qualitative differences in the composition of the commissions, in the research conducted, and in the policy recommendations made" (Tutchings 1979, p. 16).

He defines the nature of the commissions in his study by the demands for the commissions (subdivided into means of creation, issue area involved, and temporal variations in demand), information costs (consultants, research, and actual information costs), and decision costs (for which his proxy variable is degrees of dissent). These constitute organizational dynamics (Tutchings 1979, pp. 17-33). In addition, he defines the nature of the commissions by (1) the degree to which they include members of policy elites, (2) by the nature of the policy outputs or recommendations – whether distributive policy, redistributive policy, self-regulative policy, or regulative policy – and (3) by policy results (Tutchings 1979 pp. 37-47, 51-52, 76). Our study is substantially simplified by the fact that we are holding a number of these variables constant.

We have a single issue area and a set of commissions for which "temporal variations in demand" (variations in length of commission life) were only from more-than-two to less-than-four years. We have held information costs as constant as possible, given our lack of information, by considering only those small commissions whose members were their own experts. Given the degree to which size of commission is correlated with amount of dissent (the Tutchings proxy for decision costs), this will also have the effect of making our determination of decision costs rather better than his, though this was not its purpose (Tutchings 1979, p. 33). We also have a single policy output or recommendation, which is tax equity and thus distributive or (in the absence of equity) redistributive (Tutchings 1979, p. 51). Our typology of results has already been given: it will be compared with the typology suggested by Tutchings as we consider the work of the individual commissions. The variables of particular concern to us are thus the means by which the commissions were established, the degree of dissent, the inclusion of members of policy elites, and the policy results. In looking at results, we will be considering two of the three kinds of outcomes suggested by Tutchings (leaving out "Administrative Action") and adding a third ("Increased Equity").

Because of our relatively narrow scope, we are not looking at outcomes falling within the categories "symbolic" or "knowledge/plan" (that is, further study, by this commission or another), or "augment" (have an agency do what it's been doing, only moreso). We are looking only at regulative (legislative) outcomes for distributive or redistributive purposes (typology from Tutchings 1979, pp. 59-67). As we go through our five specimen commissions, we will find that we may disagree with the claim, advanced by Professor Tutchings, that the "articulation of a demand, the information costs allocated, and the permissible range of decisions made are highly predictive of the likely results" (p. 120). If that comes to be, the cause may lie in the fact that our commissions precisely mirror the larger political arena for the question at hand. Professor Tutchings suggests that "the frequency and regularity of the use of the commission method demonstrates innate incapabilities on the part of the routinely organized branches [of government]" (p. 121). But if our tax revision commissions are routinely unsuccessful, that may demonstrate innate incapabilities of the commission system.

All of that will be dealt with in the Conclusion, and a fuller discussion of the commission model, for those desiring it, will be given in Chapter II. Before we come to that, we should look at the milieu in which our commissions were operating – not so much the Progressive spirit of the times (discussed in the Preface) as the financial conditions of the state governments in the years when our first commissions were conceived, and the ways in which those state governments raised their funds. In the words of the era's premier financial historian, in "1860 the fiscal practices of American governments and their extra-legal counterparts which had grown up around the financing of political parties were still simple, democratic, and congenial to the peoples of an agricultural society; in 1880 these practices were in decay and under fierce attack; before 1925 they had been brought into closer consonance with the requirements of modern government and the realities of urban industrial life" (Yearley 1970, p. xi).

25

In large part, the impetus for tax reform in the United States did not differ from the impetus for tax reform elsewhere.  But only in the United States did the impetus act on a dual fiscal system.  On the one hand, there was (in 1870) "the official machinery inherited from antebellum days" which "centered its operations around some form of general property tax" and assumed (as the author says, "specifically, and from critical perspectives naively") that taxation was to be democratic.  Therefore, it was accordingly assumed that "all taxable property should bear public burdens equally; that equal taxation was feasible because all property could safely be treated as if it were tangible or corporeal – that is, that it could be discovered readily, valued easily, and taxed fairly" (Yearley 1970, p. 12).  But on the other hand, as one observer noted in 1887, "Political power has a great affinity for public revenues, and seeks alliance with that organism which can most readily furnish it" (Tucker 1887, p. 628).

The political parties thus counted on – in effect – dining at the public trough, or (in the historian's words) "financing themselves primarily by tapping public power and the fiscal resources of government" (Yearley 1970, p. xiii).  As a result, there was argument between or among different elites as to whether funds were needed, the reasons they were needed (if they were), and the sources from which they should come.  No one wants to gore his own ox, and much of the history of tax revision in the latter part of the last century and the beginning of this can be read as conflict among rural elites, urban elites, and the urban machine elites.

The atrophy of traditional public mechanisms for taxing, spending, and borrowing proceeded apace after the Civil War, in town and country both, but much more in town.  Pressures of growing city populations, with their need for sanitation, transportation, education, and public

26

health and safety, put heavier and heavier burdens on a tax base where properties "changed form with dismaying frequency" and seemed to flourish (as the Grange charged of the railroads) just, and illegitimately, beyond the range of the tax-gatherer (Yearley 1970, p. 3). "'Responsible' citizens . . . were presented with the broad picture of a dramatic and sustained upward trend in the burdens of taxation . . . Moreover, on the basis of their experiences it was a picture they accepted" (p. 9). They were thus open to "experts" who called for reform.

It is true they were most open to the experts who called for reforms that protected certain parts of the status quo, but the work of such pioneers as David A. Wells (Wells 1871), Ely, Seligman, Henry Carter Adams, received more than a merely respectful hearing (Yearley 1970, pp. 167-191). At the beginning and indeed throughout much of the period, the chief questions within the argument for equity were whether farmers were paying too much (or, occasionally, too little) in taxes, what should be the place of corporations (and particularly, in the earlier part of the period, of railroads) in the tax system, and (as we have already noted) income taxes as against the old-line taxes on property (Yearley 1970, pp. 77-95 and 299-303). Since income taxes are now known to be capable of yielding much greater revenue than property taxes, we might expect to see city residents (given the cities' need for money) lined up behind the income tax: whether that is the case for our specimen commissions will become more evident as we go on.

There was, however, another and quite important argument, not entirely divorced from the matter of equity and not fitting easily within it, yet highly important throughout the period of our concern: who should collect the taxes? We have already noted the question about the separation of state and local taxes, which is a part of this, but the dispute

27

went much further and touched the very possibility of reform. Because the segregation of revenues is not a lively present issue, even to the degree that agricultural taxation is (and certainly far less than the income tax), we may be well advised to discuss it here.

This was, in fact, generally considered the main route along which all progress in tax reform would have to begin (Yearley pp. 193-196). David Wells was moving along that route when – for the sake of "efficiency, uniformity, and equality of assessments" – he argued that railroads in particular and corporations in general should be taxed by the State of New York rather than by its local governments, but that was only a harbinger of things to come. The abandonment of the general property tax, a goal agreed upon by virtually every tax reformer by the end of the nineteenth century, was (as Clifton Yearley notes) "implied by the application of the principles of segregated revenues locally" (p. 194). More, the abandonment of the general property tax in turn implied segregation. And segregation became almost a cure-all for the ills of the state tax systems: the California Tax Commission of 1906, for example, argued that "complete separation will abolish at once the expense, friction, and annoyance of the vain attempt to equalize between the different counties. Partial separation will lessen this evil" (quoted in Yearley 1970, p. 196).

This segregation of revenues would lead to centralization of state revenue systems (since only local taxes would be collected locally): that was the key, all arguments about Federalism not withstanding. The advocates of revenue segregation were not supporters of local governments against the state governments but quite the reverse. (There were some exceptions, but they were minor.) In addition, they were largely advocates of state taxation of corporations: Pennsylvania, as we will see, had been largely supported by corporate wealth taxes in the

28

1880s, but Pennsylvania was virtually alone in this, and the increasing use of taxes on corporations was part of the history of state tax revision in our period (Yearley 1970, p. 197).

After the over-all transformation of fiscal policy between the Civil War and the 1920s, there ensued, as we know, high prosperity, low Depression, and World War II. By the time we get to the 1947 Commission the pressure of events has overtaken the (relatively) rational system of taxation in place by 1929 and brought in such anomalies as the "temporary" taxes of the 1930s, re-enacted every two years and still in effect. But for the most part they are only an appendix to our story.

Or perhaps "story" is not quite the right word. This is a study in applied history: that is, it is explicitly designed not so much to tell what happened as to use what happened as a guide for what is likely to happen in similar circumstances in the future. (This is a much oversimplified definition, but for the moment it will do.) It turns out that virtually all the currently accepted modes of applied history are present in the study – which is interesting, to me at least, since exemplifying the modes of applied history was not at all my purpose in writing a made-to-order work for the Pennsylvania Tax Revision Commission of 1979-82. These modes (once again we are oversimplifying) are analogy, trend assessment, the provision of perspective, historical induction, the use of history in evaluating national myths, and the use of history to prove (that is, test) the policy rule by looking for the exception -- history being capable of greater singularity than (other?) social sciences (Stearns 1981, pp. 533-37, Fiske 1981, pp. C1, C4). Let me briefly summarize the ways in which this study participates in all six of these historical modes.

First, though on the surface weakest, we are here considering five tax revision commissions (with some supporting evidence from others),

29

as part of an argument for what might be expected of future commissions, if any: this sounds like, and to some extent is, an argument from analogy. However, because we are looking at these commissions within a theoretical framework based in part on public choice and public policy, as well as on the behavioral theories of Herbert Simon, the opportunities are both less limited and more exact than might initially seem to be the case.

Second, we are assessing, in a kind of semantic study, trends in the meaning of certain key words (one might, using present slang, call them buzzwords) in the arguments over taxation. We might call this applied intellectual history, and it seems to me it would be a promising area of the field, though its results here are limited. Still, we do discover that the key words are from time to time not quite synchronized with what we have subsequently decided was the reality when they were uttered.

Third, we are seeking to apply the techniques of history to a particular policy problem. For example, let us consider – it is one of the mainstays of the present "scientific historical" approach – the question of periodization. By this is meant the way the historians deal with the "age" (*Zeit*) before dealing with the "spirit of the age" (*Zeitgeist*). Thus, if the age (or period) is the Progressive Era, we can reasonably use other historians' studies of that era to illuminate our research (Wiebe 1967 for example) – always assuming we can agree on what defines the period and when it began and ended, and always assuming we do not let our "periodization" trap us into arbitrary separations or arbitrary lumpings-together. In the present case, definition of the Progressive Era is complicated by the fact that Progressives like Gifford Pinchot (specifically in his second term) held power in Pennsylvania long after most of the nation (Wisconsin excepted) had returned to normalcy. Perhaps we should use Wiebe's term and call the period the Era of the

30

Search for Order, and in fact we will do just that. Four of our five commissions (the 1947 Pennsylvania Commission is the exception) may be considered to fall within this era.

Fourth, we have the mode of historical induction, meaning the development of theory from past events. There is a question here in connection with historical significance: can we have enough cases, in history, to draw statistically significant conclusions? And although the answer would seem to be no, it has been argued that a restricted comparative technique can be used to draw conclusions even when the evidence is (technically) statistically insignificant: this comparative technique has been applied, generally, in the field of diplomatic history (among the early examples being George 1979), but it can be used in others and is used here. From our few examples, in a controlled comparison, we are led into some general conclusions about the way things – or, in our case, tax revision commissions – work. Or fail to work.

Fifth, we are evaluating a myth: indeed (though this was not my intention when I came to the topic back in 1979), we are evaluating the foundation myth of our Era of the Search for Order – the Goo-Goo Myth, or Blue Ribbon Myth, the myth (call it what you will) that a group of the best citizens, working together, can set the world aright. In this case, I believe, the myth (in the Aristotelian or sociological sense) turns out to be a myth (in the popular sense of "what is not true"). A sociological or Aristotelian myth may well be factually true, but its symbolic truth is more important than its factual truth. Nevertheless, if a myth is demonstrably factually untrue, then its symbolic truth is compromised and may be ended (Checkland 1980 for the best discussion when I first wrote this). This study might have had some slight effect in

31

this direction if it had been published when written, but I am not sanguine at this later date..

Sixth and last, if we are to draw policy rules from our past experience – which is, in the final event, all we ever have from which to draw policy rules – we must determine whether the past is sufficiently like the present for the rules to be even putatively valid. This brings us to the matter of testing for exceptions to "prove" the rule, and though I have put this last among our modes of applied history, in fact it is part of the fabric of the whole approach. As we look at each commission, we will be looking to see whether time and chance have left our present world sufficiently like the world in which the commission functioned for the lessons of the past (whatever they are) to be applied to the present. After all, it was no less than Abraham Lincoln who was supposed to have issued, and acted in accordance with, the dictum that the dogmas of the quiet (quiet!) past were inadequate to deal with present storms. And whether he did or not, the point of view he is supposed to have expressed is not at all an uncommon one. Part of the test for singularity – perhaps the entire test – can only be made, I believe, by an historian.

Before I turn to a fuller development of the policy commission model, I think it would be well to sketch briefly the five commissions that are the subject of Chapters III through VI. These are the McCamant Commission of 1889 (Pennsylvania), the Kennan Commission of 1897-8 (Wisconsin), the Mercur Commission of 1919-21 (Pennsylvania), the Edmonds Commission of 1923-7 (Pennsylvania), and the Matthews Commission of 1947-9 (Pennsylvania). I have given each commission the name of its chairman, except the Kennan Commission, which was chaired by Burr Jones of Madison but which was the brainchild, first and last, of Kossuth Kent Kennan of Milwaukee, its secretary (Philipp 1973, pp. 100-05).

The Pennsylvania Revenue Commission of 1889 came into being under Governor James Beaver with the Pennsylvania Auditor-General, Thomas McCamant, as chairman. Its purpose was, at least in the public mind, to shift the burden of taxes on to the railroads and off the land, especially off the agricultural land (Pennsylvania 1889, pp. 1-36, 136, Tax Conference 1892, passim, Olmsted 1892-96). Its members were appointed to represent various interest groups, and some of them were appointed by the interest groups themselves (Pennsylvania 1889, Introduction). Thus State Master of the Grange Leonard Rhone was appointed by the Grange to represent the state agricultural interests, and Erie County Commissioners' Clerk Giles Price was appointed by the Association of County Commissioners to represent their interests.

Taking the question to be whether taxes should be shifted from the people to the corporations, the Commission answered with a *yes* so resounding (and so biased) that the Legislature chose to pass McCamant's substitute report. Indeed, the three most knowledgeable members of the Commission filed dissenting reports, and though it was McCamant's that was passed, those of John Armstrong Wright (1820-1891) and Professor Albert S. Bolles (1844-1935) are much more interesting. Wright's, in my view, deserves republication along with Richard Ely's dissenting report on the 1888 Maryland Commission.

The Wisconsin State Tax Commission of 1897 was appointed by the governor, but it was not quite a public commission: indeed, not until Kossuth Kent Kennan had said he would serve without pay, and the Legislature had eliminated financial support for the Commission, was the bill authorizing it passed and signed (Philipp 1973, pp. 102-03). The body was given a six-part mandate: (1) to make a careful compilation of state laws and court decisions relating to taxation; (2) to collect and classify data on taxation in the state; (3) to investigate complaints of

33

unfair taxation; (4) to collect information from other states, and particularly from the reports of other state tax commissions; (5) to recommend revisions of old laws or enactment of new; and (6) to "embody the results of their investigation in a report which shall be as plain, concise and comprehensible as possible" (Kennan 1898, pp. 5-6). In the event, it particularly emphasized the first, second, fourth, and sixth of these, and recommended by way of legislation only the establishment of a permanent state tax commission with a similar mandate (Kennan 1898, pp. 8-10, 181-83). It should be noted that this commission was the smallest of all tax revision commissions, having only three appointed members, Burr Jones, K. K. Kennan, and George Curtis (Kennan 1898, pp. 6-7).

The Pennsylvania Tax Law Revision Commission of 1919 (the date of the law authorizing it, though the members were not appointed until 1920) was appointed by Governor William Sproul, under the chairmanship of Rodney Mercur (1851-1933). It reported in 1921, was renewed and expanded the same year, but apparently never reported again (Pennsylvania Legislature 1919, p. 229, Pennsylvania Legislature 1921, p. 1077). Its purpose was to achieve fairer land taxation by altering the method of choosing assessors and the frequency of valuation. All the members but the chairman seem to have been appointed with some kind of scheme of geographical representation in mind – one piece of evidence for this being the presence of the Chairman of the Allegheny County Commissioners, Addison Gumbert (1868-1925), though Allegheny and Philadelphia counties were specifically excluded from the Commission's purview by the enabling act (Pennsylvania Legislature 1919, p. 229). A form of the law the Commission recommended was twice introduced into the Legislature, overwhelmingly defeated, finally (1931) passed in a modified version

34

applying only to five counties, and then, ten years after Chairman Mercur's death, extended in that modified form to the rest of the state (*Pennsylvania Handbook* 1933, p. 875, *Pennsylvania Legislature* 1943, p. 572). If this be success, we will make the most of it.

The Pennsylvania Tax Commission of 1923, on the other hand, was appointed by Governor Gifford Pinchot, with a singularly broad mandate, and under precisely the sort of chairman one would have expected Pinchot to appoint: he was Franklin S. Edmonds (1874-1945) of Philadelphia, one of several City Club members on the Commission and a tax expert in his own right. Like the McCamant Commission, the Edmonds Commission was seeking a proper balance between personal and corporate taxation. Like the Mercur Commission, it was dealing with assessment practices, and in fact it took over Mercur's recommendations verbatim as part of its preliminary report in 1925. Its preliminary and final reports contained more than twenty specific recommendations, many of them minor. The preliminary report included a plan proposed by John Penman Wood (1861-1927), also of Philadelphia, not unlike the plan proposed by John A. Wright back in 1890. This commission, by the way, was the only one of our four Pennsylvania commissions to have a member found in the *Dictionary of American Biography*, Judge James Reed of Pittsburgh (1853-1927), better known as Andrew Carnegie's lawyer.

Finally, the Tax Study Committee of the Joint State Government Committee (of the Pennsylvania Legislature), appointed in 1947, though included because it satisfies our criteria in size and self-expertise, thus holding information costs constant across time, is organizationally anomalous. It was a body provided for by a legislative enabling act, appointed wholly or in part by the Governor, and having at least some "public" (non-legislative) members (Pennsylvania 1949, Introduction).

But it was a (sub)committee of a legislative committee, despite the presence of its public members. It was chaired ex officio by Commonwealth Secretary of Commerce Orus Matthews. Four of its six members were legislators (all Republicans, as was Matthews), one was an ex-legislator (also Republican), and the sixth was Frank W. Main of Pittsburgh, the first professional accountant to serve on a Pennsylvania commission. The Matthews Commission had as its purpose the establishment of a more equitable system of taxation – as, of course, did the McCamant, Kennan, Mercur, and Edmonds commissions – and in the scope of its mandate fell between its two immediate predecessors (though its mandate came from the Joint State Government Committee, and only two of its members were appointed by the Governor).

The Matthews Commission is particularly interesting because it came at a time when the nature (though apparently not the incidence or burden) of Pennsylvania taxes was shifting substantially, for reasons having little or nothing to do with the recommendations of any commission. Indeed, it may be noted, as a general rule, that the greatest changes in the Pennsylvania tax system, at least in this century, could more accurately be adduced to laws passed in a temporary fit of absence of mind (or of desperation) than to the work of commissions or their members, jointly or severally. Thus, for example, the 18-percent Liquor Store Sales Tax has been referred to as an "emergency" tax for half a century: its presence surely affects tax incidence, but no study of its equity has yet been made, so far as I know. The longstanding (and highly confusing) distinction between the Corporate Income Tax and the Corporation Income Tax was finally ushered in to oblivion not because a commission had recommended its demise but because of a decision of the U. S. Supreme Court (*1980 Guidebook*, pp. 11-12). And the highly important section of the Pennsylvania Tax Code authorizing local

36

governments to levy new kinds of taxes was not recommended by a single commission before its passage (*Pennsylvania Legislature* 1947, p. 1145, *Pennsylvania Legislature* 1965, pp. 1257ff).

None of these statements is designed to cast doubt on the efficacy of tax revision commissions, since the test for efficacy is whether the commissions produce change, not whether change also comes from other sources. It is, however, at least arguable that the Matthews Commission was an anomalous throwback to an age believing in both the efficacy of commissions and the (relative) inefficacy of other approaches. That part of the "New Order" tradition – if it is indeed a part (as suggested in Yearley 1970, p. 207) – will be dealt with *seriatim* in Chapters III through V. That will come after we have constructed a model of commission behavior, which is the subject of Chapter II. But before we construct that model, I should explain in brief one of the theoretical underpinnings that underlies my whole enquiry into the matter of tax revision commissions. The theory involved goes under the general name of Bounded Rationality and is particularly connected with the name of Herbert Simon (Simon 1957, Simon 1976, Simon 1981). Since the early versions of this study were written at and for Carnegie Mellon University, explaining Simon would have been an extreme case of carrying coals to Newcastle (or Pittsburgh), but perhaps there is a need to do so now.

No one, not even the most brilliant among us, can effectively program all the data necessary for a fully rational decision, even if those data were available at a reasonable search cost – which, generally, they are not (Simon 1981, p. 41). We do, as it happens, make rational decisions, but only within the bounds imposed by data availability and data processing limitations – by search costs and processing capacity. To limit these costs (or, in other words, to limit our search space), we take certain things for granted. The things we take for granted are, roughly speaking, what Simon calls decision premises (Simon 1981, p. 48, and Simon 1976, pp. xxxvi-xxxviii). Before we decide, we set up the rules for our deciding (or, in some cases, have them set up for us). And once they are set up, we do not generally go back over them. This is particularly true of one subset of these decision premises – the one determined by our role in whatever decision-making organization we are involved in. It should be noted that, the less the importance of roles (in tax revision commissions or elsewhere), the smaller must be the percentage of the decision premises encompassed in these roles, the greater must be the open search space (all other things being equal), the more expert must the decision-makers be – or alternatively (other things not equal), the more circumscribed must be their mandate. The relevance of this point will become evident when we consider the relative success of the Kennan and Mercur commissions. With this brief discussion of bounded rationality in mind, we may turn to our model of commission behavior – not of state tax revision commissions only, but of all "policy" commissions in general. The application of the model comes in Chapters III-VII.

# CHAPTER II: THE POLICY PROBLEM OF COMMISSIONS

In the early days of *The Public Interest*, Daniel Bell wrote a short "Comment" in which he set out a typology of government commissions – advisory, evaluative, fact-finding, public relations, and policy recommendation commissions (Bell 1966, p. 6). These commissions, he suggested, represented something new in the Executive Branch: they provided for the direct representation of "functional constituencies" in the advisory process; they permitted the government to explore the limits of action by taking soundings; they served as a direct public relations device to call attention to certain issues; and they fostered "elite participation" in government policy. Bell's point was that, in terms formulated by Bertrand de Jouvenel, the purpose of such commissions was to make the future a matter for public opinion (Bell 1966, pp. 7, 9).

Bell's typology is not nearly so clear as his short piece suggests, inasmuch as advisory, fact-finding, and policy recommendation commissions tend rather to slide into one another, but – characteristically – he put his finger on two points of major importance. First (as in his typology), commissions may be characterized by output (recommendations, factual reports, public relations. Second (as in his list of "new functions"), commissions may be categorized by inputs (the participation of "functional constituencies" and political elites. His statement of purpose, however, though intriguing, seems (as we would expect from a "Comment") somewhat incomplete.

Also in the 1960s, a considerable degree of attention was being given to the problems of "committees" (in part as a form of the problem

39

of "legislatures"). This attention, at least insofar as I am examining it here, grew out of a set of attempts to apply economic rules and economic reasoning to political problems (Tullock 1981, pp. 47-57). One set is called public choice theory and is particularly, in its origins, connected with the name of Duncan Black (Grofman 1981, pp. 11-46). Another, bearing the more wide-ranging name of social choice, is connected particularly with the work of Kenneth Arrow (Arrow 1951). Both trace their putative origins to the work of the Marquis de Condorcet in the eighteenth century and that of Charles Lutwidge Dodgson (who was also Lewis Carroll) in the nineteenth (Condorcet 1785, Dodgson 1876). Both deal with the question of the way in which a political body comes to conclusions, and whether those conclusions represent the will of the body or of the constituents it is supposed to represent. And both, because a commission is a restricted form of a committee, are of some value to us. Of them, the public choice approach – because it deals more narrowly with political choice, rather than social welfare – seems to me the more valuable tool for our purposes (Grofman 1981, p. 41).

Duncan Black set out, back in the 1940s, to develop a pure theory of politics as a ramified theory of committees (Grofman 1981, p. 12). Our concern here is not with the science of politics so much as with the theory of committees, or rather with that part of it which can be adapted to the peculiar and limited form of committee that constitutes a commission. At the time I was writing the original version of this paper, my friend Kenneth Koford noted that "the relatively subtle connections among committees that an 'exchange' theory of legislatures would suggest have not yet been looked for in the empirical committee literature. And it is difficult to rule out the possibility that committee and floor leaders are making bargains across committee boundaries"

(Koford 1982, pp. 11-12). Doubtless they are, but we are fortunately spared this consideration in looking at commissions not made up of legislative members (though the comment suggests a difficulty for the 1947 Commission). We are not, however, spared the problems arising from the fact that members of commissions, like members of legislative committees, are representatives of some constituency: we are in fact (as will become apparent even with the "blue-ribbon" 1923 Pennsylvania Commission) dealing with decision-making by representatives, which is the essential subject of public choice (Mueller 1979, pp. 97ff).

It turns out, however, that the dice ought to be loaded in our favor, for reasons I will try to explain here. Let me quote Duncan Black's description of his original moment of insight into committee voting. "I was 'firewatching' in case of air raids, late at night in the green drawing-room at Warwick Castle, which . . . was strewn with civil service tables and paraphernalia. *Acting apparently at random, I wrote down a single diagram and saw in a shock of recognition the property of the median optimum.* This could be got by interpreting the diagram I had drawn, in terms of a committee using a simple majority, whose members' preferences, in regard to the motions put forward, could be represented by a set of single-peaked curves. Grant that, and the decision of the committee would correspond to the median optimum" (Grofman 1981, p. 19). That is, Black saw (what has since been systematically proven) that, if committee members have preference rankings that rise steadily to a single peak and then fall steadily away from it, then there is a single unique outcome capable of receiving a majority in pair-wise competition against other alternatives, and *this unique outcome will always be the median voter's most preferred alternative* (Grofman 1981, pp. 19-20).

This rule can be generalized to multi-dimensional issue spaces – that is, the "property of the median optimum" (the fact that the outcome

41

will be what the median voter most wants) will hold even if more that one issue is at stake, but only if there are single-peaked preferences on every issue. It turns out that the greater the number of issues, the less likely this is (Plotz 1967, pp. 787-806, Bernholz 1981, pp. 59-78, and subsequent work built on these). Accordingly, by restricting our commissions to those dealing with tax equity, we have increased the likelihood of fully operative single-peaked preferences, and we have therefore made it more likely that Black's "median optimum" property will apply. This is what I mean by loading the dice in our favor. We have then a theory of committees into which our commissions may be fitted. We have (from Daniel Bell) an initial typology of commissions. We have (in Chapter I) a brief discussion of bounded rationality and a brief outline of a theory of commissions formed by Terence Tutchings. What we are going to do now is put all these together.

First, we will set out the Tutchings theory in greater detail as a political-science model. Second, we will note the correspondences between his model and Bell's brief typology. Third, we will suggest ways in which public choice theory (in the theory of committees) and Simon's bounded rationality can work together to illuminate and make more rigorous the commission model Tutchings has proposed. We will also, as an exercise, deal briefly with three U. S. national commissions (not taxation commissions), to see how our model works for them. These are the 1919, 1935, and 1943 U. S. commissions dealing with race riots, conveniently summarized by Platt (Platt 1971). Then we will go on, in Chapters III through VI, to look at our specimen tax commissions.

Tutchings developed his theory initially from David Easton's model of political process (Easton 1965). In the model's simplest form, inputs (in the form of demands and supports) enter the political system, which then (through authoritative decisions and acts) produces outputs,

42

which then (through their outcomes) act upon the environment (defined inclusively rather than exclusively), producing feedback and thus inputs (in the form of demands and supports), which enter the political system . . . and so on, cyclically (Tutchings 1979, pp. 4-6). In the form presented by Salisbury and Heinz (Salisbury and Heinz 1970, pp. 39-42), the supports are defined in terms of cost, and the environment is more or less considered as a demand system, balancing the political system: that is, the political system's outputs are inputs to the demand system, and the demand system's outputs are inputs to the political system. In both models, evidently, the feedback loop is either complete or can be made complete, and in both the political or decisional system is a "black box" not opened for inspection.

Tutchings also appeals to a model developed by Dye (Dye 1976). This model (which Tutchings gives as "The View from the Top" because of Dye's concern with élites) has a more detailed process component, but restricts commissions to the "opinion-making" function and leaves the internal processes of both policy-making and opinion-making bodies in the black box (Tutchings 1979, pp. 14, 16). What Tutchings tried to do – and the reason his modelling is particularly germane to our purposes – is to use his own typology of commissions by inputs and outputs to glimpse the inside of the black box (Tutchings 1979, p. 2). If we find that commissions with particular sorts of inputs tend to make particular sorts of recommendations both as to what should be done and as to how it should be done, we should be well on the way to reducing the box's blackness. Tutchings, more than any other modeller, is looking at both the *what* and the *how*.

The inputs may be divided into organization ("organizational dynamics") and personnel, with organization further divided – as we noted in Chapter I – into demands, information costs, and decision costs,

43

and personnel (though Tutchings does not make much of this) into types of elites (Tutchings 1979, pp. 17-33, 38-47). The demands may be further subdivided into circumstances of creation, issue areas, and temporal variations. Policy outputs (recommendations) may be classified according to *who* (actor) is to do *what* (action) for *what* (end)? Both action and end may be classified into redistributive policy, distributive policy, self-regulative policy, and regulative policy (Tutchings 1979, pp. 51-52). Policy outputs, in the Tutchings study, are tabulated by three-digit codes – thus a recommendation that Congress pass laws to ensure equitable access to public education would be a 3-1-4, with the "3" for Congress, the "1" for legislative action, and the "4" for redistributive ends (Tutchings 1979, p. 53). Tutchings studied ninety-five U. S. Presidential commissions in the years from Truman to the end of Nixon's first term, with a total of 5,053 recommendations (Tutchings 1979, pp. 13, 52, 123-142). Though his years overlaps ours only (so to speak) by courtesy, the model he forms should be sufficiently broad to encompass our concerns.

His possible *what* outputs (that is, the "action") he divides into (1) specific actions, (2) regulative actions, (3) self-regulative actions, (4) distributive actions, (5) redistributive actions, (6) symbolic actions, (7) further study ("Knowledge/Plan"), (8) increased level of present action ("augment"), (9) unspecified change, and (10) "Other" (meaning mostly "nothing in particular"). Note that a recommendation of specific new laws (or amendments to old laws) is a "specific" action, while an expression of the view that the law should be changed is not. (Tutchings 1979, pp. 60-61.)

The regulative/self-regulative/distributive/redistributive quartet is taken over from Salisbury and Heinz, who use it with a typology of fragmented and integrated decision- and demand-systems. In this analysis, a fragmented demand-system with an integrated decision system will produce a policy of regulation, an integrated demand-system with an integrated decision-system will produce a policy of redistribution, a fragmented demand-system with a fragmented decision-system produces self-regulation, and a fragmented demand-system with an integrated decision-system produces a distributive outcome (Salisbury and Heinz 1970, p. 43, Tutchings 1979, p. 94). I am not entirely convinced by this, but there is ore in the vein, and I, like Professor Tutchings, have mined it for most of what it is worth. Even so, the quartet seems to fit a trifle awkwardly with the other six categories. But perhaps only a trifle awkwardly.

From his studies of these ninety-five commissions and their 5,053 recommendations, Tutchings draws a set of conclusions, which in turn leads him to classify commission recommendations according to a "manipulability" factor. For our purposes, we should note that the *least* manipulable by commission report, of all actors that national (that is, Presidential) commissions might want to manipulate, is the U. S. Congress (Tutchings 1979, p. 69). The analogue for our study – that is, what we might expect on the basis of this finding – is that the least manipulable of all actors on the state level would be the state legislature in question, which (with the possibly exception of the Kennan Commission) would be the actor all our commissions would want to manipulate. (The Kennan Commission was manipulating the Governor as much as or more than the Legislature.)

Tutchings, of course, draws other conclusions quite as relevant to our study, if not necessarily to our conclusions. He divides his commissions by membership into (1) corporate/governmental, (2) public interest, and (3) mixed (Tutchings 1979, pp. 97, 99-100). These correspond roughly to the categories under which I grouped tax revision

45

commissions in my initial study – to wit, "blue ribbon" commissions, "interest group" commissions, and (as an afterthought) "political commissions." Roughly speaking, I would argue that my "blue ribbon" commissions share with the "corporate/government" elite commissions a Hamiltonian ("the rich, the well-born, and the able") and centripetal character, my "interest group" commissions share with the "public interest" commissions a populist and centrifugal character, and my "political" are like the "mixed" commissions – in-between. Because our research here ends not much past the point at which Tutchings began his, I think my terms somewhat more applicable, but the underlying reality and the essential typology remain pretty much constant. In any case, from this division, and his division of outcomes, Tutchings begins to shine light into the box.

Of the 5,053 actions recommended by the commissions, only 368 were for the Congress. Of these, there were three specific, 223 regulatory, three distributive, one redistributive, one symbolic, seven "knowledge/plan" (or further study), two "augment" ("same only moreso"), 119 for general change, and nine for "other" (or for "nothing in particular"). Of them, 47 had specific ends, 114 regulatory ("regulation") ends, 27 distributive ("distribution") ends, 37 redistributive, one symbolic, 33 "knowledge/plan" ends, 13 "augment," 70 general change, and 26 other (Tutchings 1979, pp. 62, 65). Evidently (for example), it was more likely that a commission recommend Congress pass laws to attain a specific end, than that it recommend specific laws to be passed.

Tutchings next constructed his manipulability indices, with actor, action, and end each rated from 1 (least manipulable) to 4 (most). For our purposes, we should note again that Congress was the least manipulable actor; we should note that the least manipulable actions

46

were redistributive and specific; and we should note that the least manipulable ends were redistributive, specific, and self-regulatory (Tutchings 1979, pp. 69, 71). Most manipulable were the symbolic and knowledge/plan actions and ends.

Legislative (that is, in his case, Congressional) responses to the ninety-five commissions show that the combination of specific recommendations for specific ends (in other words, action to be taken by the Congress) was virtually the kiss of death (Tutchings 1979, pp. 84-86). But this depressing finding is to some extent balanced by the findings on the impact of commission membership on the type of recommendations made and the likelihood of their success. Specifically, Tutchings concludes (given thirty-nine commissions with "high demand" and fifty-six with "low demand") that achieved coalitions within the commission were more likely to be associated with regulative outputs for low-demand commissions than for high-demand commissions, that corporate/governmental commissions (by fourteen to ten) and mixed commissions (by thirteen to ten) were more likely to produce regulative recommendations than were public interest commissions (twenty-one regulative to twenty-seven non-regulative), and that new legislation came about for thirteen of twenty-four corporate/governmental commissions, nineteen of forty-eight public interest commissions, and twelve of twenty-three mixed commissions (Tutchings 1979, pp. 95, 99).

The joker in this, however, is that new legislation came about for only five of fourteen corporate/governmental commissions, seven of twenty-one public interest commissions, and six of thirteen mixed commissions with regulative recommendations (ibid.): in other words, the best way to get legislation was not to recommend it, but the presence of corporate/governmental commissioners did help.

47

The "achieved coalitions"/"low demand" finding noted above can be roughly interpreted as saying that high-demand issues ("important" issues, though that is my word and inexact) are more likely to lead to regulative recommendations in the absence of consensus than are low-demand ("relatively unimportant") issues. Commissions appointed from the corporate/governmental elite are more likely to make regulative recommendations and moderately more likely to have their recommendations accepted than are public interest commissions. Commissions with achieved coalitions are slightly less likely to recommend regulative action (twenty-five of fifty-two or 48.1 percent) than commissions without achieved coalitions (twenty-three of forty-three or 53.5 percent) – but this does not seem to be the determining variable. If anything, the determining variable is degree of demand. (Tutchings 1979, p. 95.)

These findings provide us with a kind of lead-in to our discussion of the internal workings of commissions, but before we get to that, I should like to suggest the ways in which Tutchings has added both insight and rigor to Bell's typology – partly because Bell's short piece is better known than *Rhetoric and Reality*, partly to indicate some fundamental similarities, and partly to show that Bell's observations from within the system corroborate observations by Tutchings from outside. Besides, I hope I will be able to provide additional insight, and perhaps rigor, from within the framework of the Tutchings model, *explicitly*, as Tutchings did from within Bell's framework, *implicitly*. What I have to say should fit well within both.

Bell, it will be recalled, divided commissions by output (advice, evaluation, fact-finding, public relations, and policy recommendations) and input (interest groups or "functional constituencies" along with elite participation and government pressures or "p.r."). It turns out that his advisory commissions are statutory bodies with fixed-term memberships, like the Labor-Management Advisory Committee, and it is to such bodies as these that government pressure or "p.r." will be applied (Bell 1966, pp. 6-7). These are not within the Tutchings purview, nor generally is the use of commissions for government "fronts" (another of Bell's categories. Bell's four relevant outputs have become ten, with policy recommendations divided into seven categories (eight if we include "other"), public relations into two ("symbolic" and "change" -- or three if we count "other"), while his evaluation and fact-finding fall into the undifferentiated "other" (Bell 1966, pp. 6-7, and Tutchings 1979, pp. 60-61). Note that these output categories, like those of Tutchings, are "end" categories – indeed, Bell may well have thought of them more as ends than as actions.

In addition, Bell's two kinds of inputs are the guiding categories for the Tutchings personnel classifications and for mine, since the third classification ("mixed") is a balance between the other two. What Bell, however, does not provide, except anecdotally, while Tutchings does, is anything on the organizational dynamics (Tutchings "inputs") for the commissions. These would be questions of demand (subdivided into circumstances of creation, issue area, temporal variations), information costs, and decision costs. We may note that Bell's prime example, the National Commission on Technology, Automation, and Economic Progress (Tutchings no. 41), was a low-demand, high-information-cost, medium-decision-cost commission, with no legislative result and not even much support from the President who appointed it (Bell 1966, pp. 3-5, Tutchings 1979, p. 78). It fits neatly within the Tutchings typology, with the expected Tutchings results, at least in terms of demand factors. (Note, by the way, that this was a "mixed" commission, though perhaps more "blue ribbon" than "interest group" in my terms – though these may grow increasingly less useful as time goes on, being much more suited to 1889-1949, our primary period, than to the 1960s and thereafter.)

But what is it about the nature of the commission process or dynamic that makes these the expected results? To that question we will now turn, by way of our Theory of Committees.

The problem that gives rise to the literature on committees may be set out in a three-person three-alternative example. Suppose person no. 1 prefers alternative A to alternative B to alternative C (1: ApBpC). Suppose person no. 2 prefers alternative B to alternative C to alternative A (2: BpCpA). Suppose person no. 3 prefers alternative C to alternative A to alternative B (3: CpApB). Now if all we have are these ordinal rankings, without any cardinal values attached, a committee consisting of these three persons (1, 2, and 3) and faced with these alternatives (A, B, and C) will vote 2-1 for A over B (ApB: 2-1), 2-1 for B over C (BpC: 2-1), but 2-1 for C over A (CpA: 2-1). That is, the 2-1 preference for A over B and B over C will not produce (transitively) a preference for A over C. Indeed, as noted, C will be preferred over A, 2-1 (Arrow 1951).

This is very much a simplified case (and indeed is a paradox noted by Condorcet more than two centuries ago), but it presents the difficulty in no uncertain terms. What Duncan Black did was to show that the difficulty was not always insuperable (though it is fundamentally so in our simplified case). Under some conditions, there can be a stable equilibrium solution, and when there is, it is the most preferred alternative for the median voter (Black 1948, pp. 23-34, Black 1958). Various criteria for determining "majority will" had been proposed by Condorcet ("any alternative which is preferred by a majority to each and every other alternative"), Jean-Charles de Borda ("assigns to each alternative for each committee member one point for each alternative to which it is preferred by that committee member" – with the alternative that gains the highest point total being selected), and C. L. Dodgson ("choose the element that would become maximal with the fewest changes to existing preference orderings"). The first two of these classical criteria cannot solve the "intransitivity" problem presented above, nor is there any median voter, which is why the "median optimum" solution cannot hold. What the eventual solution to the problem may be (a Dodgson variant, probably) is not so important here as the fact that the problem exists, and what its existence portends for the Tutchings findings.

Specifically, can we see some kind of correlation between any of the Tutchings actor/action/end types, on the one hand, and the probable presence of a Condorcet, de Borda, straightforward Dodgson, or Black solution on the other? Evidently, since this is not something Tutchings reported on, we will be arguing largely on *a priori* grounds, just as we will argue subsequently for connections between the committee problem and bounded rationality on *a priori* grounds. We will, however, test both our sets of *a priori* connections by examining the three U. S. race-riot commissions (1919, 1935, 1943), before going on to apply them to our five specimen tax revision commissions.

We would expect to find our strongest connection between and among the make-up of the commission, the difficulty of reaching a decision (decision cost), and the likelihood of a stable preference solution. We discover from Tutchings that commissions made up from the corporate/governmental elite are significantly more likely than either public-interest or mixed commissions to come up with regulative recommendations, with the difference between public-interest and mixed commissions insignificant (Tutchings 1979, p. 108). We discover that both corporate/governmental commissions and mixed commissions are

51

more likely than public-interest commissions to have their recommendations passed into law, with the difference between corporate/governmental and mixed commissions insignificant (Tutchings 1979, p. 111).

The public-interest (or "functional constituency" or – in our period – "interest-group") commission is least likely to have a single preferred alternative (Condorcet solution). It is least likely to have real de Borda rankings (that is, to have preferences arranged at uniform intervals on a preference schedule). It is perhaps least likely – and certainly not very likely – to have the possibility of a Dodgson solution (because existing preference orderings are unlikely to have significant overlapping). It is certainly least likely to possess a median optimum. The presence of public-interest members on a mixed commission will have pretty much the same set of effects.

On the other hand, so far as having recommendations passed into law is concerned, we are at least partly out of the black box and into the policy process. In that process, of course (and especially if one adopts Dye's model), the presence of elites on a commission could be expected to produce support for that commission's recommendations. But having recommendations enacted is not merely a function of elite support, or public support, for the ideas. It is also (as the 1889 Pennsylvania Commission will remind us) a function of the form in which the recommendations are drafted, which I would consider an "in-the-box" question, and one subject to the same majority-vote problems we noted above.

In one way, commissions (with a few exceptions) are far more restricted than (legislative) committees in what they can do to get their recommendations accepted, and indeed in what can be done to hammer out recommendations within the commission. To see why, let us consider the possibility of reaching a Dodgson solution within a legislative committee suffering from a problem of intransitive preferences. What we need to do is make the fewest possible changes in preference orderings. The question is how. And the usual answer is along the lines of "you scratch my back – I'll scratch yours." This is known, in the literature, as log-rolling (Mueller 1979, pp. 49-98).

Suppose the members of the committee have preferences of different intensities on different issues, either in this committee or (as we noted earlier) coming up before different committees with overlapping memberships. Suppose in our A/B/C case above that person no. 1 would "give anything" to defeat alternative C, while person no. 3 would give anything to defeat alternative B: person no 2, on the other hand, prefers B to C to A, but does not really care very much. A minor change in no. 2's preferences can be assured by no. 1 or no. 3 or both, at low cost, provided there is another issue available for trade (an issue in which no. 2 is perhaps more involved). In fact, trading (log-rolling) of this type might produce de Borda, Condorcet, or median optimum solutions from the revised preference schedule (Mueller 1979, p. 50). That it might not produce social welfare, though true, is not our present concern.

Now consider the state tax revision commission, with (generally) only the single issue of tax equity at stake. It is true that there might be trading off among various specific alternatives – as, for example, specific portions of a recommended law, or specific laws among a recommended set. But we have mostly eliminated the possibility (or at least substantially reduced the probability) of log-rolling within the box. We could still have a Dodgson solution without log-rolling (granting different intensities of preference) or a de Borda solution (but not a "real" de Borda solution if there were differing intensities). With single-peaked preference schedules we might have a median optimum solution.

With a single preferred alternative we would have a Condorcet solution. But – and this is the point – whatever solution we reached, we would be forced to reach it without the aid of log-rolling (Mueller 1979, pp. 49-58).

Moreover, the commission is similarly limited in getting its recommendations passed, since it does not have and its members need not have anything to offer in the way of trade-offs after the report is made. It is, I believe, this factor that leads to the greater effectiveness of corporate/governmental commissions – that is, leads both to their recommending effective laws and to the laws they recommend being passed. Members of corporate élites and members of governmental élites (and some commission members are both simultaneously) are both likely to have at least some carrots to dangle for future exchange. On the other hand, our own specimen commissions suggest this factor may be overestimated – or perhaps things have changed since 1927, when the bluest-ribbon commission of all reported.

The question may now be asked whether commission members are likely to have preferences of different intensities, whether they are likely to have single-peaked preference schedules, whether they are likely to include an actual median member – in short, whether all this is merely abstraction or whether it decribes the way particular human beings (commission members) behave? We can begin our attempt to answer that question by appealing to an early, but still valid, study by Herbert Simon on interaction in small groups (Simon 1952).

In his paper, Simon proved formally that, given a particular group structure and set of interactions, in groups containing subgroups or cliques, the equilibrium value of whole-group activity will decline as the clique activity increases – external goals being held constant – and that, in addition, there may well be no equilibrium activity point for the group as a whole (Simon 1952, p. 210). In other words, there is no guarantee the group will fulfill any set portion of its assigned tasks. We will come back to this shortly.

We might actually begin even earlier in Simon's work, in fact where he himself began his theories of bounded rationality, with his discovery – in Milwaukee, Wisconsin, back in the 1930s – that two rational men, each with the best interests of the community at heart, and apparently agreeing on the objectives of a recreation program, were in a state of "continual disagreement and tension . . . with respect to the allocation of funds between physical maintenance, on the one hand, and play supervision on the other" (Simon 1982, p. 481). His conclusion, then and later, was that this was a case of *subgoal identification*: "When the goals of an organization cannot be connected operationally with actions . . . then decisions will be judged against subordinate goals that can be so connected."

In this lies the kernel of Simon's theory of bounded *procedural* rationality: the two men in question had adopted simplified models of the real situation, to permit them to work with goals that could be operationally connected to actions. The principle of bounded rationality is that the capacity of the human mind for formulating and solving complex problems is very small compared with the size of the problems whose solution is required for "objectively rational" behavior in the real world, or even for a reasonable approximation of such behavior. The consequence is that the "intended rationality of an actor" requires him to construct a simplified model of the "real situation" in order to deal with it (Simon 1957, pp. 241-43, 256).

To predict the actor's behavior (as, for example, the behavior of Simon's two men, or the members of the Tutchings commissions, or of ours), we must understand the way in which the simplified model is constructed, and we know its construction will be related to – if not fully determined by – the actor's properties as a perceiving, thinking, and learning animal. Thus the principle of bounded rationality lies at the very core of organization theory, and also (as Simon specifically points out) at the core of any theory of action that purports to treat human behavior in complex situations (Simon 1957, p. 256) – including the complex situations involved in commission behavior.

Simon's two men in Milwaukee were the head of the school board and the head of the public works department: their subgoals were formed in accordance with their roles (Simon 1982, p. 481). In Simon's terms, the specification of a role is in fact the specification of some subset of the premises that are to guide the decisions of the actor as to the correct course of behavior (decision premises, in short). The principle of bounded rationality tells us that many or most of the premises of rational choice will be determined by the social and psychological environment of the subject making the choice. The "role hypothesis" asserts that many of these premises will be obtained from the socially-defined role in which the actor (in our case the commission member) is placed.

Hence, if we take the premise as the unit for role description, we can accept both the idea that behavior is rational and the idea that it is, to a considerable extent, role-determined. It is, however, necessary that roles (so as to be enacted) be specified in such a way as to bring them within the actors' computational capabilities (Simon 1957, pp. 241-43). The two men in Milwaukee could not conceive of their roles as "making economic decisions at the margin" (that is, acting as that grand abstraction, Economic Man), because the computation – indeed the whole computational framework – that required was beyond their capabilities (Simon 1982, p. 481).

56

We must therefore take into account the simplifications made by (in Simon's term) the "choosing organism" so as to bring his or her model of the situation within the range of the organism's computing capacity. The environment in which decisions are made thus lies in part within the skin of the organism: constraints that must be taken as "givens" in the equation for choice may be the organism's physiological and psychological limitations. Most important among them are likely to be limitations on computational choice (Simon 1957, p. 256).

These limitations require simplifying decision processes by adopting – in accordance with one's role (one might say, *as* one's role) – certain subsets of decision premises that are thereafter left unexamined, and that must be left unexamined if work is to be done. But to the degree that the same subsets are adopted by more than one member of a group, there will tend to be factions (cliques, subgroups) within that group: this will lead to unstable activity and questionable output.

Different decision premises will lead, as in our Milwaukee example, to different and even diametrically opposed conclusions on important issues. If, in our original A/B/C model, we were to have three three-person cliques rather than three single persons, the model would still hold: indeed, inasmuch as there would be activity within cliques, lowering the level of the group activity as a whole, the preferences of the cliques might be even more intractable than individual preferences would be. To the degree that log-rolling would be a between-clique rather than a within-clique activity (and of course it would be), there would be less time for log-rolling in a commission with cliques than in a commission without.

Moreover, in addition to producing unstable and diminished over-all activity levels, and making log-rolling less likely, cliques in any voting group (including a commission) will reduce the applicability of de Borda solutions, somewhat reduce the probability of a median optimum, and likewise reduce the probability of a Condorcet solution. Activity within cliques will, as Simon's model indicates, lead to better interrelationships within cliques, strengthen member identification with clique desires. It will thus (1) tend to set preferences at irregular intervals along preference schedules (with the clique's preferred alternative way ahead of others), and (2) tend to establish clique allegiance to increasingly different sets of preferences. This latter will both reduce the chances that there will be a true median optimum and (somewhat more obviously) reduce the chances that any single alternative action, however minor, will be preferred to all other alternatives (Simon 1982b, p. 41).

All this deals with the difficulty of making decisions, or what Tutchings includes as part of decision costs, and with the personnel question (corporate/governmental elites, public-interest membership, and so on). We have yet to consider the ways in which our theories of committees and bounded rationality can illuminate demands, which is to say, can illuminate circumstances of creation, issue areas, and temporal variations. Note that we have eliminated the second Tutchings variable, information costs, by considering only commissions of self-expertise. Note also that we have held the "issues area" variable more or less constant, by considering taxation revision commissions with a mandate to pursue tax equity. Temporal variation of any significance occurs only with the Edmonds Commission of 1923, and this could be neutralized by considering the interim (1925) rather than the final (1927) report. (We will take this up in Chapter V.) Let us, for the moment, look at the effect of our back-up theories in connection with our "circumstances of creation" variable.

Suppose there is considerable public pressure for tax revision – pressure of the sort that was unquestionably present for the 1889 Pennsylvania and 1897 Wisconsin commissions. We would expect single-peaked preferences in such a case – to the extent that public concern for an issue generates well-defined preference schedules, which it will, and to the extent that these will be single-peaked, which is probably more likely than not. We would expect, on much the same grounds, that de Borda and Condorcet solutions would both be unlikely. We might expect that public pressure could generate log-rolling in order to bring about a Dodgson solution in the real world, but our understanding of the bounds to rationality does suggest limitations even here. And we should emphasize that the bounds apply to procedural rationality: it will probably be the case that the differing subsets of "role" decision premises will generate differing preferences as to final recommendations, and the fact that these subsets exist may limit the ability of one commission member to follow another's logic. Experiments with computer chess have suggested just how important this problem is -- differing algorithms lead to widely differing strengths and weaknesses in patterns of play (Simon 1982b, pp. 412-18).

We have not yet considered one highly important point in the public choice literature, the "agenda" question. It has been widely agreed that he who sets the agenda (in this imperfect world) determines the outcome (Koford 1981, pp. 5-6, Kramer 1977, McKelvey 1976, and subsequent work developed from these). What is not agreed is whether there exists any reasonable way around this. Controlled (laboratory) experiments have shown that groups of decision-makers do not, in fact, act in such a way as to produce a lack of stable equilibrium in their decision-making. But they still seem to show that equilibrium, whether real or apparent, is a function of agenda-setting (Fiorina and Plott 1978,

59

pp. 575-598, though since that time most studies of agenda-setting have concentrated on the media). In our context, it appears that restrictive agenda-setting can assure equilibrium – that is, an agreed-upon decision –, but cannot assure a "best" equilibrium – that is, in economists's terms, Pareto-optimality (Koford 1981, p. 6). To take our A/B/C case, if the agenda-setter stops after the second pair-wise vote, we have a solution (ApB and BpC, with the false implication that ApC). But the equilibrium is only apparent, since in fact, if we voted, C would be preferred to A.

Now we are arguing (*via* Simon) that commissions will perforce seek "satisficing" solutions (that is, they will at some point adopt as recommendations the best-looking alternative to come along, without looking to see if there exists a better yet), which means we are accepting the absence of Pareto-optimality. The question for us then becomes the restrictiveness of the agenda-setting, and I will argue that only the 1919 Pennsylvania Commission (the Mercur Commission) had an agenda significantly more restricted than any of the others. What is also important, however, is the question *who sets the internal order of the agenda*: to this question we have, except by inference, no answer, but we can set out a general principle.

To the degree that the same person (or body) appoints the members and sets the agenda, the members ought to be such that the agenda is suited to them, and to the goal of the commission, unless the person (or body) making the appointments has failed to match them because of computational or information bounds (Simon 1982b, pp. 344-350). The exception would occur under conditions of insincere appointment or agenda-setting with concealed goals (Grofman 1981, pp. 30-36). In each of our cases, the (internal) agenda we can deduce seems fitted to the membership and putative goals of the commission, though there may be

60

one exception (see Chapter V, *infra*). Whether this would hold true with larger "p.r." commissions of the sort popular in Pennsylvania after 1950, and especially whether there would not be concealment and insincerity, is not our concern here. So long as we have (even though for other reasons) limited ourselves to "self-expert" commissions, this will not be a problem.

Now the first three commissions in Platt's compendium on race riots fall within this "self-expert" category, once we eliminate the 1917 Commission as being, in fact, a legislative committee, consisting of four Congressmen (Platt 1971, pp. 83-89, esp. 87). In Bell's typology they were fact-finding and policy-recommendation commissions, or at least that is what they were announced as: the 1943 Detroit Commission had a concealed goal and insincere agenda, although the 1919 Chicago and 1934 Harlem commissions were straightforward and sincere (Platt 1971, pp. 120-25, 161-62, 229, 249-50). They were "élite" commissions, in Bell's sense, but they were also designed to include one special functional constituency: black people (Platt 1971, pp. 123-24, 161, 249).

In Tutchings terminology, all these were high-demand commissions, created while rioting was going on, under public pressure, and all had the same issue area. Demand would have varied among the three, if at all, only temporally – that is, things might (so to speak) have sorted themselves out before the commission reported, if the commission took a particularly long time to report, or if the apparent problem turned out (or seemed to turn out) to be less intense than it first appeared, or over sooner (Tutchings 1979, p. 23). This may have been the case with the 1935 Harlem Commission (Platt 1971, p. 162), and (given its four-year life) we may find it to be a relevant consideration with our own 1923 Edmonds Commission. By looking at self-expert

61

commissions in our tax inquiry, we have limited, if not entirely eliminated, the information cost problem: though the commission members would have to find out *what* had happened, they should have a very good idea *how* to find it out (low search costs) and also *why* it might have happened. The two variables with the greatest variability – or the prospect of the greatest variability – would thus seem to be decision costs and personnel (whether corporate/governmental élite, or interest group, or mixed). How does this apply with the race-riot commissions?

Granted that a biracial commission meeting on racial matters will have some of the characteristics of an interest-group commission no matter how the members are picked, there are still some personnel differences. And since decision costs would be high for any regulative recommendations– especially redistributive regulative recommendations (including redistributive specific) – in all three race-riot commissions, any differences in outcome we should probably be able to trace to the mode of choosing personnel. Although the 1943 Detroit Commission, as I have suggested, had concealed goals, it turns out this comes to light in an examination of the appointment process, and its effect is created through personnel choice (Platt 1971, pp. 199, 249ff).

The reason for going over this here is that these are relatively well-known commissions for which the necessary information is independently and conveniently available (well-known relative to state tax revision commissions, certainly) – though perhaps better known when I started writing the first draft of this study in 1982 than now in 2006. The reader wishing to check the suggested approach can thus find out whether the approach works to the degree I claim it does. Moreover, going over these commissions in brief will provide a background for our discussion of the tax revision commissions, inasmuch as the reader will have been reminded what kinds of things to be looking for.

We should note that one way in which decision costs may have varied, or may have been perceived to vary, between Chicago 1919 and Harlem 1935, on the one hand, and Detroit 1943 on the other, lies in the fact that the Detroit riot was in time of war, and among the white rioters were soldiers and sailors in uniform (Platt 1971, pp. 240, 251-53). The in-uniform part applied, though not strongly, to Chicago 1919, but not the time-of-war part. In the wings to the Detroit stage was, among others, Congressman Martin Dies and his House Un-American Activities Committee (Platt 1971, p. 230). We would expect to find, all other things being equal, that the Detroit Commission would be less likely to come up with regulative recommendations than either of the others, since (from the Salisbury-Heinz model, as Tutchings uses it) we know that commissions with high decision costs and high demand will shy away from regulative recommendations (Tutchings 1979, p. 50).

There remains the question of personnel. We fortunately have some notes made by Francis W. Shepardson, who (in Governor Frank Lowden's name) chose the members of the commission in 1919 (Platt 1971, pp. 121-23). It is evident that this was an elite commission, but it was not a corporate/governmental elite: to find a member of the black elite in either corporation or government in Chicago in 1919 would have been impossible (the church and the law were the most likely spots), so this commission was technically mixed (Platt 1971, pp. 123-25). We do not have comparable notes on the 1935 Harlem Commission, but we know enough about Fiorello LaGuardia, who appointed it, enough about Harlem in the 1930s, and enough about the members who were appointed (such as Countee Cullen, Morris Ernst, A. Philip Randolph), to see the same kind of selection process at work (Platt 1971, p. 161). If the process was slightly more politicized for the Harlem commission, that made no difference, so far as the nature of the "mixed" commission was concerned (Tutchings 1979, pp. 96-112). At least it made no difference in its mixed-ness.

The 1943 Detroit Commission (the commission appointed by the Governor, not the twelve-member, biracial, and quite useless commission appointed by the Mayor) consisted of four members: County Prosecutor William Dowling, Detroit Police Commissioner John Witherspoon, State Attorney-General Herbert Rushton, and State Police Commissioner Oscar Olander (Platt 1971, pp. 201, 249). This commission does not fit neatly into the Tutchings paradigm, but it might be considered a restricted form of an "interest-group" commission (Bell's term) or a "public-interest" commission – though the idea of a public-interest commission composed entirely of lawmen is a bit paradoxical. It can be seen why this commission may be said to have had concealed goals.

Certainly this commission had an integrated decision system, high demand, and would by the Tutchings model be expected to come up with self-regulative or symbolic actions – though this typology is, as Tutchings recognizes, somewhat artificial (Tutchings 1979, pp. 50, 95). Note that the members' preferences were presumably single-peaked, with pretty much the same peak, that we might therefore expect a Condorcet solution identical with the median-optimum solution, but that this solution is unlikely to be Pareto-optimal (Koford 1982, p. 6). This brings up a point we should consider briefly before going on to the first of our taxation revision commissions. Unanimity of role – that is, agreed-upon decision premises (at least so far as the "role" subset is concerned) – is no guarantee of a "best" solution, only that a solution will be agreed upon. In the case of a white lawmen's commission on a race riot, this point may be evident: we will have cause to recollect it in a less-obvious context in Chapter V.

Meanwhile, we can summarize our tentative application of the model to these commissions, though the application has been sketchy – rather like running through scales on an instrument before settling down to play the piece. We have two significant Tutchings variables not held constant, decision costs and personnel inputs. As the Tutchings model suggests, these together are sufficient to predict the differing outcomes: self-regulative or symbolic in the Detroit case, regulative in others, though that is something of an oversimplification. The 1919 Chicago Commission, for example, made fifty-nine separate recommendations, none of which were for new laws, but a number of which were for the enforcement of laws or use of regulatory powers already in place (Platt 1971, pp. 106-119). For reasons suggested by our model (including bounded rationality), the Detroit outcome, though agreed-upon, was evidently non-optimal. If the role identification for Detroit had not been so very restrictive, perhaps there might have been a Pareto-optimal outcome, but what follows on our tax revision commissions suggests that Pareto-optimality is unlikely in any case.

Finally, we should note that time swallowed the Harlem Commission's recommendations (this is the "temporal demand variable" from Tutchings), a point we should keep in mind. And perhaps we should note that, for all we have tried to meld our various approaches together, a certain eclecticism still exists. Also, and far from unimportant, we have been speaking of Pareto-optimality without saying what, in the riot circumstances, it would have been: when we come to our tax revision commissions, we will be looking only for local optimality, recommendations that would "work" as we have defined that term in Chapter I. In the Detroit case, however, the locally optimal solution -- or equilibrium solution – was not a working solution in our terms. We shall see how important this kind of divergence may be for our commissions.

# CHAPTER III: THE PENNSYLVANIA COMMISSION OF 1889

The first Pennsylvania tax reform commission was created by act of the Legislature June 27, 1889 (Pennsylvania 1890, p. 5). It was originally to have seven members: the Auditor-General, by virtue of his office, a member selected by the Association of County Commissioners, a member appointed by the Governor to represent manufacturing interests, two members each having "given special study to the subject of taxation and who may be considered an authority on the same" -- one to be chosen by the Senate and one by the House, one member to represent financial and mercantile interests to be chosen by the House, and one member to represent agricultural interests to be appointed by the State Grange. The Senate passed the bill to establish the Commission with these seven members. The House amended it to provide for an eighth member, to "represent the wage workers of the Commonwealth" and to be appointed by the Governor. Evidently the eight-member Commission was viewed more as a meeting-place for the representatives of divergent interest-groups than as a blue-ribbon body representing the citizens of Pennsylvania as a whole.

In our last chapter we argued that if the person who appoints the members also sets the agenda, then the members and the agenda ought to be suited to each other. We also argued that the mere existence of differing subsets of "role" decision premises may limit the ability of one commission member to follow another's logic. And we noted that in groups containing subgroups or cliques, the equilibrium value of whole-group activity will decline as clique activity increases and that (with clique activity) there may be no equilibrium activity point for the group as a whole.

All of this (which may seem a technical way of expressing a common-sense truth) suggests that a commission chosen in accordance with the legislative mandate might in this case not have made any recommendation. Whatever may have been its reasons, the House of Representatives did not take the chance: instead, it appointed two of its former members, Austin L. Taggart and Samuel McClure [or McCune] Wherry, to the place of the authority on taxation and the representative of financial and mercantile interests, though both Taggart and Wherry were farmers. Which of them was supposed to fill which position I have been unable to determine. Both had been members of the House committees on Appropriations, on Federal Regulations, and on Ways and Means. Wherry was also a member of the committees on Counties and Townships, on Judiciary (Local), and on Revision and Reform, Taggart of that on the Bureau of Statistics (Smull 1887, pp. 683, 685, 709-15).

Of the two, Wherry had the more distinguished career, though that may not be saying much. He was born in Cumberland County on January 5, 1840 (or January 5, 1839), making him forty-nine years old (or fifty), had graduated from Princeton in 1860, studied law in Carlisle, been admitted to the Bar, served as a member of the Constitutional Convention of 1872-73, and edited the *Carlisle Volunteer* in 1877-78, before being elected to the House for the term beginning 1887. He was the losing Democratic candidate for Speaker in 1889. His biography describes him as a farmer "for revenue only" – which certainly does not place him as a representative of the mercantile or financial interests (Smull 1887, p. 685). Perhaps, as a lawyer and newspaperman, and

68

Constitutional Convention delegate, he had studied taxes. That is a supposition. What is sure is that he was a farmer.

Austin L. Taggart was Representative from Montgomery County in the 1887-88 session. He had been born at Tamaqua, Schuylkill County, on November 21, 1836, making him fifty-two, had been educated at the common schools, and had been all his life a farmer when he was elected to the House for that session. He died in 1894. Nothing in the available information suggests any mercantile or financial interests, or any *expertise* in taxation (Smull 1887, p. 683). It is hard to escape the conclusion that Wherry and Taggart were chosen by the House because they were ex-members known to be sympathetic to the agricultural interests. It is only a slight oversimplification to say that the contestants in the tax battle were the railroads and the farmers (Yearley 1970, pp. 39-41, 53-56, 62-66, 72-74). Here we should perhaps pause to note that when Yearley quotes the Report of the 1889 Pennsylvania Commission (pp. 51, 64-65, 66-71), he is in fact quoting John A. Wright's Minority Report, and to that extent the over-all Report will not bear the interpretation he places on it. It remains the case that the conflict was essentially between the farmers and the railroads.

In that conflict, Wherry and Taggart were not on the side of the railroads. That much is clear. Taggart's subsequent activities in the matter of tax reform can be traced in part through Olmsted (Olmsted 1892-96) and in the records of the Pennsylvania Tax Conference (Tax Conference 1892-96). What Wherry did after 1891, I do not know. In any case, the conflict between the House appointees and the Senate appointee is obvious, as we shall see.

The Senate's appointee could quite reasonably be considered a railroad man, though he had certainly "given special study to the subject of taxation" – as his notable minority report (Wright 1890) and earlier memorandum to the Commission (Wright 1889) both testify. This was John Armstrong Wright, far and away (in my view) the most accomplished and most interesting member of the Commission, and a man who should be in the *Dictionary of American Biography*. He was born in Philadelphia, on October 7, 1820, and was thus sixty-eight years old at his appointment and seventy when he filed his Report. (He died on November 2, 1891, so his service on the Commission was his swan song.) Even before his graduation from Dickinson College in 1838, he had been hired to join "an engineering corps" under H. Hage, surveying for a rail route to connect Philadelphia and Pittsburgh. After a short time with Hage, he went down to Georgia, working with J. Edgar Thomson, surveying an extension of the Georgia Railroad between Madison and Atlanta. His return to Philadelphia in the mid-1840s was marked by a series of articles in the *North American*, calling attention to the surveys he had worked on in 1838. (Montgomery 1923, pp. 85-88.) This series has been considered instrumental in the decision to grant the Pennsylvania Railroad a charter in 1846 (Watkins 1896, p. 337).

Wright was made a member of the Pennsylvania Railroad Board of Directors and was instrumental in Thomson's being hired as Chief Engineer (Ward 1980, p. 71). Two years later, Wright became head of the Freedom Iron Works in Mifflin County, where he was among the earliest (and virtually the only one unsuccessful) of the converts to the Bessemer Process (Morison 1966, pp. 191, 203). It was at Wright's house at the Freedom Forges, in 1851, that Thomson was persuaded to become President of the Pennsylvania, and for the rest of his life, Wright was considered as part of the "Philadelphia interests" surrounding Thomson (Ward 1980, p. 88). He retired from the Works in 1868, was thereafter appointed (1874, when Thomson died) as a member of the Commission to Investigate the Affairs of the Pennsylvania Railroad, served (1876-78) with a similar commission on the bankruptcy of the New York, Lake Erie, and Western, and then (1879) became a member of the Board of Railroad Arbitrators. It was Wright who laid out the City of Altoona (on what was originally his property), and at one time the Pennsylvania Railroad works there bore his name (Montgomery 1923). Short of naming someone in the active management of the Pennsylvania, it is difficult to see how the Senate could have picked a member more identified with railroads. That identification is evident in his minority report, but in very large part he rose above it – if indeed it was something that needed to be risen above, of which I am not sure.

Wright was the real "star" of the commission, both in background and in the quality of his thought. His dissenting *Report*, with his original *Memorandum*, deserves reprinting alongside Ely's 1888 Maryland Commission *Minority Report* for the detailed application of a theory of political economy to a specific "real world" case. Some distance behind Wright, but still men of considerable achievement and knowledge, were the Governor's "manufacturing interest" appointee, Albert Bolles, and his representative of the "wage workers of the Commonwealth" of Pennsylvania, William Martin – and perhaps his *ex officio* member, Auditor-General Thomas McCamant, subsequently chosen as Chairman of the Commission.

Albert S. Bolles was at this time Chief of the Bureau of Industrial Statistics at Harrisburg. He was forty-four years old, having been born in Montville, Connecticut, March 8, 1845, and admitted to the Bar there in 1865. Like Wherry, he was both lawyer and newspaper man – he was editor of the *Norwich* (Connecticut) *Bulletin* from 1875 to 1880. But at that point his career took a sudden turn: he became editor of the *Banker's Magazine*, and that led to his appointment as Professor of Mercantile Law and Banking at the new Wharton School of Commerce and Finance in 1883. Four years later he left Wharton to head the Bureau of Industrial Statistics. He wrote, among other books, an *Industrial History of the United States* (Norwich 1881), a *Financial History of the United States* (three volumes, New York 1894), a study on *The Conflict between Labor and Capital*, and (later) a *History of Pennsylvania*. After his service with the Bureau of Industrial Statistics, he taught at Drexel Institute of Technology (1895-97), now Drexel University, in Philadelphia, and then at Haverford College, Haverford, Pennsylvania (1897-1917). He died in retirement at Williamstown, Massachusetts, on May 8, 1939. (Cheyney and Oberholzer 1902, pp. 386-87, and *National Cyclopedia*, vol. 30, p. 270.)

Just as he appointed the Commissioner of the Bureau of Industrial Statistics to represent the manufacturing interests, so Governor Beaver appointed his Chief Factory Inspector "to represent the wage workers of the Commonwealth" – apparently acting (though not consciously, I assume) in accordance with that form of Progressivism given the name of the Wisconsin Idea, in which practical experience, government service, and intellectual understanding are and of right ought to be thoroughly intermixed. In any event, William H. Martin, who had been the first Factory Inspector of the Commonwealth appointed under the law of May 20, 1889, was appointed (late) to the Commission. After his service on the Commission he was a resident of Pittsburgh and active in labor affairs there: his papers (disappointingly meagre for the period 1889-91) are in the Darlington Collection at Pittsburgh. They deserve further study.

Auditor-General Thomas McCamant had the curious distinction of being the only member of the Commission to have seen active service in the War of the Rebellion, a very curious distinction indeed twenty-four years after a great civil war whose greatest battle was fought within the state. (John Armstrong Wright, serving as a Colonel in the Militia, had however been involved in matters of supply in the Gettysburg campaign.) McCamant, a graduate of Tuscarora Academy (Juniata County) and of Lafayette College, Class of 1861, had promptly volunteered and had served three years in the 125th Pennsylvania Volunteer Infantry (Smull 1887, p. lxxi, as also for what follows). He was admitted to the Bar in 1864. After the War, from 1867 to 1881, he was Chief Clerk in the Office of the Secretary of the Commonwealth, and then from 1881 to 1888 Chief Clerk in the Auditor-General's Department, before being appointed Auditor-General himself, to fill the vacancy created by the death of A. Wilson Norris. He was elected in his own right for the term beginning 1889: in that year (also, of course, the year in which he chaired the Commission) he was forty-nine. An associate of Republican political boss Matthew Quay, he was removed from office by Democratic Governor Pattison in 1891 (effective 1892). His son, Wallace McCamant, by the way, went west and was the Delegate who surprised the 1920 Republican Convention by upsetting the bosses' applecart and nominating Calvin Coolidge for Vice President.

Thus far we should have had the Commonwealth's own fiscal expert (the Auditor-General), two students of taxation, a representative of the manufacturing interests, a representative of the mercantile and financial interests, and a representative of the laboring interests or wage workers of the Commonwealth. In fact, we have three bureaucrats (one of them an academician as well) of whom one did well and truly represent the wage workers, we have two farmers, and we have one railroad man. Still to come to our attention are the representative of the County Commissioners (appointed by the Association of County Commissioners) and the representative of the Grange (appointed by the

73

Grange). If we assume (quite reasonably, under the circumstances) that wage workers and farmers would unite in opposing the "Philadelphia interests" or the Pittsburgh interests, and that the-farmers-against-the-railroads was the game being played, we should expect to find Wherry, Taggart, and Martin on one side, Wright on the other, and – given the proclivities of academicians – Bolles somewhere off on his own. He was, by the way, "a man of great versatility, possessed of a great fund of general information. Personally, he was cheerful, optimistic, witty, and humorous. . . . Travel was his chief recreation and he made numerous trips abroad" (*National Cyclopedia*, p. 270).

Now the Association of County Commissioners appointed one of those jacks-of-all-trades commoner in the nineteenth century than in the twentieth. His name was Giles D. Price: he was fifty years old, and just at this time he was Clerk in the Office of the County Commissioners for Erie County, and indeed had held that position since 1883. Before that he had been six years (1876-82) as Prothonotary of Erie County, and before that he had been – reading backwards in time – a miller in Venango County (for ten years), a prospector near Pike's Peak during the Colorado Gold Rush (for five years), and a salesman in and around Erie County, going back to the time he was sixteen, which is to say 1855 (Warner and Beers 1884, p. 340). Whatever the specific nature of his likes and dislikes, it must certainly be fair to conclude that Giles Price would be for the little man and the countryside, against the big man and the city (Price and Rhone 1890, pp. 1, 14-17).

Finally, the Grange chose as its representative its own leader, the Master of the Pennsylvania State Grange, Leonard Rhone. He had been born of an old Pennsylvania German family, on the family farm near Centre Hall, Centre County, on July 21, 1838, making him a month older than Price, or just short of fifty-one when the Commission was

74

appointed. Though he had taught for one year at the Tusseyville School (1858-59), he was a career farmer, Master of the Pomona (Centre County) Grange 1875 and re-elected five times, Master of the Centre Hall Grange 1877, Overseer of the Pennsylvania State Grange 1878, and Master of the State Grange and Trustee of the State College 1880, the year he declined the Greenback nomination for Congress. In 1892 he was an official of the National Grange. (Beers 1898 pp. 113-15, Yearley 1970, p. 209).

If indeed this was a commission whose members would vote in accordance with the desires of the "interests" they were representing, we could reasonably expect five of the eight members (Wherry, Taggart, Martin, Price, Rhone) to vote with the farmers and against the railroads. But because the members were not all appointed by the Governor (only three were), there is no reason to assume they would be well suited to the Governor's agenda. Moreover, if the "role" decision premises were strong, as they should be with the strong agriculture/countryside loyalties we discern, it is unlikely that the presumed five-member majority (perhaps Wherry?) would be able to follow the logic of the minority, or any one of its members. On the other hand, if this five-member majority is considered a clique (and we may so consider it), then by virtue of its size, it will substitute clique activity for whole-group activity. In other words, it will ram its own desires down the throats of the minority (Simon 1982, p. 481).

And so it did. In the event, the Commission's Majority Report was signed by ex-Representative Wherry (farmer), ex-Representative Taggart (farmer), Grange Master Rhone (farmer), Giles Price (ex-everything), and William Martin (for the "wage workers"). It was opposed in part by Chairman Thomas McCamant (who was at least knowledgeable on the subject of taxes), in much greater part by Albert

Sidney Bolles (who may have been more knowledgeable), and entirely by John Armstrong Wright (who was admittedly a railroad man, but who may have known more about state and national tax structures than everyone else on the Commission put together, and certainly more than everyone else but Bolles put together). The severity of Wright's opposition may well have come from his railroad experience, but it was justified and intelligent opposition, as several of his opponents later admitted (Tax Conference 1894, pp. 8-18).

The majority bill contained three major sections (17 through 19) dealing with transportation companies. The general flavor of these can be gained from the requirement that the chief officer of every transportation (read "railroad") company should report *on oath* "all matters and things pertaining to its property or its business, necessary to give a full and complete knowledge of the total aggregate value of all lands, buildings, superstructures, bridges, tunnels, viaducts, aqueducts, tracks, embankments, cuts, turntables, tools, implements, instruments, furniture, batteries, rolling stock, and all other property" (section 17), and the provision that any officer neglecting to make the report shall be automatically fined $1000 (in 1889, mind you), with any officer willfully making a false report – and no way is provided for determining what is "willfully" done – to be "adjudged guilty of perjury" apparently without a trial (section 18, with this being the purpose of the oath in section 17). In a phrase, sock it to 'em. (Pennsylvania 1890, pp. 25-27). Note that this is before the day of the Certified Public Accountant (Carey 1969).

Moreover, if the Auditor-General, under this law, were to decide the chief officer's valuation was wrong, he could fix his own. To paraphrase all this, by way of an example, if the President of the Pennsylvania Railroad could not provide the data necessary for a full and complete knowledge of the value of everything from the conductor's chair in the caboose (furniture) to the embankment or cut for the never-used or even never-built spur (embankments, cuts), to the screwdriver used to prop the window open in the freight station at Chester (tools), why then, make it possible for the Auditor-General to fix his own value, and declare the President to be guilty of perjury (never mind trial by jury – the report says "shall be adjudged guilty"). Lock him up and throw away the key. It is not perhaps surprising that the Auditor-General wanted no part of this (McCamant 1890, pp. 32-36).

This commission, as Wright felt it incumbent on himself to remind the commissioners, was established "to prepare a uniform revenue law covering both State and local taxation" – not to resolve the longstanding dispute between farmers and railroads (Wright 1890, pp. 37, 63). But the bill recommended by the majority made no reference to State taxes, and rather than adding uniformity it merely added new taxes on the local level. Moreover (and here one may suspect Wright of a rhetorical trick), the Constitution of the Commonwealth required the titles of bills to present an accurate view of their contents, but this report proposed the taxation of income from trades, occupations, or the investment of money or capital: in addition, it provided for an addition of county funds equal to about two thirds the annual amount of State and county taxes, thereby unbalancing the relationship between State and county taxes. These secondary points were doubtless true, but they were only secondary. The real gravamen of Wright's charges against the Majority Report lay in its attack on the railroads (Wright 1890, pp. 74-84).

"This bill" (he wrote) "is unjust in principle, impracticable in its provisions, and at many points illegal; it is unduly inquisitional . . . and contains no provisions by which its requirements may be made equally operative throughout the taxable districts of the state." Besides, "if its

77

provisions could be carried out, the bill would raise an amount far in excess of any possible claim that real estate owners could, with any pretence to justice, fairly demand" (Wright 1890, p. 37). This last point may be considered his response to the preamble of the bill recommended by the Majority Report – "whereas, It is desirable to largely increase the State appropriation for the support of the public needs, out of an increased taxation upon the capital stock of certain corporations . . ." (Pennsylvania 1890, p. 9). By which, of course, was meant certain railroad corporations, and (this being Pennsylvania) one railroad corporation in particular.

The lines, then, were well and truly drawn: the majority on one side, Wright on the other. And that was unfortunate, because Wright had what the majority did not, a clear view of the whole process of taxation – clearer, I believe, than the view of Albert Bolles, and certainly clearer than the view of the public at large. Despite the fact that no one on the Commission was listening, and indeed that our theory tells us no one could have been listening (or at least it was unlikely they could have been), Wright's views are worth rehearsing here. We will hear some of them again, and in general they provide a framework for considering the mandate not only of this commission but of succeeding commissions.

Wright draws a distinction between the purposes of State taxation and those of local taxation. "The objective point of State taxation is to enable the different departments of the State government to carry out and enforce the provisions of the Constitution of the State, to execute the laws of the Commonwealth, and broadly to care for the people" (Wright 1890, p. 39). Thus the State raises money to pay the expenses of the Legislature, of the Executive, of the Judiciary, of the public schools, public orphanages, insane asylums, houses of correction, prisons, and the State's military organizations (Wright 1890, p. 40). On the other hand, the tax laws for counties, cities, boroughs, and townships "should be confined and limited to raising the moneys necessary for the care and support of the respective local interests" – these being health, local courts, police, jails, poorhouses, streets and roads, bridges, sewers, water mains, lights, public parks, and (perhaps curiously) higher education.

In Wright's view, all state taxes should be levied on earnings, from the workings of all capital, all labor, and all real property, by whomsoever owned or provided – not on the capital, or on the labor, or on the real property but on their earnings, specifically their net earnings (Wright 1890, p. 41). Contrariwise, local taxes should be levied first on "the real estate within the bounds of a municipal body" (real estate whose protection and enhancement is one of the responsibilities of the municipal body) and then on retail liquor licenses (which tend to provide business for the courts, police, jails, poorhouses, and so on), and then on "horses, mules, oxen, wagons, carriages, omnibuses, stages, and all vehicles used locally for the transportation of persons or freight" (Wright 1890, p. 58). Finally, there is to be a local tax on amusement licenses. The principle is one of suitability: roads are local, so a local tax for their support is levied on local vehicles; the municipality cares for its sick or its poor or its drunks out of locally-raised revenues because they are local problems; property whose value is enhanced by sewers is taxed to pay for the sewers. And meanwhile, the state pays for matters which are statewide concerns, out of a uniform tax levied statewide.

But such theorizing could not be heard by the majority. It was heard, and to some extent answered, by Bolles, who argued that the State's principal tax should be precisely on those railroads Wright was defending. The "principal revenue for the State should be from railroads" (he argued) inasmuch as "a railroad company is a creation of the state, and lives by its permission" so that "the entire State ought to share in the tax or return made by the company" – which would have meant State rather than local taxation of the railroads (Bolles 1890, pp. 154-55). This seems to have made quite as much impression on the majority as Wright's arguments made, which is to say, none at all.

Even when Wright was clearly arguing from experience, as he did on Section 17, no one was listening. "In the first place, it is questioned if the officers of any railroad company could answer the questions named in that section of the bill. This will be evident to any one acquainted with the details of the cost of railways, and secondly, if the questions could be answered, no Auditor-General and no State Treasurer could fix 'a (proper) value upon all the property of such . . . companies" (Wright 1890, p. 77). Perhaps McCamant listened here: he did, after all, propose his own bill without this provision. But the majority clearly did not listen, and by our hypothesis could not.

Even when Wright pointed out the nearly self-evident fact that no Auditor-General, or anyone else, could be expected (within any reasonable time) to check the values of "two hundred and fifty (250) railway corporations in the State, with property and assets valued at some seventeen hundred millions of dollars ($1,700,000,000), some seventy-five (75) passenger railway companies costing nearly thirty millions of dollars ($30,000,000)" – to say nothing of seven canal companies and "numerous other transportation and transmission companies" – no one (except, again, perhaps McCamant) was listening. (Wright 1890, pp. 77-78.) The roles of the Commission members as interest-group representatives left no hearing space for what Wright was saying.

In the end it was McCamant, who seems to have disagreed with everyone, who wrote the Minority Report that was eventually passed into law by the Legislature, with an appropriately agricultural preamble

80

and a few additions and amendments (Pennsylvania 1890, pp. 167-70, Pennsylvania Laws 1891, pp. 229-43). Since McCamant was the Governor's man, and since the Governor signed the bill, and since the Governor's party controlled the Legislature, it is not unlikely that the bill, or something very like it, was what the Governor intended for the Commission's agenda all along. The Commission got out of hand, so to speak, but not disastrously out of hand.

But what of our view that the interest-group commission is least likely to have a single preferred alternative (Condorcet solution) or to have a Dodgson solution inasmuch as existing preference orderings are unlikely to have significant overlappings. The improbability of a Dodgson solution, as we noted, does not hold if only a few parts of the "public interest" are being represented, and a Condorcet solution will occur whenever there is a built-in majority. After all, a Condorcet solution is "any alternative proposed which is preferred by a majority to each and every other alternative" (Grofman 1981, p. 24). Thus, when the House of Representatives chose farmers Wherry and Taggart, rather than a tax expert and a representative of the mercantile interests, it short-circuited the interest-group requirement in such a way that a Condorcet solution could be achieved (which would be equivalent to a Dodgson solution if there was a trade-off for Martin or Price). But there was a cost involved.

Specifically, the cost was that the Majority Report did not propose a law designed to solve the particular problem for which the Commission was given its mandate – preparing "a uniform revenue law covering both State and local taxation" (Pennsylvania 1890, p. 3). Nor – and this may be considered a second cost – did the Majority Report find its way into law. Nor – which may be considered a third cost – did the Commission's majority succeed in rectifying the situation which caused

81

the Commission to be assembled, or even the situation which the majority seemed to think had caused it to be assembled. In other words, what they recommended was irrelevant to their mandate; it was not passed into law; if it had been passed into law it would have made little or no difference (being utterly impracticable); and, in any case, the perceived imbalance between the tax burden on farmers and the tax burden on railroads did not in fact exist. (I will return to this last point shortly.) To put the matter briefly, the 1889 Pennsylvania Commission, as a commission (through not perhaps as a smokescreen laid down to get what the Governor wanted before the Legislature), was a failure. Its success was that it came to a conclusion. And if the House had not violated its mandate, quite probably even that limited success might not have been achieved.

It is, of course, possible that the presence of, say, another member of the "Philadelphia interest" (in the unlikely event the House had appointed one) and of another bureaucrat (in the unlikely event the House had appointed one of those) could have allowed for log-rolling and some kind of preferred outcome. There would then have been a three-farmer/three-bureaucrat/two-railroader line-up. But given the paucity of possible trade-offs, I should not care to bet even then on a preferred outcome. (The line-up here counts William H. Martin as being allied with the farmers – that is, with Price and Rhone.)

Admittedly, it could be argued that the Commission did finally have one of its recommendations passed into law, albeit it was the recommendation made by McCamant in his dissenting opinion. Perhaps we should ask whether the law did redress the balance between "moneyed capital" and local property holders. If taxes on moneyed capital were only about 10 percent of total taxes in 1888-89, as claimed in (Pennsylvania 1890), was the situation any better in 1898-99 or 1908-

82

09? For answering these questions we may seek two kinds of evidence. First, did the agricultural interests, and their allies, rest content with their success – did they even deem it success – or did they keep trying new ways to reach the same goal? Or did they perhaps decide, improbably, on future reflection, that the goal had been achieved before the Commission came into being? Granted that achievement may breed discontent – as with "revolutions of rising expectations" – it should be possible to tell whether continued discontent is feeding on achievement or the lack thereof. Second, did the incidence of taxation in fact undergo any significant change in the relevant period? Did taxes on moneyed capital provide a greater portion of total tax revenues after the bill than they did before? This is not, to be sure, the best way to ask this question: we should ideally be asking whether the burden of payment (presumably relative to the ability to pay) was shifted from property holders to corporations, which is to say moneyed capital. But if we assume that economic fluctuations altering the real burden of taxation were in fact unpredictable, then we can take the amounts paid in the various taxes in 1888, 1898, and 1908 as fairly representing the bill's success in altering the tax burden – or at least as the best proxy we have for that success.

In answer to the first question, whether the agricultural interests were content with McCamant's bill – in a word, no. The Tax Conference of Pennsylvania Interests, a private group whose members included Leonard Rhone and Austin Taggart (both representing agriculture) and Giles Price (representing the county commissioners), was established in 1891-92: "This conference" (reported the Harrisburg *Patriot*) "has grown out of the defeat of the Taggart tax bill by the last Legislature and a desire to harmonize the great interests of the state" (Olmsted 1892-96, February 5, 1892). The convention was urged by

83

State Senator John Price of Scranton after McCamant's substitute bill was passed, its purpose being to formulate a plan "on the basis of which the tax lines could be equitably adjusted" (Yearley 1970, pp. 21-23, quoting C. Stuart Patterson) – so much for the McCamant bill.

Before answering the second question by appeal to the relevant statistical data, we may profitably follow the tergiversations of the Tax Conference of Pennsylvania Interests during the 1890s, since these give support to our initial conclusion that the McCamant bill did little or nothing to correct perceived inequities – or, if one prefers less emotionally-charged language, to alter the incidence of taxation. The Tax Conference appointed a committee "to examine the Tax Laws of other American States and report an opinion for or against the governing principles embraced therein" (*Tax Conference* 1892, pp. [unnumbered], 1). This, by the way, John A. Wright had done in 1889-90 as part of his preliminary memorandum to the Commission members. The tax law examination committee of the Tax Conference was to have as two of its members Leonard Rhone and Giles Price.

The committee's report seems to show some impatience with the kind of approach through political economy that Wright had taken: "As we understand the resolution, our duty seems to be not to find theories with which to construct an ideal tax system . . . but to show the trend of opinion among practical men, who are in touch with the every day life of the American people. Theories, however symmetrical or logical, are apt to go to pieces when brought into contact with the stubborn realities of taxation" (*Tax Conference* 1892, p. 14). (What a beautiful illustration of the difference between Populists and Progressives!) But it concludes, meekly enough, that there ought to be uniform assessment, and that it might be reasonable to set certain property aside for state assessment, certain property for county assessment, and certain property for purely

84

local assessment *(Tax Conference* 1892, pp. 14-17). The committee members were still opposed to an income tax, but they are more moderate than the majority on the 1890 Commission, only two years before.

Indeed, the whole of the 1892 Conference Report is highly instructive for our purposes. Like the 1889 Commission, the Conference was an interest-group meeting-place. Like the Commission, it had five major interests – agriculture (five members), transportation (four members), county commissioners (four), manufacturing (eight), and labor (four, of whom only one stuck with it). Like the Commission, it was weighted against the railroads, though not so strongly. But unlike the Commission, it had no easy answers, and its committee on railroad valuation was set up to study the matter further, which it did – and in 1894 it reported that "the railroads of Pennsylvania paid on the average at least as high a millage rate of taxation as the average millage of all classes of property in Pennsylvania" *(Tax Conference* 1894, p. 18). This sounds rather like a recantation, if indeed Rhone and Price subscribed to this report – rather like saying the perceived inequity had never existed in the first place. The 1892 Report had concluded that the assessed valuation of Pennsylvania real estate generally was just under 70 percent of actual value, while nowhere in the state did the assessment of rural realty rise above one third of the true (Weeks 1892, *passim*).

Even so, we may still ask whether the incidence of taxation (or our proxy variable, the percentage of revenues from various sources) changed between 1888 and 1898 or 1908. In 1888-89 total state tax revenues were just under $8.5 million, of which just over $4.5 million were from corporate sources, or roughly 53.6 percent. In 1898-99 total state tax revenues were roughly $15.5 million, of which just over $8.0 million were from corporate sources, or 51.9 percent. In 1908-09 total state tax revenues were just under $28 million, with just under $17 million from corporate sources, or roughly 60.4 percent. The changing percentages would seem to be attributable for the most part to economic fluctuations rather than to any changes in tax policy: thus, for example, in 1909-10, with no changes in the tax laws from 1908-09, the figures were roughly $16.3 million from corporate sources, and $12.2 million non-corporate, with the corporate percentage being less than 58.0 (*Pennsylvania Auditor-General* 1898, 1908, 1909). We can state with some assurance that the corporate burden rose somewhat after 1900, and that the rise had nothing to do with the activities of the 1889 Commission.

If our concern were solely with the success or failure of the Commission, there might be little more to say. But a comparison between the activities of the Tax Conference and those of the Commission reveals something about the reasons for the failure, beyond what we have already revealed. The difference in tone between the Taggart bill of 1891 (recommended by the *Majority Report* signed by Rhone and Price as well as Taggart) and the Conference reports of 1892 and 1894 (subscribed to by Taggart and Rhone and Price) is instructive, and I think it may be traced to a difference in mandate.

Here is the Permanent Chairman of the Tax Conference of Pennsylvania Interests, Joseph D. Weeks (a railroad man, by the way), speaking to the members in the 1892 Report (*Tax Conference* 1892, p. 2): "I express the hope – in which I think I am joined by you – that nothing piecemeal shall be done, but that any action that is taken by this Conference, shall be, not in detail, but broadly, generally. We should seek a revision of our taxing system, not a detailed amending of our present laws." But of course it was precisely a detailed amending of the present laws that the members of the 1889 Commission believed

86

themselves to be seeking (*Pennsylvania* 1890, pp. 9-31). This brings us back to the question of the body's mandate.

When the body's mandate is specific – a legislative action, for example, with redistributive goals – experience teaches us that the desired outcome is unlikely. Much more likely would be what Tutchings has called symbolic or knowledge/plan actions, which were on the Conference's agenda, but not on the Commission's (*Tax Conference* 1892, pp. 1-2, *Pennsylvania* 1890, pp. 3-5). Moreover, as we noted, a fit between members and agenda is much less likely if they are not chosen by the same agent than if they are: the Tax Conference, as a body, chose itself and its agenda, while the Commission had the Governor's agenda combined with appointment by five agents. It might be argued, of course, that a limited mandate (to pass a law) would reduce search space and render commission members more likely to move out of their accustomed "role" decision premises: indeed, we shall see that something very like this happened with the 1919 Commission. Contrariwise, it might be thought that the less-defined mandate of the Tax Conference would have expanded search space requirements and tied the members more closely to their roles.

It did not, at least not so far as the roles in question were those of "farmer" or "railroad man" or "labor leader" – because, it may be suggested, there was no time limit on the desired goal, and because there was no pre-existent majority representing one "interest" (as with agriculture on the 1889 Commission), and because the size of the Tax Conference (twenty-five members) moved it out of the realm of decision-making into the realm of conversation, and would have so moved it even if it had a limited-time mandate to come up with specific amendments to Pennsylvania law. If the 1919 Commission is adduced as evidence that a narrowed mandate, and therefore narrowed required search space, will allow a relaxation of "role" decision premises, it must be remembered that the make-up of the 1919 Commission was substantially different from that of McCamant's Commission – and specifically that Governor Sproul chose the 1919 members on geographic rather than ideological grounds, so far as we know.

Even though the Tax Conference was designed, indeed self-designed, for "knowledge/plan" outcomes, which are generally the easiest to achieve, it did not in fact come up with much in that line. A little plaintively, Rhone and Giles Price noted that "The members have sought to obtain the facts asked for by their appointment, but the time at their command has not been sufficient to enable them to effect a complete harmony of views" (*Tax Conference* 1892, p. 17). And it is worth recalling here, lest we think of Pennsylvania as having more than ordinarily difficult tax problems, that this was all taking place in a state widely regarded as possessing "model fiscal machinery, complete with an extensive system of general corporate taxation" and extracting from its corporations more than twice the revenues extracted by New York or Massachusetts, its closest rivals (Yearley 1970, p. 208).

It would appear that when Rhone and Price were released from the roles (that is, the decision premises) provided them by the mandate for the 1889 Commission, they grew less sure of their ground. When they were asked, not to contend with John Wright's data and ideas, but to come up with their own, they seem to have retreated temporarily. This does not mean that the Commonwealth of Pennsylvania ceased to be riven by the struggle of farmer against corporation, or even that the Tax Conference failed to reflect that struggle: in 1895 the Conference supported, indeed was the motivating force behind, the so-called Riter Bill (H.R. 230), which crystallized "that bitter controversy which has been waged for so many years between the corporate and agricultural interests of this Commonwealth" (Yearley 1970, p. 208, quoting Stuart Patterson). But it does suggest that the decision premises enforced by the mandate and method of selection for the 1889 Commission were what operated to produce its *Majority Report*. We noted at the end of Chapter I that the less the importance of roles, the smaller must be the percentage of the decision premises encompassed in these roles, the greater must be the open search space, the more expert must be the decision-makers, or the more circumscribed their mandate. In this case, the relaxing of the roles revealed the inexpertise of the presumed experts in question.

It remains to be asked whether there was any functional relationship between the elite members of the McCamant Commission and the passage of its recommendations into law (or their failure to be passed). We may reasonably consider as elite members of the Commission John Armstrong Wright, Albert Sidney Bolles, perhaps Thomas McCamant, perhaps William H. Martin, perhaps Leonard Rhone, but not Price, not Taggart, and not Wherry (even though he went to Princeton). In other words, the elite members were far from agreeing among themselves, and the only members then or thereafter fitting Digby Baltzell's definition of a Philadelphia gentleman were strongly against the Majority Report (Baltzell 1958, *passim*). If there is, as Tutchings suggests, a positive correlation between the passage of commission recommendations into law and the presence of élite members, we should expect to find that the Majority Report was not passed into law, as of course it was not.

We have four commissions still to consider, and as we consider them we should be using what we have found out about the 1890 Commission as a set of benchmarks to measure our theories and hypotheses against. Would a narrower mandate lead to greater success?

Would such a mandate have to be combined with less ideological grounds for the choice of members? Would an élite (or "blue-ribbon") commission have better success with a broad mandate than this interest-group commission had? Would a two-part agenda, with the first part involving only symbolic or "knowledge/plan" goals, have a better chance of success than an open single-stage agenda? Can commissions whose membership does not include a ready-made majority even come up with a Condorcet or even a Dodgson solution? Does a divorce between agenda-setting and power of appointment always lead to failure (always in our experience that is)?

The 1889 Commission was indeed a failure, by the standards we set out in Chapter I. It failed to recommend a law that would have produced greater tax equity (if anything it would have lessened it). It failed to produce a law that was passed. The *Minority Report* that was passed into law did not, so far as we can measure it, have any noticeable effect on the incidence of taxation on the state level. In fact, the major effect of any law on the incidence of taxation in our period may have come from the tightening of the five-mill capital tax in 1907 (*Pennsylvania Laws* 1907, pp. 431-32, 441). We have not the data to measure the effect of McCamant's law on the incidence of local taxation, except to say that McCamant himself did not believe there had been any (*Auditor-General* 1898, p. vi).

Moreover, it is worth noting that the McCamant Commission apparently did not even serve propaganda purposes, at least not successfully: in the remote event that its true agenda involved educating the Legislature to the need for a kind of reform, rather than getting a particular bill passed, it was still a failure. (Recall that Tutchings found significantly greater success for commissions recommending the passage of laws to a specific end than for those recommending the passage of specific laws.) Four years after the Commission reported, the Riter Bill – designed not merely to rationalize railroad taxation but to levy taxes on "a large amount of valuable property" that was escaping state taxation (Yearley 1970, p. 211) – was defeated, not passed, by the Legislature. It is true that this failure was unimportant in itself, since the railroads were already busily changing the foundations on which the Tax Conference's criteria for taxing them were based, but it is important for telling us something about the McCamant Commission's success in public, or legislative, relations.

Before we go on to the other Pennsylvania tax revision commissions falling within our purview – 1919 (the Mercur Commission), 1923 (the Edmonds Commission), and 1947 (the Matthews Commission) – we should turn aside to look at a commission widely thought to be a model, widely considered successful, and highly relevant to our inquiry. This is the Kennan Commission in Wisconsin in 1897-98. Before we look at the Kennan Commission, we should remind ourselves of what appears at this late date a somewhat curious fact: it is not accidental, and certainly not out of the ordinary (as Chapter I should have made clear) that the business man on the McCamant Commission, John Armstrong Wright, supported a general income tax, while the Greenbackers or Populists (large-P or small) or the "agricultural interests" were all thinking along the lines of a land-based or property-based tax. To propose an income tax (especially if it is not a graduated income tax, but even if it is) is to argue that it does not make a difference whether income is derived from capital or labor or even land. To propose a tax on wealth is to reduce the earning power of capital by taking some of the capital away, while leaving the earning power of labor intact. And when the capital (as with the railroads) blends into real property, the Populist can attack both kinds of wealth in one breath.

91

Let us now turn to Kossuth Kent Kennan and the Wisconsin State Tax Commission of 1897-98.

# CHAPTER IV: THE WISCONSIN COMMISSION OF 1897

We come now to another state and to the apparent exception that tests the rule, what I have called the Kennan Commission, officially the Wisconsin State Tax Commission of 1897 (Wisconsin 1897, p. 5). This had its origins – not coincidentally – in the same year that the McCamant Commission was formed, that is, in 1889 (Philipp 1973, p. 100). In that year, Kossuth Kent Kennan, then thirty-seven years of age, the tax commissioner of the Wisconsin Central railroad company, had drawn up a bill creating a State Tax Commission, and had arranged for Representative Peter Leonard of Price County to introduce the bill into the State Legislature. The bill did not pass, but as Emanuel Philipp (later Governor of Wisconsin) observed in his history of tax reform in the state, the seed was planted that bore fruit eight years later (Philipp 1973, p. 101).

Kennan believed (in Philipp's words) that "if a commission of competent men were employed to compile statistics relating to the taxes collected, together with facts concerning the operations of the laws, the inequalities and injustice necessarily attending upon the enforcing of the illogical, conflicting and uncertain statutes by taxing officers with elastic consciences, the consequence would be a speedy attempt to remedy the defects in the system" (Philipp 1973, pp. 100-01). Compare John A. Wright's views in his "Memorandum" – especially his statement that "no one will claim that the revenue laws of any State are wholly based on equitable principles. . . . revenue laws are unfair and unjust. . . . our present system of taxation is an aggregation of partial remedies applied at various times" (Wright 1889, pp. 38-39). The complaint is certainly a common one, as Clifton Yearley's history makes clear (Yearley 1970, pp. 37-95, *passim*).

But Kennan had more than a little trouble in convincing the Governor and the Legislature that the project was worthwhile. For one thing, he was out of the state during the 1891 and 1893 sessions, though a bill similar to his was passed by the House in 1893, before dying in the Senate (Philipp 1973, p. 101). For another – and this one more important – the Governor either had no faith that a commission would work, or else he was afraid it would: which of the two was his reason is not entirely clear, though I would lean to the second, for reasons given below. I suspect that Kennan was playing Peck's bad boy to the Governor. In any event, another Kennan bill, this one introduced by Representative William O'Neal of Bayfield County, passed the House in the 1895 session, before it too died in the Senate.

At this point Kennan was convinced the problem lay in the appropriation for the commission's expenses, or so Emanuel Philipp tells us (Philipp 1973, pp. 102-03). Whether for that purpose, or simply to rally public opinion to his side, after his bill (introduced by Representative Merriam of Rock County) had once again passed the House – in 1897 – and once again failed in the Senate, Kennan decided to amend the bill by cutting out the appropriation – whereupon the bill passed both House and Senate, and whereupon Governor Schofield threatened to veto it. "He frankly stated that he would not be put in the position of asking men competent to perform so important a work for the benefit of the state to give their time and pay their own expenses while in the state's service" (Philipp 1973, p. 103). Whatever the Governor's motives (and I am profoundly suspicious), Kennan promptly assured the Governor that private funds could be raised to pay the estimated $4,500 cost of the commission, and the Governor thereupon signed the bill into law.

I am taking Emanuel Philipp's word for it that what Kennan wanted was a fact-finding commission. We should note, however, that the Kennan Commission mandate was not restricted to fact-finding: besides compiling laws, statistics, complaints, and information on what other states were doing, the commissioners were to "make such recommendation as to the revision of the lax laws of Wisconsin, or as to the enactment of new laws, as they may deem necessary, in order to simplify, condense and improve the present system and equalize the burden of taxation upon all classes of property" (*Wisconsin* 1897, p. 6). Here we are with equalization and property taxes once again -- the key words for virtually all efforts at tax reform in those days (Yearley 1970, pp. 193-223, *passim*). There were exceptions, as we noted before, and one of these, curiously enough, was Wisconsin, though not in 1897 (Brownlee 1971, pp. 41-64 and 123-34).

Indeed, the history of tax reform in Wisconsin in the years from 1889 to 1911 is the history of a revolution in the hearts and minds of men, and it was a revolution begun by Kossuth Kent Kennan. This is not the opinion of recent historians of the Wisconsin income tax: Elliot Brownlee, for example, refers to Kennan only as a "Milwaukee member of the 1897 Tax Commission" (in a footnote) and as "a Milwaukee proponent of steeper utility taxation" with only a passing mention of Kennan's historical study of income taxation (Brownlee 1971, pp. 124, 47, 53). But Brownlee's reconstruction of events does not really explain how it was that only five years passed between the Kennan Commission's report and the beginning of the drive for state income taxation. I would argue that it was precisely the widespread acceptance of Kennan's report that led to the successor Tax Commission's enjoying

95

"extraordinary prestige and confidence" (in the words of the late Harold Groves). But that is getting ahead of our story. (Groves n.d., p. 1.)

Besides Kennan, the other members of the Commission were Burr Jones of Madison and George Curtis of Merrill (*Wisconsin* 1897 p. 7). It might reasonably be asked why, if the Commission was Kennan's brainchild (as I have suggested it was), he was not chosen as Chairman. The answer is hinted at by Governor Scofield's equivocal response to the bill without the appropriation: he wanted to make sure the Commission did not get out of hand, and so Burr W. Jones of Madison became Chairman. Jones was a Gold Democrat, and the Gold Democrats were in a somewhat uneasy alliance with the conservative or Stalwart Republicans in Wisconsin (Margulies 1968, pp. 29ff).

Jones was at this time almost fifty-two (he was to die in his eighty-ninth year, in 1935). He had been born in Evansville, Rock County, Wisconsin, graduated from the Evansville Academy, and then taught school before attending the University of Wisconsin at Madison, where he took his B.A. in 1870, his LL.B. in 1871, his M.A. in 1874, and was eventually given his LL.D. *honoris causa* in 1916 (*Congress* 1971, p. 1202, *Who Was Who* 1942, p. 646). He was Dane County District Attorney 1872-76, member of the Forty-eighth Congress 1883-85 (as a Democrat), and in 1885 became Professor of Law at the University. He was Chairman of the Democratic State Convention in 1892 and Delegate to the Gold Democrats' National Convention in 1896. After his retirement from the Law School he was Associate Justice of the Wisconsin Supreme Court 1920-26 (*Congress* 1971, p. 1202, correcting *Who Was Who* 1942, p. 646). The Kennan Commission represented his sole foray into the tax field, though he was the author of a notable study on *The Law of Evidence in Civil Cases* (fourth edition, in six volumes, 1926), and his name is still remembered in Madison, though Burr Jones

96

Field there is named after Burr W. Jones, Jr. It is hard to escape the conclusion that Jones was not appointed to the Commission because of his tax *expertise*.

The third commissioner appointed by Governor Scofield was George Curtis, Jr., of Merrill, an ally of the Governor. He was subsequently appointed First Assistant Commissioner of Taxation on the Wisconsin Tax Commission appointed for ten years beginning May 1, 1899 (*Wisconsin* 1901, pp. 5-7). A lawyer for the lumbering interests, he was born in 1851 and died in 1922 (*Wisconsin Bar* 1924, pp. 8-9). When he was First Assistant Commissioner, the Commissioner of Taxation then appointed was Michael Griffin of Eau Claire, and the Second Assistant Commissioner was Norman S. Gilson of Fond du Lac. But when Griffin died on December 29, 1899, Governor Scofield passed over Curtis and appointed Gilson as Commissioner (*Wisconsin* 1901, p. 7). The distinctions of Tax Commissioner, First Assistant, and Second Assistant were in any case abolished when the Commission was made permanent in 1905, but this is to get ahead of our story (Phelan 1908, p. 343).

The very fact that the 1897 Commission had only three members (two Chiefs and only one Brave, so to speak) sets it apart from all other state tax revision commissions both before and after 1897. No other commission had less than five members. The fact that the Commission passed almost directly into existence as a continuing body also and especially sets it apart, and we shall turn to this shortly. But for the meantime, we should look at the size of the Commission, in connection with what we have said so far about the behavior of commissions. After that, we shall talk about its mandate, the mandate of the successor Wisconsin Tax Commission of 1899, and the degree of continuity between the two, and indeed between the Kennan Commission and the permanent Wisconsin Tax Commission of 1905-39.

It was Professor Northcote Parkinson who suggested that the ideal size for a policy-making committee was five, "allowing for two members to be absent or sick at any one time" (Parkinson 1957). But with the Wisconsin State Tax Commission of 1897, it is arguable that only Kennan was really needed, inasmuch as the Commission had decided to restrict its activities to fact-finding, except for what was virtually its single recommendation (Kennan 1897, pp. 181-82, and Phelan 1906, p. 341). "Meetings to hear complaints and suggestions of tax-payers and to study the needs of special localities" were held "at various points in the state, including Milwaukee, Madison, La Crosse, Eau Claire, Chippewa Falls, Superior, Ashland, Merrill, Wausau, Marinette and Oshkosh" (*Wisconsin* 1897, p. 7). But there is no indication that the report would have differed significantly in its final form if not one of those meetings had ever been held. The report begins with the Danegeld (Kennan 1897, p. 11) and ends with a review of tax commissions in other states (Kennan 1897, pp. 169-81). Much of the work can be paralleled by parts of Kennan's study of the income tax (Kennan 1910), and the whole is clearly almost entirely his. The testimony at best provided corroborative evidence.

That Kennan wrote the report we know, and we know that he was one of Wisconsin's three chief experts in taxation. Neither of the other two, Richard Ely (whom we have met briefly in connection with the Maryland Report of 1888, and in the Introduction and Dedication) and Delos Kinsman (a student of Ely's at Wisconsin), was much involved with the 1897 Commission. The question may reasonably be asked, "Why?" The answer would seem to be that this was, despite its small size, an interest-group as well as a blue-ribbon commission – a railroad man (who had virtually forced the Commission into being), the Governor's man as Chairman (as with McCamant in Pennsylvania), and Curtis as agriculturalist (lumberman) to counterbalance Kennan's presumed railroad sympathies. Note that the Commission was required to have one lawyer, but since Jones, Kennan, and Curtis all fitted that bill, the requirement was not what kept Ely or Kinsman off.

Although the "Wisconsin Idea" had already come into being by the 1890s, it had apparently not yet taken as firm root as it had by the 1920s and 1930s, when it was University men like Edwin Witte and Paul Rauschenbush, and women like Elizabeth Brandeis Rauschenbush, who drew up plans for Social Security and Unemployment Compensation. By the Wisconsin Idea, it will be remembered, I mean the idea that professional experts, from varying backgrounds, working through commissions, can determine proper courses of action more efficiently than they can be determined by ordinary political process. Both the Kennan Commission and its successor should be considered in connection with this idea, and indeed the Wisconsin Idea itself is interesting as representing a midpoint between the interest-group approach of the 1890s and the blue-ribbon approach of the 1920s. I may note that I have come to this view as the result of writing this paper: initially, despite eight years' residence in Wisconsin (six in Madison), I had thought of the Wisconsin Idea as virtually synonymous with blue-ribbon Progressivism.

Though it was Charles McCarthy, as we noted in the Preface, who wrote the book called *The Wisconsin Idea*, it was men like Richard Ely, John R. Commons, and Charles R. Van Hise, at the University end of State Street, and Robert La Follette at the Capitol end, who gave it form (Thelen 1976, pp. 108-09, Margulies 1968, p. 131). The description by Herbert Margulies is worth quoting. "Madison's State Street was a

99

much-used thoroughfare during the Progressive Era, for it connected the University of Wisconsin with the state Capitol. Traffic moved in both directions. John R. Commons, Balthasar Meyer, Richard T. Ely, Charles R. Van Hise, and many other scholars gave advice and sometimes administrative service to the state. La Follette and many of his lieutenants, in turn, as devoted alumni of the University of Wisconsin, tried to use their power to help their alma mater and to make fullest use of the services of faculty and students in the business of government. The relationship became known as the Wisconsin Idea." (Margulies 1968, p. 131.)

That sounds very much like an intellectual or University version of the blue-ribbon idea. But in juxtaposition to this should be set the words of John R. Commons, that "leading representatives of conflicting interests" should determine what was best (in the instant case, the conditions of labor) without pressure from politicians or consumers (quoted in Thelen 1976, p. 109). Commons was very much the leading example of an academician in service to the State of Wisconsin, as a member of the Industrial Commission, which one historian has called the "most famous feature of the Wisconsin Idea" (Thelen 1976, p. 109). If Commons thought, as he evidently did, that the salient feature of the Wisconsin Idea was the presence of representatives of leading interests, then it would seem that the Wisconsin Idea is indeed a bridge between the interest groups and the blue ribbon commissions.

The Wisconsin State Tax Commission of 1897, which I have called the Kennan Commission, though non-partisan at the time, has become a partisan historical (or historiographical) football. David Thelen, for example, has summarized the creation of the Commission in these words: "At the state level, the insurgents, led by the Milwaukee Municipal League, had trebled utility taxes, repealed a special

100

exemption law for utilities, and created a statewide commission to redistribute the tax burden" (Thelen 1976, pp. 26-27). But this is surely a very strange way of saying that an old-line Republican Governor was bullied by the Tax Commissioner of the Wisconsin Central Railroad into appointing a fact-finding commission consisting of that Commissioner, a prominent Gold Democrat, and a minor Republican ally of the Governor – and that this Commission then published its Secretary's report, recommending the establishment of a permanent commission.

The fact is, Robert La Follette and his partisans so colored the perception of Wisconsin history that we are only now beginning to see how much more complex the reality was than the picture developed by Progressive historians. And it is necessary to do some clearing away of Progressive preconceptions here because what Kennan did provides an object lesson in the management of a policy-making commission of the interest-group type – though Jones and Kennan – and probably Curtis – were at the very least "blue-ribbon"-class representatives of their groups.

The old-line Republicans and the Gold Democrats were allies, and Burr Jones could be relied upon not to upset any applecarts: like McCamant on the 1889 Pennsylvania Commission (or, as we will see, Bernard Myers on the 1919 Pennsylvania Commission), Jones was there to see that things did not get out of hand. Kennan was, like John Wright, a thoughtful railroad man, though of a younger generation and a family with wider interests: his name "Kossuth" might be considered a tip-off, even if we did not know that his brother wrote a distinguished book on *Siberia and the Exile System*, and his son, George Frost Kennan, was even into the twenty-first century the grand old man of foreign affairs, author (as "X") of the containment doctrine and the last of the Seven Wise Men. And George Curtis of Merrill may be considered to have represented not the agricultural interests in the usual sense of that word

101

but the 1890s equivalent of agribusiness, to wit, the lumbering interests, who indeed counted Governor Scofield as one of their own (*Wisconsin State Bar* 1924, pp. 8-9, Margulies 1968, p. 32).

This scarcely insurgent body was not, on the face of it, likely to come up with any sweeping revision of the Wisconsin tax system. Nor did it, at least directly. But it opened the door by recommending a permanent Wisconsin Tax Commission, whose Commissioner was to "have a general supervision of the system of taxation throughout this state . . . have power to make a thorough investigation thereof, and . . . report to the legislature . . . the results of his supervision and investigation, and . . . formulate and recommend legislation for the improvement of the system and for the equalization of the taxation of the state" (Kennan 1898, p. 182, *Wisconsin* 1901, p. 4). This mandate differed only marginally from that of the members of the 1897 Commission.

But then after starting "as a purely investigatory body, the successor Commission rapidly acquired wide supervision and control of the tax system. The ad-valorem assessment of railroads was placed in its hands, and gradually it was granted full power of assessment of public service corporations operating within more than one district. In two transitional steps it was made the State Board of Assessment to determine values upon which to apportion the state property tax and to arrive at an average state rate for application to public service corporations" (Groves n.d., pp. 1-2). Eventually it became the agency for property tax appeal, as well as the agency that administered the inheritance tax and the income tax.

Quite probably this whole line of development was not in Kossuth Kent Kennan's mind when he proposed a state tax commission back in 1889. Moreover, because we are treating limited-term tax revision

102

commissions, rather than permanent tax administering commissions, these later changes are not, strictly speaking, part of our subject. But the fact remains that the 1897 Commission did, through this process, bring about substantial and largely successful revision of the state tax laws (just how successful we will try to determine shortly). Given the general lack of success of tax revision commissions, and particularly of the major Pennsylvania commissions (1889 and 1923), Kennan's apparent end run around his opposition is worth some study.

We know, to be sure, that the smaller the commission, the more likely it is to come to a conclusion. Moreover, with a three-man commission, the problem of clique activity arises only in the special form where the clique is in fact a majority of the commission. But I still affirm that the 1897 Commission was constructed in such a way as virtually to preclude any successful outcome: Governor Scofield (or his mentors) had no intention of bringing about significant change, or even of rocking the boat at all (Philipp 1973, pp. 100ff). The Commission (in the Tutchings terminology) was midway between being corporate/ governmental and being public-interest in membership, so perhaps we can consider it a "mixed" commission – as we would expect, given our (revised) understanding of the Wisconsin Idea. We recall from Chapter II that neither public-interest nor mixed commissions are as likely as corporate/governmental commissions to come up with "regulative" recommendations, but that both corporate/governmental and mixed commissions are more likely to have their recommendations passed into law. In short, then, if Governor Scofield knew then what we know now, he would have appointed a mixed commission of this sort if he wanted a non-"regulative" recommendation (a "knowledge/plan" or symbolic recommendation) – or rather, we might say, to guarantee that if anything were passed into law, this is what it would be.

103

The Kennan Commission (again, in the Tutchings terminology) was a high-demand, low-information-cost, high-decision-cost commission, with a limited issue area (though no more limited than the McCamant Commission) and a fixed term – specifically until December 31, 1898 (*Wisconsin* 1897, p. 5). This suggests that, without coinciding single-peaked preferences (and thus a Condorcet solution), the expected outcome would be no achieved coalition, thus no recommendation – but if a recommendation, one for "regulative" (here read "legislative") action that would fail. Even though mixed commissions that recommended specific legislation did better at getting it than corporate/governmental commissions (by 6/13 to 5/14), nevertheless, with high demand and high decision-costs, no coalition for legislation could be expected.

But in the event, this is not what came about. What came about instead, I would suggest, is that Kennan convinced Jones and Curtis (whose single-peaked preferences were for doing little or nothing) that compiling a report and recommending a ten-year Wisconsin Tax Commission to do very much the same things this temporary commission had been doing were outcomes that did not contravene their preferences. Notes and minutes have apparently not survived (though Professor George Kennan promised to let me know if any ever surface in his father's papers, apparently they never did), so my supposition cannot be immediately checked. By this reading, Kennan's statement (Kennan 1898, p. 8) that no commission of this sort could be expected to straighten out Wisconsin taxes might seem almost Machiavellian: perhaps we should look at the statement in full.

"There has seemed to be a popular impression that the present tax commission would furnish the legislature with an elaborate and complete system of taxation, ready for adoption and embodying all needed reforms. But the utter impracticability of forestalling or even

104

materially influencing legislative action in this manner must be apparent to any thoughtful person. The highest measure of economy and equality in taxation cannot be reached at a single bound. The necessary reforms are not likely to be brought about by the work of any one commission or legislature. Public sentiment must be educated to a clearer and truer view of the province and limitations of taxation, before it can be expected to advance in the direction of genuine reform."

Note particularly the statement that no one commission is likely to bring about the necessary reforms, which suggests that they might in fact be brought about by several successive commissions, engaged *inter alia* in educating public sentiment. We will see this education of public sentiment in action in a different way when we come to the Pennsylvania Commission of 1919 (the Tax Law Revision Commission), but for the moment we should note that the use of a commission as a step in this process of education would appear to fall within the opinion-making rather than the policy-making area. But what if the opinion-making is only the recognized first step (recognized by the members of a commission) toward the policy-making? And what if it is not the body in question, but its successor, that was principally engaged in opinion-making? The questions are in fact rhetorical, and what Kennan did was create a continuous presence for a tax commission in Wisconsin, in line with the impossibility for "any one commission" to change things.

There is no doubt that the commissions were considered as a continuous presence. From Raymond Phelan in his *Financial History of Wisconsin* (Phelan 1906) to Elliot Brownlee in his *Progressivism and Economic Growth* (Brownlee 1971), no distinction is made between or among the temporary Wisconsin State Tax Commission of 1897-98, the successor (longer-termed but still temporary) Wisconsin Tax

Commission created for ten years in 1899, and the permanent (until 1939) Wisconsin Tax Commission into which it was converted in 1905 (Brownlee 1971, pp. 124, 126, in particular). We have yet to see how the major tax revision of 1911 – the State Income Tax – came into being, but we shall find that it quite probably would not have come into being without the work of Kossuth Kent Kennan.

On our reconstruction, Kennan (tipped off perhaps by the Governor's reluctance to appoint the Commission until Kennan forced him into a corner) decided that a detailed factual report and a continuing commission were the best that he could hope for as outcomes of the 1897 Commission's deliberations. It is apparently not possible, at this date, to determine whether he converted the other two commissioners to the view that these were desirable outcomes (as Curtis's presence on the successor commission might suggest, in his case at least), or whether – in the vernacular – he pulled a fast one, or if you prefer, sneaked a pitch by them.

It is possible that what we have for the 1897 Commission is a Dodgson solution, in which Curtis could be brought around to Kennan's view with very little offered to bring him around (the Dodgson solution, it will be remembered, is to choose the element that would become maximal with the fewest changes to existing preference orderings). There is no Minority Report for the Kennan Commission, and it is difficult to find out what went on in the Commission meetings, other than the taking of testimony. But Kennan did produce his *Report*, which all subsequent commentators praised, which both Jones and Curtis signed, whose recommendations were followed, and which led to a virtual revolution in Wisconsin's tax laws, in the not-very-long run.

It has been said that Kennan himself did not favor a State Income Tax, so that it would be a trifle suspect to hail him for his achievement

106

in bringing one about (Brownlee 1971, pp. 47, 53). This seems to me to rest on a misapprehension. It is true that the "Kinsman and Kennan histories of income taxation . . . concluded that the states had been largely unsuccessful in their scattered efforts at income taxation" (Brownlee 1971, p. 47). But it is also true that Kennan quotes with manifest approval Kinsman's conclusion that "One of the fundamental principles of taxation is that the subjects of a state ought to contribute to the support of the government in proportion to their respective abilities, and it is generally agreed that these abilities are best measured by income. Therefore . . . an income tax is the fairest system yet proposed" (Kennan 1910, p. 236). The failures, Kinsman goes on to say (and with him Kennan), have "been due to the administration of the laws" (Kennan 1910, p. 236). To say this is a far cry from saying that the income tax should not be adopted – indeed, it would seem that Kennan thought it should be adopted, if only it could be made to work.

Much has been made of the fact that the Wisconsin Tax Commission that was active when the State Income Tax was passed was appointed by La Follette (Brownlee 1971, chapter 3). But this may be misreading history. Not only was the Commission under La Follette not enthusiastic about the Income Tax, but it has been claimed (and with some justice) that the "people of the state . . . were practically united in the desire to bring about needed changes in the laws" (Philipp 1973, p. 107). Our experience with Pennsylvania (and Clifton Yearley has found this to be true in a great many cases) has taught us that it was likely to be the industrialists, or at least the railroad men, who favored the income tax: Kennan would have been acting somewhat out of character had he opposed it, just as Ely (once his alliance with the Progressives was cemented) would have been acting somewhat out of character had he supported it. He never did, in fact, even after Governor La Follette's

107

historiographic inventions had converted the tax to a Progressive issue. I am not saying Kennan set out to bring about the tax: I am saying that he recognized a need which could be met by such a tax (a tax he believed fair), and that he went about arranging things so as to meet the need – however the meeting was made.

And I am saying that, in doing so, he provided an object lesson in how to triumph over the commission structure – though to be sure, he had only a three-man commission to deal with, so that he only needed to convince one man. If he had been forced to deal with a larger commission, his fate might have been different – but then he had written the law calling for the three-man commission, and had managed the appropriation question in such a way that no one was likely to want to add anyone else to the commission (Philipp 1973, pp. 100-01).

I have been saying pretty much throughout our discussion that the Kennan Commission restricted its recommendations to the establishment of a continuing tax commission. That is not strictly true, and it might be argued that one of the other recommendations made was of some importance in the fiscal history of the State of Wisconsin. The Commission made, in fact, some eight recommendations, of which three dealt with town taxes (two of the three being essentially administrative), two with supervision of taxes, and only three with broader questions of what kind of tax should be levied (Kennan 1898, p. 182).

Of these three (numbers 3, 7, and 8), one dealt with the abolition of the poll tax, or rather of the power to levy it, one with the establishment of an inheritance tax, and one with corporations, of which the most relevant portion (for our purposes) was Kennan's refusal to recommend specific changes – with the sole exception of an end to railroad mileage taxes – and his encouraging further study (Kennan 1898, pp. 181-83). Some claim might be made that the inheritance tax constituted a significant reform: in my view, it may have constituted a significant addition to tax revenues; it may even have altered the incidence of taxation later on; but it was not a reform, or even particularly a matter of tax policy (*Wisconsin* 1929, p. 6, *NICB* 1924, pp. 117-34). The success of the Kennan Commission in altering the tax policy of Wisconsin came with the establishment of its successor commission.

It is for that reason that one of the two recommendations on supervision of taxes, noted above, might be considered a sleeper. The straightforward recommendation was a minor one on the process of reassessment. The sleeper was the recommendation that "the entire administration of the tax laws" be placed in the hands "of capable and disinterested agents of the state" (Kennan 1898, p. 182). It turned out, when the sleeper awoke, that the capable and disinterested hands were those of the permanent Wisconsin Tax Commission.

The Kennan Commission was successful in the first and second senses of the word. That is, the Commission was charged to address a particular problem and came up with a proposal that (to the best understanding then current -- Kennan's) would solve the problem, and the proposal was passed into law. (So, by the way, was the Inheritance Tax.) But was the Commission successful in the third sense? Did the proposal in fact produce the desired result? Was the tax burden equalized?

It does indeed appear that there was some equalization of the tax burden through the State Income Tax. In this connection we should note the view that "the outstanding innovation and contribution of the Wisconsin law was its provision for centralized administration" -- thus producing the efficient and relatively impartial enforcement that other state income taxes had lacked and that the Kennan Commission had called for generally (Groves n.d., p. 17). It should also be noted that this

109

tax was closely integrated with the property tax, with a personal property tax offset. And it should be noted that the 1911 Income Tax did not bring about a significant shift away from the importance of either land in particular or property in general in the Wisconsin tax system (Groves n.d., p. 18). But there was nevertheless some equalization from the State Income Tax.

For example, in 1901, the general property taxes in the State of Wisconsin produced revenues of $19,376,402, the special property taxes (on railroad rolling stock) $24,204, other special taxes (on transportation companies, trust companies, and insurance companies) $2,130,411, and the Inheritance Tax $30,939 (Wisconsin 1929, p. 6). In 1911, just before the Income Tax, the general property taxes produced $30,675,518, the special property taxes $3,755,550, other special taxes $867,104, the Inheritance Tax $916,793, and motor vehicle license fees $15,740 (Wisconsin 1929, p. 11). And in 1921, the figures were $96,268,625 for general property levies, $8,579,653 for special property taxes, $2,030,642 for other special taxes, $1,368,061 for the Inheritance Tax, $3,650,029 for motor vehicle license fees, and $6,034,628 for the Income Tax (*Wisconsin* 1929, p. 16).

As these figures suggest, Wisconsin residents were subject to a quite considerable tax burden by the early 1920s. Indeed, from 1913 to 1922, the per-capita tax burden in Wisconsin rose from $17.35 per annum to $45.94 per annum (*NICB* 1924, p. 38). For persons gainfully employed, the comparable figures were $46.63 and $123.39 (*NICB* 1924, p. 39). The question, of course, is whether the burden, though increased, fell more equitably in Wisconsin than it would have without the Income Tax – or, as a surrogate measure, failing the data for determining the counterfactual ("what would have happened if . . ."), whether the burden was borne more equitably in Wisconsin than in other states. Note that 1913 was the first year in which the Wisconsin State Income Tax operated, so that it was in operation for the entire 1913-22 period.

Certainly the period of the agricultural depression of the 1920s showed sharply reduced revenue from income taxes, with no comparable sharp reduction in revenue from property and other taxes: if taxation should be levied according to the ability to pay, then the income tax acted equitably in shifting the incidence from farmers to manufacturers and city-dwellers. But we cannot claim a success for an 1897 commission, producing a 1911 law, if the effects of that law were not initially equitable, but only became so in 1921. Or if we can, it would be a very limited success.

No, what we need to do is find out whether the tax produced equitable results in the period, say from 1913 (imposition) to 1922 (for the sake of gathering a decade's figures). Or, if we cannot quite do that directly, then we ought to find out whether the over-all tax system in Wisconsin was more (or less) equitable than the system in any comparable states. In both cases, the answer seems to be that the personal property offset (by which personal property tax receipts could be used as payment for income tax) and the more steeply rising rates on corporate taxation combined to produce an incidence for this income tax only slightly different from the incidence of property and other taxes (*NICB* 1924, pp. 81-96, Groves n.d., pp. 17-18). To this statement the chief exception may lie in the incidence of motor vehicle license fees and of the Inheritance Tax – the latter being subject to random shifts (*NICB* 1924, pp. 114-30, 131-37).

The relative incidence of taxation on agricultural and manufacturing areas for Wisconsin was about average for the seven-state Midwest/Great Lakes area containing Minnesota, Wisconsin, Iowa,

111

Illinois, Michigan, Indiana, Ohio (*NICB* 1924, pp. 40-48). The over-all burden was greater, but the part borne by each sector was not out of line. The chief advantage of the Income Tax turned out to be not its equity but its flexibility, though the equity (as noted) came into play during the agricultural depression. In 1920, the Income Tax (with two surtaxes, one for veterans' aid) produced $15,144,308: it is difficult to see how this money could have been raised without this tax already on the books (*Wisconsin* 1929, p. 15).

It is not, I think, accidental that the benefits of the Income Tax, thus of the permanent State Tax Commission, and thus (if perhaps indirectly) of the Kennan Commission, were not what anyone had in mind in 1897. The Commission was successful – that is, it proposed legislation, which was passed, which did lead to (slightly) more equitable and more efficient taxation. But the line is tenuous. The Income Tax did exhibit those difficulties in administration which Seligman had seen in 1894, and 1911, and which Kinsman and Kennan had seen as well. As late as 1922, the permanent State Tax Commission was lamenting the ease of concealing income from the eye of the tax-gatherer (*NICB* 1924, pp. 97ff). The advent of the automobile provided an unplanned, and possibly equalizing, source of tax revenues.

The line from 1897 to a more equitable and efficient taxation in the 1920s is, as I say, tenuous – and I would claim that, far from being accidental, this will occur with virtually any "successful" commission. The next chapter will provide some corroborative evidence from the 1919 Pennsylvania Commission (the Mercur Commission), but let us here look at why this might be the case. Why, that is, can we not expect a direct passage from commission to tax reform?

With the Kennan Commission there was, we decided, something like a Dodgson solution, where Curtis (perhaps) gave up a weak

112

preference for doing nothing, and Kennan a weakened preference for immediate change, to reach a consensus – or else where Kennan perceived that their single-peaked preferences could be made to seem to match his. But this only explains why he was able to write the report he wanted: it does not explain what happened thereafter. The report made a recommendation, the recommendation seemed relatively innocuous, and the Legislature accepted it. We do not know how much Kennan foresaw: we assume the Legislature did not foresee what would eventually happen. The important point is that commissions (especially if appointed almost in despite of the Governor) have no way of ensuring that their recommendations will be passed into law.

Even the McCamant Commission, loaded for bear by the appointment of Taggart and Wherry (both former legislators), could not get its Majority Report even up to the Governor for his signature. And I suspect Governor Scofield in Wisconsin in 1899 would no more have been likely to sign legislation proceeding from the Kennan Commission than Governor Beaver in Pennsylvania in 1891 would have been willing to sign the initial legislation proceeding from the McCamant Commission, had it ever reached him. Tax legislation Governor Scofield did sign in 1899 (apart from the bill creating the ten-year Tax Commission) was composed of the "Whitehead bills" for taxation of transportation equipment companies, and these bills passed both House and Senate with all members present voting in the affirmative (Philipp 1973, p. 114). Governor Scofield was not prone to taking chances.

Or to put it another way, he (like Governor Beaver) knew which side his bread was buttered on, and tax revision commissions tend to be short of butter for application to the gubernatorial – or indeed the legislative – bread. The *sine qua non* for log-rolling is to have logs to roll. What Kennan did was to convert a policymaking commission (or, in Bell's terms, a policy-recommending commission) into an advisory commission. In the terms used by Terence Tutchings, he converted a "3-1-4" commission into a "9-6-9" (or at most a "9-6-4") commission: that is, he changed a commission designed to recommend to the Legislature a specific law or laws for equitable or redistributive purposes into a commission that said there should be a study of the problem (by a new commission), either for unspecified purposes ("9" in the Tutchings three-digit code) or for tax-equitable purposes (Tutchings 1979, pp. 54-55). Since the "3-1-4" code defines the set of commissions least likely to succeed, and the "9-6-9" virtually the converse, what Kennan did was well done – depending on the definition of success (pp. 75ff).

Granted that all this helps explain why the specific act recommended by the Kennan Commission was passed into the laws of Wisconsin, why did this act in the end produce (or help produce) tax reform, while the more specific recommendations of the McCamant Commission and the 1923 Edmonds Commission did not? And not only did not but probably would not have, even if they had been passed *in toto*? To try to answer this, let me essay an apparent digression.

The canons of modern tax theory were laid down by Adam Smith in 1776: taxation should be equitable, certain, convenient, and economical (Groves 1974, pp. 18ff). In essence, even more than all philosophy is a footnote to Plato, it may be said all taxation theory is a series of footnotes to Smith, and this is especially true for that part of taxation theory which argues whether equity is determined by ability to pay or by benefits received. The commissions we are dealing with lived and moved within that series of footnotes.

They also lived and moved within a particular historical context in the history of the United States as well as this particular historical context in the history of ideas, as indeed we noted in Chapter I. We

114

should not place overmuch emphasis on the "spirit of the times" or (more or less the same thing, in this case) on the Progressive Era or the Era of the Search for Order. But there is a clue here, suggested by the double meaning we noted for the Wisconsin Idea. Not only would *expertise* intermingle with democracy (which is to some extent a mark of the spirit of the age), but in a continuous two-way passage up and down State Street, the commission process substituted for the democratic process (the "blue-ribbon" idea) while the commissions themselves were made up of experts representing the various interest groups (the "interest-group" idea). The point is that the traffic was two-way and continuous, and those involved in it both representatives and experts.

The commission – the ad-hoc body like the Kennan Commission of 1897 – could not itself produce reform, but being representative, it could (by Duncan Black's definition) act as a committee, and not being purely representative, it would not always be bound by those unarguable decision premises constituting the roles of its members. Because it was both these things, it could be part of the process of reform.

The available evidence will not permit us to determine whether it could have been both these things if this were not the era of the Wisconsin Idea – or indeed whether this was the era of the Wisconsin Idea precisely because it was the era when such a commission could, though indirectly, be part of the process of reform. Nevertheless, I would argue that this individual commission "success" is inextricably tied to the two-way traffic and the two-natured commission. And certainly our next chapter suggests that indirection is a key element

Wisconsin is, in Clifton Yearley's words, "popularly acknowledged as the pioneer in experiments with modern state income taxation" in Yearley's period (Yearley 1970, p. 236). Yearley quotes Kossuth Kennan's remark that "the advocates of the law seemed to be guided not so much by any wild enthusiasm for the income tax as by a desire to find some substitute for the iniquitous personal property tax" (Kennan 1912, p. 171). Quite so, but as Yearley also points out, it required some kind of shift in attitudes for the people even to think of an income tax as an alternative. Kennan noted with surprise that the people of the state "viewed with complacency" the repeal of the personal intangible property tax, "a step which usually aroused a storm of indignant protest from those who look upon any such move as being in the interest of the wealthier classes" (Kennan 1912, p. 171). We have seen that businessmen supported and the (presumably Populist) farmers opposed the income tax in the 1890s: what happened between 1900 and 1910?

Yearley suggests that the farmers simply had their resistance worn thin (Yearley 1970, p. 237). That it was worn thin is presumably true, but the efforts of Governor Robert La Follette to increase the personal intangible property tax in 1901, coupled with his attack on that same ten-year commission which some time later produced the Income Tax, suggests that for Wisconsin at least, the matter is not this simple. Emanuel Philipp goes so far as to claim that the strengthening of this ten-year (subsequently permanent) commission was a move made for factional party purposes, by La Follette, after the defeat of the Primary Election bill in 1901 (Philipp 1973, p. 134). It is noteworthy that La Follette's first commission appointee, Nils Haugen, supported the Income Tax, going so far as to quote Richard Ely's 1888 endorsement without his subsequent recantation – though Ely was just down at the other end of State Street (Brownlee 1971, pp. 127-28). It is noteworthy that Philipp himself had no great love for the Income Tax (Philipp 1973, p. 153). There seems to have been a shift, induced by the La Follette faction, wherein the Income Tax came to be identified with agrarian rather than business interests in the state (Philipp 1973, pp. 115-151).

But perhaps we should not make too much of this. The fact that income taxes were publicly (if confusedly) discussed in the 1890s may have led to acceptance no so much of their merits as of their possibility. We will discover in the next chapter that the recommendations of the 1919 Mercur Commission in Pennsylvania gained acceptance after long, if not interminable, public discussion (and public pressure) by the Chamber of Commerce and the League of Women Voters. We will also discover that these recommendations, repeated by the 1923 Edmonds Commission (appointed by Governor Pinchot in his 1923-27 term), were in part passed into law in 1931 (in Governor Pinchot's "Little New Deal" 1931-35 term). It looks rather as though commission success, in addition to being indirect, may also be fortuitous.

Negatives are notoriously difficult to prove, and – as I noted before – to consider all state tax revision commissions would be to send my prospective readers (if any) away in droves, but I have found no commission as defined in this paper that had any direct success in producing laws designed to reform taxation, said laws being immediately passed, and said taxation being thereby reformed. The best I have been able to do is find the Wisconsin Commission of 1897, which produced one law designed eventually to reform taxation, said law being immediately passed, and said taxation being eventually more-or-less reformed. And the best I have been able to do in Pennsylvania is to find the 1919 Commission, which produced recommended laws designed to reform taxation, said laws being in part and for a limited area passed ten years later and in part for the rest of the state twelve years after that, and said taxation being slightly reformed. Of that, more in the next chapter.

Let me quote Kennan again: "it must be remembered [that] for ten years the Permanent State Tax Commission had been carrying on a campaign of public education by means of their public reports and otherwise ... calculated to bring out ... the gross inequities and general ineffectiveness of the tax on intangible personal property" (Kennan 1912, p. 171) – for which, as Yearley notes, an income tax was the major alternative, whether personal or corporate (Yearley 1970, p. 237).

Claims can be made, indeed claims have been made, that the problem with the intangibles tax was not its inequity but the impossibility of its calculation: that is, it was inequitable not in theory but in practice (Groves 1967, pp. 128-29). One might perhaps be forgiven for asking what the value of theoretical equity may be if theory also tells us that correct collection is impracticable. Be that as it may, the process of education, which from the original commission's point of view is an indirect process, would seem to be the key here.

By the Tutchings typology, this Kennan Commission was of mixed membership, relatively high demand (created by Governor Scofield over his own objections, in response to outside pressure), single-issue (like all our commissions), limited term (ditto), low information-cost (ditto), and medium or possibly high decision-cost. Its output was, so to speak, supposed to be of the kind with the least chance of success (see the "3-1-4" discussion above). High-demand commissions are more likely to recommend specific laws (make "regulative" recommendations) than low-demand commissions – as also with mixed as against interest-group commissions – and less likely to get them passed. In short, if ever the cards were stacked against a tax revision commission, they were stacked against Kennan's. But his succeeded while others failed. We may now turn to the Pennsylvania quasi-success, the 1919 Mercur Commission, to see if its lessons add to those suggested in this chapter, and then to the 1923 Edmonds Commission, for further contrast.

# CHAPTER V: THE PENNSYLVANIA TAX COMMISSIONS OF 1919 AND 1923

This chapter is divided into two parts, the first covering the Mercur Commission of 1919 and the second the Edmonds Commission of 1923. These were separate commissions, with separate mandates, appointed by separate governors. But most of the Mercur Commission's mandate, and many of its recommendations, were carried over into the Edmonds Commission's mandate and (preliminary) recommendations. Hence we have a variation in procedure for this chapter.

## PART I: THE MERCUR COMMISSION

In 1909, the Pennsylvania Legislature created the Joint Committee of the Senate and House of Representatives of the Commonwealth of Pennsylvania to Consider and Report upon a Revision of the Corporation and Revenue Laws of the Commonwealth (*Pennsylvania* 1909, p. 1). This, as a legislative committee, is beyond the scope of our inquiry, but it is worth noting (and perhaps the activity of a committee is in inverse relationship to the length of its title) that this committee did not find much wrong with the situation it surveyed. Not only did it make "no recommendation with respect to laws in general governing the organization and conduct of corporations" but it also proposed "no extensive alteration of the present system of taxation" (*Pennsylvania* 1909, p. 13). Instead, it recommended that taxation be extended "along present lines" to correct abuses, provide more revenue, and equalize burdens (*Pennsylvania* 1909, p. 44).

Exactly how doing the same thing one is doing now, only more so, will correct the failures in what one is doing now, is something the Joint Committee did not explain, and fortunately something we need not explain here either. The committee is mentioned here primarily to introduce one of its members, State Senator William C. Sproul of Chester, first elected to the State Senate in 1896 (at age 26) and President pro tem from 1903 to 1907. And State Senator Sproul is introduced because it is (I believe) highly likely that his experience on this committee led to his referring the tax problem that surfaced during his term as Governor (1919-23), not to a legislative committee, but to a commission (Smull's 1903, p. 923, for Sproul's biography).

The 1909 Joint Committee heard testimony and did nothing very much but hear testimony. When, shortly after he succeeded Governor Brumbaugh, Sproul was pressed to do something about the problems of assessment, he appointed a commission rather than seek help from a legislative committee – a commission containing one State officer, one representative of the counties, one State legislator, and two distinguished lawyers (*Pennsylvania* 1921, p. 3). It was subsequently enlarged to seven members *after* it had made its report (*Pennsylvania Laws* 1921, p. 1077). What happened after that is in part the story of another commission, but we will disentangle it all in due time.

The Tax Law Revision Commission was created by act of the Legislature of July 18, 1919, "authorizing the appointment of a commission to supervise the raising, amending, consolidating, and simplifying of the laws relating to the assessment, levy, and collection of taxes for local purposes" (*Pennsylvania* 1921, p. 3). It was to have five members, at least two of them lawyers familiar with tax law theory: others, presumably, could be lawyers unfamiliar with tax law – in the event, four of the five commissioners were lawyers. The Legislative

120

Reference Bureau was to prepare the report for the Commission, and a representative of the Bureau was to be present at the hearings the Commission conducted. But it was the Commission, not the Bureau, which was to conduct the hearings – which, in due course, it did.

In a way, the 1919 Commission might seem to violate our initial canon that these be commissions doing their own work with their own *expertise*. I do not think it does, and in any case, the effect of that canon was to limit information costs. If we consider the Bureau's representative, John H. Fertig, as simply a sixth member of the Commission, the effect would remain and the canon be unviolated (see *Pennsylvania* 1921, p. 15). Whatever we do, this remains a low-information-cost commission, as well as one whose purpose was not public relations but policy-making.

The 1919 Commission that Governor Sproul appointed had the appearance of a work of art, a paradigmatic commission, appointed admittedly in 1920 (he was in no hurry), but equally likely to have been appointed at any time in our period. The players' names would have been different at other times, to be sure, but the principal characteristics of each of the five would have been much the same. Which of the four lawyers were particularly expert in school and local tax law I have not determined, but it does not much matter. The point to be made here is that the Commission was appointed by someone with a clear picture of the ideal commission in his mind – perhaps unsurprisingly, given the number of Pennsylvania Governor's commissions operating at the same time. There were thirty-seven of these, ranging from the Commission for the Erection of a Statue or Memorial of General George Gordon Meade at Washington to the Commission to Provide for State Acquisition and Maintenance by the Commonwealth of Pennsylvania

121

and the State of New Jersey of Certain Toll Bridges over the Delaware River (Pennsylvania Laws v.d., *passim*).

The Commissioners were appointed April 5, 1920 (*Pennsylvania* 1921, p. 4). The Chairman (elected May 27, 1920) was Rodney A. Mercur, of Towanda, in Bradford County, in that region of the Commonwealth where neighboring cities in New York State may be of greater day-to-day importance than any in Pennsylvania. Mercur was almost sixty-nine years old – he was indeed almost exactly of Kossuth Kent Kannan's generation –, a graduate of Phillips Exeter Academy and Harvard College, had spent his adult lifetime practicing law in Towanda, was a charter member of the Pennsylvania Bar Association, had been many years on its Committee on Law Reform, was President of the Bradford County Bar Association, had been an Alternate Delegate to the Republican National Convention in 1888, but had never – perhaps because of his lifelong stutter – sought the political career that certainly would have been open to him (*Bench and Bar* 1903, s.n. Mercur, Bradford Letter n.d.). His father, Ulysses Mercur (1818-87), had been on the Pennsylvania Supreme Court (1860-65), then Congressman (1865-72), and eventually Chief Justice of the Commonwealth of Pennsylvania from 1882 till his death in 1887 (Bradsby 1903, *passim*). Rodney Mercur was virtually the perfect blue-ribbon lawyer.

The Secretary of the Commission, Bernard Myers, was correspondingly virtually the perfect State (or Commonwealth) bureaucrat – not a civil servant so much as a Governor's servant. The presence of such a servant on a tax commission is, by now, something that we should expect. He was forty years old, born in Lancaster County, a graduate of Lafayette (Class of 1901), had been admitted to the Bar in 1903, became City Solicitor of the City of Lancaster in 1910, and had been appointed Deputy Attorney General of the Commonwealth of Pennsylvania in 1919. From being Secretary of the Commission he moved to being Secretary of the Commonwealth (ordinarily referred to as Pennsylvania's Secretary of State) on July 20, 1921 (Smull's 1921, p. 12). One assumes this functionary's chief function in the Mercur Commission was to keep an eye on things for the Governor.

The other three members of the Commission were Addison C. Gumbert of Pittsburgh, Reuben A. Zimmerman of Scranton, and State Representative John Marshall of Beaver (*Pennsylvania* 1921, p. 4). Gumbert was Chairman of the Board of Commissioners of Allegheny County, and there was once a school named after him in Pittsburgh. Though he does not seem to have left any great mark on the Commission's work, and never reached a position beyond that on the County Board, he is nonetheless a figure deserving more study than he has had. Addie Gumbert was, so far as I can tell, the very first to parlay a major-league sports career *directly* into political success (*Pittsburgh* 1922, p. 314, Reichler 1982, p. 1716) – though John K. Tener had gone eventually from playing Major League baseball to being Governor of Pennsylvania.

When the Mercur Commission was appointed, Gumbert was fifty-one. He had gone to work in the Prothonotary's office in Pittsburgh in 1885, when he was sixteen (working offseason), continued there off-season during his entire baseball career, switched to the office of the Clerk of Common Pleas when he returned home for good in 1896, aged twenty-seven, had been elected overwhelmingly as Sheriff of Allegheny County in 1906 (serving through 1909). When he was elected County Commissioner in 1915 he was promptly made Chairman, and he served in that position until his comparatively early death in 1925 at the age of fifty-six (*Pittsburgh* 1922, p. 314, and *Fact Book* n.d.). He was a Republican. In the meantime, his pitching career, if it did not scale the heights, was at least moderately distinguished, highlighted by a 22-11 record with Boston in the rebellious Players' League season of 1890, and the same number of victories with Cleveland (National League) two years later. He pitched for Pittsburgh in 1893 and 1894.

Gumbert's over-all career records are such as to suggest that his baseball career may have aided rather than created his political career. For nine years, from 1888 through 1896 (not counting minor league ball in Zanesville, Ohio, in 1887), his won-lost record was 122-101 (Reichler 1982, p. 1716, Schneider 1983, p. 285). In any case, to go with his blue-ribbon lawyer from Towanda and his Secretary from Lancaster, Governor Sproul had appointed a non-lawyer sports figure/politician from (where else for a sports figure?) Pittsburgh. And while this may seem a disproportionately long potted biography for a minor figure, it remains true that there was no institutional reason for Gumbert's presence on the Commission, as the mandate specifically excluded Pittsburgh from the Commission's jurisdiction. It is therefore worthwhile to assemble whatever evidence we can to determine why he was appointed, and particularly evidence dealing with his place in the Pennsylvania political system. For this reason (if for no other), it is important to determine whether he worked his way up or played his way up, or a unique combination of both. The data suggest the combination.

Governor Sproul also appointed a second blue-ribbon lawyer, almost as old as Mercur, though perhaps less distinguished. Reuben A. Zimmerman of Scranton was sixty-seven, a graduate of Lafayette, who had been admitted to the Bar in Northumberland County in 1885 (when he was thirty-two), moved to Scranton the same year, and had been in practice there ever since (*Bench and Bar* 1903, p. 232). It is not entirely clear whether he was appointed from Scranton for geographic balance, or because it looked like Scranton might represent a particularly difficult

124

problem for the Commission, or both. Quite possibly the answer is *both*, inasmuch as appointment seems to have been in general geographically inspired, but every member seemed to be doing a kind of double duty – Gumbert to represent both southwestern Pennsylvania and the Counties, Myers as a State officer and to represent southeastern Pennsylvania, and so on. We shall come back to the matter of geographical representation in a little while.

The final member was John Marshall of Beaver. Like Secretary Myers, Marshall was born in 1880. Like Mercur, Myers, and Zimmerman, he was a lawyer, though he had also been a schoolteacher (having attended Grove City College, graduating in 1903) and Deputy Sheriff of Beaver County, before going to the University of Pennsylvania Law School (where he graduated in 1912) and then returning to practice in Beaver. He was elected to the State Legislature from Beaver in 1920, 1922, and 1924, as a Republican-Socialist-Prohibitionist, not entirely a fanciful combination at the time (Smull's 1921, p. 1110 – *cf* Fiorello LaGuardia).

The sixth "member" of the Commission was John H. Fertig of the Legislative Reference Bureau, who drew up the Report, and who (with at least a quorum of the Commissioners) attended every meeting of the Commission (*Pennsylvania* 1921, p. 15). There were in fact seven regular meetings and two additional presentations. Regular meetings were held at Harrisburg (three), Lancaster, Pittsburgh, Scranton, and Bedford Springs (one each). The meeting at Bedford Springs was held at the time of the Pennsylvania Bar Association meeting there, which explains why there was a meeting at Bedford Springs at all. The meeting at Pittsburgh was held there not because the Commission was concerning itself with Allegheny County (it was not), but because it was concerning itself with western Pennsylvania. In addition to these

125

meetings, Secretary Myers (who came from Lancaster) made a presentation to the Convention of Third Class City Associations at York (Philadelphia was the only first-class city and Pittsburgh the only second-class city, according to Pennsylvania law). Also, Chairman Mercur and Mr. Zimmerman appeared, both pretty much in their home area, before the Convention of County Commissioners, at Wilkes-Barre (*Pennsylvania* 1921, p. 15).

It may not be entirely accidental, and it is certainly indicative, that the Mercur Commission was in part sustained by the Legislative Reference Bureau. The first Legislative Reference Library, under the aegis of Charles McCarthy, had been one of the earliest manifestations of the Wisconsin Idea, under Governor Robert La Follette (*Pennsylvania* 1921, p. 3). I would argue that the Mercur Commission, not coincidentally, was true to the Wisconsin Idea in being part way between an interest-group commission and a blue-ribbon commission. It was not set up with specific reference to the Wisconsin Idea (though it knew of the Legislative Reference Library), and the interest groups were not those of the McCamant Commission, but I think the general conclusion holds.

The Mercur Commission was given what might be read alternatively as a double or triple mandate: that is, it was supposed to make recommendations relating to the assessment, levy, and collection of taxes, which sounds like three areas but was taken to mean two – assessment on the one hand and levy and collection on the other. Having analyzed its mandate in that fashion (*Pennsylvania* 1921, p. 3), it proceeded to concentrate on the first part, on the grounds that there were too many laws relating to levy and collection for a five-man (or even six-man) commission to be confident it had found them all in the course of the limited investigation it (or the Governor) had in mind. It did,

126

however, in the end, recommend centralized tax collection. If all this seems reminiscent of the Kennan Commission, that is because it is reminiscent of the Kennan Commission.

The Mercur Commission's work was thus substantially self-limited to the "revising, amending, consolidating, and simplifying of the laws relating to the assessment" of taxes for local purposes (*Pennsylvania* 1921, p. 3). And it was further limited by a decision to omit municipalities or districts of the first class: this eliminated Philadelphia, which was and is both a city and a school district of the first class, and it also eliminated Pittsburgh, which, though a city of the second class, was a school district of the first class. Scranton, the only other city of the second class, was and still is also a school district of the second class. When the recommended law was drafted, Scranton was allowed to come in if it wanted, but was not compelled to (*Pennsylvania* 1921, p. 5).

Apparently the Commission had no trouble in coming up with recommended legislation, unless there was some trouble involved in limiting its mandate. Whether Governor Sproul stumbled on his solution or planned it, geographic representation apparently succeeded where straight interest-group representation failed before. Had the mandate been the consideration of tax policy generally, this might not have been the case. But with the mandate restricted to local-purpose taxes, and with local purposes (schools for example) not differing widely among localities, geographic representation seems to have provided the appearance of keeping the interest groups happy while not, in fact, restricting the Commissioners to interest-group roles. The only relevant geographical distinctions were between Philadelphia and Pittsburgh (and possibly Scranton) on the one hand, which were not concerned in the Mercur reforms, and the rest of Pennsylvania on the other. But all three major metropolitan areas were represented on the Commission. We will

127

return to the matter of shedding the interest-group roles after considering the Commission's recommendations and what happened to them.

Having concentrated on its mandate relating to the assessment of taxes, the Commission, on January 24, 1921, proposed two major changes in the law on local assessments (*Pennsylvania* 1921, pp. 18-63). First, in the place of locally-elected Assessors, there would be a County Board of Assessment, appointed by the County Commissioners. Second, assessments, instead of being triennial, would be annual, with a uniform valuation standard set by the Board of Assessment. The bill itself takes up forty-six pages of the Commission's sixty-three-page *Report*, but these two provisions are the gist of it. It was duly introduced into the Legislature (in the Senate) on January 31, 1921, by State Senator Edward E. Jones of Harford, Susquehanna County, a man noted chiefly for the Jones Dirt Road Act and not particularly for work in taxes or education (*Senate* 1921, p. 109).

It may be significant that Senator Jones, like Chairman Mercur, was from the New York border country, and it may be even more significant that the same day he introduced this bill he introduced one for the benefit of the Packer Hospital at Sayre, Pennsylvania (*Senate* 1921, p. 109, Smull's 1931, p. 1379). Since he was almost certainly acting at Mercur's request on the Packer bill (Mercur being for many years a Trustee of Packer and sometime Chairman of the Board), it is not unlikely that he was similarly acting at Mercur's behest in introducing the Commission's proposal – at Mercur's behest, not the Governor's. Similarly (though this seems more in the regular course of events), it was Commission member John Marshall who finally introduced the bill in the House on February 8, 1921, at which point it was referred to the Committee on Judiciary-Local, the Senate bill having been referred to the Committee on Judiciary-General.

The unmistakable impression here is that the Governor could not have cared much less about the fate of the Commission's recommendations. If Governor Scofield was lukewarm on the Kennan Commission, Governor Sproul seems to have been distinctly chilly here. And the reason is not far to seek: there was no chance the bill, as presented, would pass, and indeed virtually no chance it would get out of committee, as subsequent events quite clearly showed.

What Governor Sproul did, faced with the Commission's unpalatable recommendations, was to have its mandate extended for two years (as of May 24, 1921) and at the same time enlarge the Commission to seven members – all this in the face of the fact that the Commission had already issued its *Report*. And in the new appointments he showed the same concern for geographic diversity that he had shown in 1920.

Charles H. English, of Erie, was thirty-seven, thus the youngest member. He had been born in Erie, October 30, 1883, received his LL.B. from Georgetown at twenty-one and his LL.M. the next year, been admitted to the Bar in 1907, been City Solicitor for Erie from 1912 to 1916, President of the Erie Chamber of Commerce in 1919, member of the Pennsylvania Commission on Constitutional Amendment and Revision the same year, and was Chairman of the Committee on Municipalities at the Pennsylvania Constitutional Convention in 1920. He was, of course, a Republican. He was also a Roman Catholic (*NY Times* 1958, obit). Geographically, in religion, and perhaps in age, he added balance, though I suspect no such addition was needed.

Benjamin H. Ludlow, described as being of Philadelphia (though in fact from Ardmore, Montgomery County), was a year older. He had graduated from Central High School in Philadelphia in 1901 and, like English, had gone straight to law school – in his case at the University of Pennsylvania. In 1909 he had moved to Ardmore, while practicing law

129

in Philadelphia, and had subsequently served as Commissioner of Lower Merion Township. The Philadelphia suburbs were now represented, and – barring the fact that Chairman Mercur came from Towanda rather than, say, Clearfield – the geographical balance was complete. But Ludlow, it turned out, did much more than merely complete the balance. In 1922 and 1924 he was elected to the State House of Representatives and there indefatigably supported, indeed introduced and reintroduced, the Commission's recommendations (*NY Times* 1957, obit., Smull's 1969, p. 345).

New members notwithstanding, and whatever effect the Commission may have had, the appointed Board of Assessment remained within the exclusive purview of Philadelphia and Pittsburgh until 1931, when the Board of Assessors was established as an instrument for counties of the third class (Smull's 1933, p. 875). By the 1919 act that defined the classes, this meant counties of populations between 250,000 and 800,000 (*Pennsylvania Laws* 1919, p. 887). In 1931 (Census of 1930), this meant Delaware County, Lackawanna County, Luzerne County, Montgomery County, and Westmoreland County (Smull's 1933, p. 875). It was not until the "Fourth to Eighth Class County Assessment Law" of 1943, ten years after Mercur's death, that appointed boards and yearly assessment replaced elected assessors and triennial assessment. Indeed, even then the replacement was incomplete, since the act provided for a Board of Assessment and Revision of Taxes for each county that would appoint county assessors and adopt rules for both county-appointed and locally-elected assessors (*Pennsylvania Laws* 1943, p. 572). In the meantime, power to appoint the County Board of Assessors had been taken from the County Commissioners (where it was vested in the 1931 act) and conferred on the Auditor-General of the Commonwealth of Pennsylvania

130

(*Pennsylvania Laws* 1937, p. 940). Nevertheless, it can be said, with some approximation to truth, that the Mercur Commission's chief recommendations of 1921 made it into law in five (of the sixty-five) relevant counties in 1931, and the other sixty in 1943.

Query – did the Commission in fact have anything to do with the revision? It turns out that, while the Jones-Marshall Act was neither passed nor even released from committee, it led a curious sort of half-life for a number of years, eventually emerging (in truncated form) as the law passed in 1931. While the Commission was in the limbo created by the extension of its own mandate and the appointment by Governor-elect Gifford Pinchot of his own advisory Citizens Committee on the Finance of Pennsylvania (noted below), the Pennsylvania State Chamber of Commerce adopted a resolution at its 1922 Meeting (Nicholson 1932, p. 274 n. 5): "Whereas the report of the Tax Law Revision Commission discloses great inequalities in local assessment, as well as excessive costs and inconvenience in the collection of local taxes; Therefore, be it Resolved, That the Pennsylvania State Chamber of Commerce urge the adoption of suitable legislation to provide a more exact and uniform basis for local assessments and greater economy and convenience in the collection of local taxes."

Similarly, and at the same time, the Pennsylvania League of Women Voters began to urge support for the Mercur Commission's recommendations (Nicholson 1932, pp. 276-77). And Representative Ludlow, who had moved from the Commission to the House, then reintroduced the Jones-Marshall bill, or a close facsimile thereof, on the House floor on March 21, 1923. It was again referred to the Committee on Judiciary-Local, but this time it re-emerged onto the floor, only to be defeated by a vote of 136 to 24 (Nicholson 1932, p. 274). After all, who on the floor (other than Ludlow or Marshall) would want to eliminate the jobs of those local members of the party faithful who just happened to be Assessors – and just happened to descend on the hapless House member in droves to argue their case? Actually, it is not the 136 nay votes but the 24 aye votes that are a little surprising.

Here we have a classic example of the inability of a commission to engage in log-rolling, and of the problems attendant on failing to have interest-group representation of the McCamant Commission sort. Failure to have that representation did permit a law to be drawn up, but – together with the attendant inability to find logs to roll – it also apparently doomed the Mercur Commission to innocuous desuetude. We have no evidence for determining the factions or cliques (if any) on the Commission: what evidence we have suggests there were none. Mercur and Marshall were responsible for introducing the original bill, and Ludlow for its successor; Mercur and Zimmerman appeared at Wilkes-Barre apparently at Gumbert's invitation; and the tone of the *Report* (and absence of a Minority Report) suggests an unprecedented harmony (*Pennsylvania* 1921, p. 17). We seem to have a Condorcet solution.

Such a solution would tend to be characteristic of blue-ribbon commissions, and this fact should concentrate our attention on our non-"blue-ribbon" Commissioners, Myers and Gumbert. Was Gumbert perhaps hoping to move up in the Republican Party hierarchy or into office in a State-wide election (a proceeding not unknown for an Allegheny County Commissioner)? Was Myers also hoping for better things, which indeed came his way? Did this provide the equivalent of log-rolling (though subtle and undeclared) in a way not generally characteristic of commissions? One can perhaps imagine the patrician Mercur or the Prohibitionist Marshall thinking, "This man Gumbert

132

really is a good sort despite his background, and I could support him for office."

We will come back to that later on. Meanwhile, we should note that the State Tax Commission of 1923, which is the subject for the second part of this chapter, "examined the provisions of the Marshall bill, introduced at the Session of 1921, and the Ludlow bill, introduced at the Session of 1923," and had little hesitation "in declaring that they would provide an urgently needed reform" – and it recommended "The enactment of a law embodying the principles set forth in the report" of the Mercur Commission (*Pennsylvania* 1927, p. 22). Representative Ludlow reintroduced his bill on February 10, 1925; it was again referred to committee, again it emerged, and this time it was defeated 170 to 29 – which led, not surprisingly, to charges of "sinister influence" from a "well-organized lobby" of assessors and tax-collectors (Nicholson 1932, p. 275). It also led to a well-organized campaign by the League of Women Voters in favor of the Mercur Report.

From June 1925 to March 1927, the League published each month in its *Pennsylvania Bulletin* reports of its volunteer tax survey workers, showing the fees accruing to local tax collectors. To be sure, the League was more interested in reducing collection costs than in rationalizing assessments, but the two were still sufficiently intertwined to make their separation difficult. The State Chamber of Commerce was working on building support for the Mercur recommendations through its Local Taxation Committee. The State Tax Commission appointed by Governor Pinchot in 1923 echoed the Mercur Commission's findings in its own report, though its mandate was far wider than that of the Mercur Commission and its Report, though not as important for what it achieved, was far longer. Supporters of the Marshall and Ludlow bills suggested divorcing tax collection from tax assessment, and a bill

133

dealing only with tax collection was introduced by Senator Horace W. Schantz on February 10, 1927: it disappeared permanently into committee shortly thereafter. (Nicholson 1932, pp. 276-81.) Despite all the efforts on its behalf, this was an idea whose time threatened to be indefinitely postponed.

Actually, as we have noted, only part of it was further postponed. Ludlow and Marshall had left the House, but the modified act applying the Mercur Commission's recommendations to five counties, including Ludlow's own Montgomery, passed both House and Senate and was signed by Governor Pinchot in 1931. Because local tax reforms were the sole charge and sole recommendation of the Mercur Commission, while only a minor part of the work of its successor, and because the line can be drawn without break (though in rather a zig-zag fashion) between the Mercur Commission and the 1931 Act, with the 1923 Commission as only one more zag, I would credit the 1931 Act (and its 1943 successor) to the original body. And here I would note a particular similarity to the history of the State Income Tax in Wisconsin after the Kennan Commission.

The similarity lies not only in the zigs and zags, but also and especially in the fact that the Commission's Report, in both cases, began or at least strongly participated in the beginning of a climate of opinion favorable to the eventual reform. We have noted that Kennan, in effect (and with the possible exception of the inheritance tax question), converted a policy-making commission into what was virtually a fact-finding commission. What Kennan did more or less deliberately, the Mercur Commission found being done to it without its own deliberation. Since these were our two more successful commissions, we might well argue that it is specifically in policy-making that commissions fail, a point to which we shall be returning. But did the Mercur Commission's recommendations, when eventually passed into law, actually bring about the desired reform?

The fact that they were passed into law in two stages provides us with the closest we can come to a laboratory test for their success. Was there any alteration in tax patterns in Delaware, Lackawanna, Luzerne, Montgomery, and Westmoreland counties from 1931, when they came under the law requiring an appointed Board of Assessors, to 1943, when the other counties in Pennsylvania came under the same requirement? If there were no change that can be tied to the goals of the Mercur Commission (principally equity in local taxation), then we will conclude the success was only skin deep: the law was passed but it did not work. Can we determine any increase in equity – fairness -- in local assessment in the five counties, from 1931 to 1943, measured against the sixty counties unaffected by the 1931 Act?

We will begin by defining perfect equity in local assessment as a situation in which assessed valuation adequately represents wealth, and by defining an equitable tax as one for which those required to make equal payments are equally able to make them. This is essentially Seligman's definition (Groves 1974, pp. 39-47). A comparison of available data shows that the correlation between assessment and ability to pay (measured by wages and product value) was greater for the counties covered by the law than for the State of Pennsylvania as a whole. Also, capital investment, which should be correlated with assessed valuation (all other things being equal – or given a sufficient number of data for the unequal things to even out), is more closely correlated for the counties covered by the law than for the rest of the State. The data for these calculations are in the Auditor-General's *Reports* 1932-44).

It is true that this last may come about from the presence of heavily industrialized counties among the five. The largest counties are, after all, the most likely to be the most heavily industrialized, and businesses are generally more accurately assessed than other holdings, besides having a closer relation between value and ability to pay. In any case, as the data show, the presence of a County Board of Assessment seems to have had a significant effect on the responsiveness of assessment to ability to pay.

We can construct a composite index of ability to pay (Seligman's "faculty"), consisting of wages, capital investment, and value of product. For the seven counties (including Philadelphia and Allegheny) with a County Board, assessed valuation declined roughly 10.5 percent in the Depression years 1931-34, while the rest of the State, and even the five largest fourth-class counties, showed no effective decrease. At the same time, the ability to pay declined 13.5 percent for the seven counties, about 10.8 percent for the other sixty, and just about 9.0 percent for the five largest fourth-class counties. This last category represents the closest approximation to a group strictly comparable to the five third-class counties.

Subsequent data show that the sixty counties had some reassessment between 1935 and 1937 and then remained relatively constant in assessed valuation, despite sharp increases in ability to pay. It might be argued that the same pattern (also evident for the five largest fourth-class counties) simply marks the counties with appointed local boards. But we should pause to note, first, that there was some upward reassessment for these counties, and second, that they had been historically over-assessed. This historical over-assessment was, of course, partly the result of the same pressures that had led to the factionalism of the McCamant Commission and the whole interest-group

136

endeavor to tax industrial rather than agricultural property. It is not surprising that there was some reassessment (of taxes and policy) under pressure of the business decline in the 1930s. Here is the Report on the Industrial Tax Survey Committee (*Pennsylvania* 1939, p. 1): "The Commission is unable to make recommendations which will immediately and definitely correct the present complaints. . . . The difficulty in which this Commonwealth finds itself lies principally in the enormous amount of revenue required and needed to carry the relief load and social security."

Whether this reassessment would have occurred without the Mercur revisions we cannot say – only that the tax reassessment happened more readily in counties under the 1931 law. It is true that one would like to have more convincing evidence, though the very immobility of assessments elsewhere in the State of Pennsylvania should be considered significant. In the long run, the Tax Law Revision Commission of 1919 is the only "success" of our four Pennsylvania commissions – for all that its record is mostly zigs and zags: Commission appointed 1920 (appointment renewed 1921), Report filed in 1921, bill sent to committee 1921, bill reintroduced 1923, killed, bill reintroduced 1925, killed, Report supported by successor Commission, bill partially reintroduced 1927, killed, bill (in limited form) reintroduced 1931, passed, and recommendations finally (more or less) passed into law in 1943. This record has enough similarities to that of Wisconsin's Kennan Commission to raise a warning flag.

First, as I have said, it was a policy-making commission converted into a fact-finding commission. Second, even as a policy-making commission it had a severely limited mandate. Third – apparently unlike the Kennan Commission before Kennan sneaked his pitch by the other Commissioners –, it was a commission whose members seem to

137

have had single-peaked preferences, which largely coincided, thus permitting a Condorcet solution. Fourth, though its members were representative, they were not solely representative of interest groups, and thus this, like the Kennan Commission, was somewhere between an interest-group and a blue-ribbon body. Fifth, significantly, it took a long time for the reform to come after the Report appeared, and then it came in a form different from the one that the Report envisioned. And sixth, it seems to have occupied a rather anomalous position in relation to the Governor who appointed it. This last reminds us of a point made by Tutchings early on in his study.

He argued that the demand for a commission – or rather, the articulation of the demand – was, with the information costs and the range of permissible outcomes – highly predictive of the eventual outcome (Tutchings 1979, p. 120). That may be, of course. But with both the Kennan Commission and the Mercur Commission, it would appear that the expected outcome (and in the case of the Mercur Commission, the actual outcome) was not within the permissible range. It would appear that the Governor's relation to the articulated demand was ambiguous (and failures from such ambiguity were the origin of Daniel Bell's "Comment"). And, though all our commissions have low information costs, these two may well have had the lowest – the difference perhaps being insignificant and in any case not to be built on, given our inexact information. The other two points, however, should give us to think quite seriously about the relation of appointer to commission appointed.

Perhaps the operative point is that Kennan, in the first case, and Mercur (perhaps) in the second, seized the agenda from the Governor. Who determines the agenda determines the outcome, and clearly Sproul (if not Scofield) disapproved of the immediate outcome of his

138

Commission. In one sense, of course, a chairman who controls the agenda is simply acting as a chairman – but Kennan, who controlled the agenda, was Secretary, not Chairman, and it is not clear that Sproul made a mistake when he made Myers Secretary and not Chairman. The very possibility of control by the Chairman may, to be sure, be limited by the nature of a commission: an interest-group commission of the McCamant sort, with strongly defined role decision premises, may not be amenable to control from outside the majority clique (if there is a majority clique), And, as we will discover very shortly, a pure blue-ribbon commission may (unexpectedly) have the same kind of problem. So also may a commission without strongly-defined roles, which brings up a different problem, as we will see in Chapter VI.

The oddest characteristic of the Mercur Commission was the apparent geographical basis for appointment. Not that there is anything especially odd about the seeking of geographical balance *per se*, but it is hard to escape the feeling that this balance was pretty much factitious: Rodney Mercur's views on tax administration did not depend on his coming from Towanda, and there was scarcely an "Erie view" or a "Beaver view" of tax collection. Why then did Governor Sproul choose one from southeastern Pennsylvania, one from the anthracite country, one from southwestern Pennsylvania, and so on? I suspect that this pattern derived from the party politician's belief that tickets, and everything else in party politics, should have this kind of balance.

This, in a way, brings us back to Governor Sproul's own experience on the 1909 Committee, whose *modus operandi* was the taking of testimony around the state (*Pennsylvania* 1909, pp. 9ff). He may have learned from this experience that committees, as opposed to commissions, may not be the way to tax reform: he almost certainly learned from it, as from his political experience generally, that geographic representation is important in making policy for an entire state. That is, of course, a truism, and part of the reason for having representatives of any kind elected geographically. The curious thing in this case was that the principle was invoked where it had no particular relevance – and yet, in my view, its irrelevance contributed to the Mercur Commission's success.

## PART II: THE EDMONDS COMMISSION

As our discussion thus far will have suggested, it is not unequivocally clear whether the 1931 Act that established the County Boards of Assessment and Review (in five counties) should be credited as the success of the 1919 Mercur Commission or the 1923 Edmonds Commission, though the weight of the evidence strongly favors the former. While the Edmonds Commission, besides taking over the earlier body's recommendations, also took over its research man at the Legislative Reference Bureau, John H. Fertig, it was in all other respects a very different body from Rodney Mercur's low-key limited-mandate group (*Pennsylvania* 1925, pp. 3-5). Briefly, it was appointed by Gifford Pinchot, Pennsylvania's own blue-ribbon Progressive, and its membership shows it.

The Chairman was Franklin Spencer Edmonds, then forty-nine years old, a graduate of Philadelphia's Central High School at age seventeen and the University of Pennsylvania at age nineteen. For two years immediately thereafter, he was Andrew D. White Fellow in Political Economy at Cornell, then returned to teach at Central High. He took his law degree at the University of Pennsylvania Law School in 1903, and the year after began a six-year term as Professor of Law at Swarthmore (where he must have known Albert Bolles, lecturing on

140

Commercial Law at Haverford), besides forming the law firm of Edmonds, Obermayer, and Redmond, in Philadelphia. In 1903-05 he was also President of the Philadelphia Teachers Association, and from 1906 to 1911 he was on the Philadelphia Board of Public Education. Author of a study on *Reciprocity in State Inheritance Tax*, he also wrote a life of Ulysses S. Grant and a history of Philadelphia Central High. He had been elected to the Pennsylvania House of Representatives in 1920 and 1922 and was to be elected again in 1924. After his service as Chairman of the Tax Commission, he went on to become President of the National Tax Association, in 1932, and somewhat later, in 1938, was elected to the Pennsylvania Senate from Montgomery County (Keator 1948, pp. 185ff). His successor in this last position, by the way, was Lloyd Wood, whom we shall meet in Chapter VI.

Even more distinguished – as the *Dictionary of American Biography* counts distinction – was Commission member James Hay Reed of Pittsburgh. Judge Reed (always called so from his service as Federal Judge for the Western District of Pennsylvania in 1891-92) was nearly seventy, and in fact he died (at seventy-three, in 1927) while the Commission was still in existence. He had graduated from the Western University of Pennsylvania (now the University of Pittsburgh) back in 1872, been admitted to the Bar in 1875, formed a partnership with Philander C. Knox (T. Roosevelt's Attorney General) in 1877, was Counselor to Andrew Carnegie, organized both the Union Railroad Co. of Pittsburgh and the Pittsburgh, Bessemer and Lake Erie (being President of both). He was also President of the Philadelphia Company (the public-utility holding company that controlled the Pittsburgh public utilities) from 1898 to 1919, and then First Vice-President. He was also President of the Reliance Life Insurance Co. of Pittsburgh from 1903 (*DAB* XV, p. 449). Though he had been a Judge, and though he had

141

served on the Pennsylvania Commission on Constitutional Revision and Amendment in 1919-20, Reed was a corporation man, a Carnegie man, a money man, rather than a Philadelphia gentleman like Edmonds. Obviously he was not without Philadelphia connections, and had he lived at that end of the state he would have qualified as a Philadelphia gentleman (Baltzell 1958, *passim*); he was also a man whose law partner was T.R.'s friend Knox – a fact which may have been important to Governor Pinchot.

If Edmonds was a Philadelphia gentleman, John Penman Wood was a Philadelphia gentleman who could have stepped out of the pages of a Richard Harding Davis novel. Wood, who gave him name to the Plan that was the chief long-range recommendation or suggested recommendation of the Edmonds Commission's *Interim Report* – but that disappeared from the *Final Report* –, was a Philadelphia woollen manufacturer, born in 1862, a founding member of the Pennsylvania Association of Manufacturers in 1911, and a member as well of the socialite Philadelphia City Cavalry Troop. He had served in the Spanish American War; he had chased Pancho Villa (the City Cavalry being part of the Pennsylvania National Guard mustered into the Federal service in 1916); and at fifty-five he had been a Captain in the American Expeditionary Force in France. At his appointment to the Commission he was sixty-one, and a Brigadier-General in the Guard. (Wood Papers, *passim*, Wike 1960, p. 21.) Back in 1915, before his adventures in Mexico, he had warned the Pennsylvania Manufacturers that it was not enough to oppose programs one did not like – it was necessary to come up with alternatives (Wike 1960, p. 257): "Let us place ourselves in the position of advocating constructive legislation and not merely opposing destructive legislation brought forward by others." In his work on the Edmonds Commission he certainly lived up to that charge.

142

Alexander R. Wheeler, the first-term State Representative from Forest County, was not from Philadelphia (he was born in Tidionte, Warren County, Pennsylvania, in 1889), but the lineaments were much the same. He graduated from Yale in 1911, took his M.A. at Oxford, drove an ambulance for the Red Cross in France in 1915-16, was Second Lieutenant, then First Lieutenant, and finally Captain with the AEF, being mustered out on August 14, 1919 (Smull's 1923). He was in the lumber business, but one suspects Yale and Oxford and the Red Cross and the AEF had more to do with his appointment than his business did – or perhaps not, if he was by way of being interested in scientific forestry. Pinchot, of course, rose to fame as Chief Forester.

Professor Marion K. McKay of the University of Pittsburgh Department of Economics, with M.A. and Ph.D. from Harvard (after a B.S. at Ohio Northern and A.B. at Ohio State), was thirty-eight years old and had come to Pitt in 1920, after three years at the University of New Hampshire. Like Chairman Edmonds, he was to go on in the study of taxation, in his case becoming a member of President Hoover's Commission on the Taxation of Houses, and eventually a member of the Subcommittee to the Committee on Finance of the Pennsylvania Joint State Government Commission in 1939-41, where we will meet him in passing in Chapter VI (*WW PA* 1939).

Archibald Foster Jones of Coudersport, forty-three, was largely self-educated (he had left high school at fourteen, read law at twenty, and was admitted to the Bar at twenty-two). He had been active in local Republican organizations while building up the mostly business-oriented law practice of Lewis, Jones, and Lewis. While winding up his service on the Edmonds Commission (in 1927) he was appointed a member of the Commission to Study the Distribution of State Subsidies to School Districts (Jordan 1913, s.n. Jones, *Pennsylvania* 1929, p. 3). Evidence

143

suggests that he had come to Pinchot's attention from his work on local tax problems.

Finally, John Patrick Connelly of Philadelphia, then forty-eight, had attended parochial schools in his native city to the age of fourteen, then went to work for Flanders and Pugh, marine attorneys, eventually studying law and being admitted to the Bar under the tutelage of senior partner Henry Flanders in 1896, at age twenty-one (*NCAB XXXVI*, p. 206). He entered private practice that same year, first a general practice, then corporation law, and eventually tax law. He was a member of the Philadelphia City Council 1905-16 and City Solicitor 1916-18. He was, predictably, a member of the Philadelphia Zoological Society, the American-Irish Historical Society, the Philadelphia Country Club, and the Knights of Columbus. Virtually all his ties (except the Zoological Society) were Irish and Roman Catholic: his wife was a Maguire and his children married, *inter alia*, a Murray, a Casey, and a Conway. Connelly died in Merion in 1948.

The Edmonds Commission issued its *Interim Report* in 1925 and its *Final Report* in 1927. For long-range policy the *Interim Report* suggested but did not fully recommend the Wood Plan. This plan, as John Penman Wood presented and explained it, had eight major provisions, some of which bring irresistibly to mind the recommendations of John Armstrong Wright. A uniform tax on business net income was to be substituted for the raft of existing business taxes. There was to be substitution of a personal income tax for personal property taxes and poll taxes and occupation taxes and school capitation tax. There were to be a single local assessment, uniform state inheritance taxes, a permanent increase in the motor fuels tax, a tax on insurance company premiums (this already existed), "separation taxes" on mineral produce, and supporting the business and personal income

144

taxes, enactment of a State Income Tax Law (*Pennsylvania* 1925, pp. 55-57).

None of this was very new, and it may be taken as the informed but not original thought of an intelligent and enthusiastic man with a general but not expert knowledge. It was of no eventual importance for the Commission, since Wood died during the Commission's term and the Wood Plan disappeared from the *Final Report*. It can, however, quite clearly be taken as representing Wood's views on taxation, as we attempt to uncover the process by which the Commission reached its final conclusions – to open the black box of what goes on inside closed bodies, in theory or practice. There are indeed Minority Reports in the Commission's *Final Report*, but the evidence on debate within the Commission can otherwise be adduced only from the fortunes of the Wood Plan.

The *Interim Report* recommended, as immediate measures, eleven tax changes (amendments to previous laws) and four Constitutional amendments: it believed these, while they would not "establish a permanent policy of taxation for the State," would nevertheless "abolish many existing ills" (*Pennsylvania* 1925, p. 42). This spate of specific changes – and there were more in the *Final Report* – may be contrasted, first, with the more limited proposals of the three commissions we have already considered and, second, with the even more limited results that these highly specific proposals produced. It is true that the Kennan Commission actually made eight proposals. It is true that the monstrosity of a bill proposed by the majority on the McCamant Commission went into exhaustive and idiotic detail on just how railroad management was to be drawn and quartered. But the Edmonds Commission proposals were still something different, and in that difference, I believe, lies the germ of their failure.

145

First, the Commission recommended discontinuing the Corporate Loans Tax on municipal debt. Second, it recommended a substantial reduction in the Capital-stock (Bonus) Tax. Third, it recommended collection of the Gross Tax from every entity engaged in providing transportation or power. Fourth, it recommended changes in the law on taxing insurance premiums. Fifth, it recommended tightening the tax on bank stock. Sixth, it recommended repealing the tax on notary public gross receipts. Seventh, it recommended eliminating taxes on the personal property of non-resident decedents (those who lived and died outside the State of Pennsylvania, but at the time they died had property within the State). Eighth, it recommended taxing privately-owned improvements on public lands. Ninth, it recommended abatement of county taxes to those living in third-class cities, or else the elimination of all abatements. Tenth, it proposed extending the tax on personal intangible property. And eleventh, it proposed restricting tax-exemption of religious property (*Pennsylvania* 1925, pp. 42-44).

In addition, it proposed four amendments to the Pennsylvania State Constitution. These were submitted as part of the *Interim Report* in order to prevent delay in the adoption of a permanent tax policy, inasmuch as amendments required passage in two successive legislative sessions. Three of these were proposed *de novo* by the Commission, while the fourth was an amendment already passed (first passage) in the 1923 Session (*Pennsylvania* 1925, p. 44).

First, the Commission recommended second passage of the proposed amendment to Section I, Article 9, of the Constitution, permitting certain exemptions from inheritance taxes. Second, it proposed a new – and much more important – amendment to the same section, to allow the General Assembly to define and impose different rates of taxation on incomes and inheritances: that is, the Edmonds

146

Commission proposed a graduated State Income Tax, which Pennsylvania had resisted for half a century from the 1873 Constitution and has continued to resist. Third, it proposed an amendment permitting income-tax and inheritance-tax reciprocity. And fourth, it proposed an amendment to Section VIII, Article 9, to increase the borrowing power of municipalities in line with the projected elimination of the four-mill tax on intangible personal property (*Pennsylvania* 1925, pp. 44-46).

Though we have since seen the United States Congress pass a 2200-page Omnibus Tax Bill which (according to informed opinion) no single person had read in its entirety, back in 1925, in the Commonwealth of Pennsylvania, this *omnium gatherum* of a bill was a stiff proposition. It was not made any less stiff by the fact that the Commission also supported and incorporated in its *Report* the Mercur Commission's recommendations (*Pennsylvania* 1927, p. 21, quoted below). This support was expressed in the *Final Report* rather than the *Interim Report*, apparently because the Mercur Commission's mandate was still in effect at the time the Edmonds Commission was established, but not at the time the Edmonds Commission was extended in 1925 (Nicholson 1932, pp. 278-79). Here is the Edmonds Commission supporting the Mercur Commission:

"No subject considered by the commission has aroused more universal interest than the assessment and collection of local taxes. In the administration of Governor Sproul, a commission was appointed on this subject, whose findings were submitted to the Legislature in 1921, 1923, and 1925." (That is, bills were submitted incorporating the findings.) "As that commission has expired, we have, after careful consideration, adopted some of its conclusions as our own, and present its recommendations in modified form." In this connection, the Commission noted a study by F. P. Weaver, Professor of Agricultural

147

Economics at the Pennsylvania State College, on the assessment and collection of taxes on farm property in Crawford, Lancaster, Lebanon, Warren, Westmoreland, and Wyoming counties. Weaver's study showed a striking lack of uniformity in realty assessment among counties (the 1924 *Wisconsin Tax Problem* study showed the same thing), among taxing districts in the same county, and sometimes among realty in the same taxing district in the same county – and it also showed a great and recently increased tax burden upon agriculture as a result of the Agricultural Depression. It supported the Mercur Commission's recommendations, since it was clear that the assessment procedure was both unfair and excessively cumbersome. To be sure, some of the unfairness was on the way out, and was gone by the 1930s, but only after some of the unfairly-taxed farms had been squeezed out.

When the time came for the *Final Report*, there were some changes made. The Wood Plan disappeared. So did the *Interim Report*'s recommendations for eliminating the Gross Receipts Tax on notaries public. The Commission was having some second thoughts about uniformity in business taxation. The problem of taxing forests seemed to have grown in importance. Other states had passed laws establishing reciprocity in the matter of inheritance taxes on the property of non-resident decedents (a source of "great satisfaction" to the Commission), and the Federal government had enacted an Estate tax (*Pennsylvania* 1927, pp. 23ff).

So, in the end (besides the Constitutional amendments already recommended), the Edmonds Commission presented to the Legislature, in its *Final Report*, twenty new bills and one resolution. We should note, at this point, that only the most minor of its eleven previous recommendations had been passed, which should perhaps have suggested something to the Commission members. Edmonds and

148

Wheeler were, after all, in the Legislature. But the Commission proceeded to make its twenty separate recommendations.

First, the Commission recommended a permanent State Tax Commission (note that even the successful Wisconsin Tax Commission proceeded to permanent status only in stages). Second, it recommended three bills essentially encompassing the provisions of the Marshall-Ludlow bill (*Pennsylvania* 1927, pp. 21-22). Third, it recommended uniformity in tax abatement, thus repeating the *Interim Report* recommendation. Fourth, and also repeating the *Interim Report* recommendation, it recommended taxation of privately-owned improvements on public land. Fifth, it recommended differential inheritance taxes, with non-resident reciprocity, and additional taxes to make up for revenues lost to Pennsylvania through the new Federal Estate Tax. Sixth, it recommended eliminating in-state probate of out-of-state wills involving in-state property in trust. Seventh, it recommended eliminating the Corporate Loans Tax on municipal obligations and the bonds of first-class corporations. Eighth, it proposed a 2-percent tax on the profits of private and investment bankers and brokers. Ninth, it recommended a payment equivalent to municipal taxes for tax-exempt State property. Tenth, it recommended taxing the land (but not the improvements) of religious, educational, and charitable institutions. These ten recommendations are in *Pennsylvania* 1927, pp. 54-56.

Eleventh (I think we should start another paragraph here), it proposed triennial reaffirmation of exemption. Twelfth, it proposed legal review of new municipal indebtedness (in all cases but Philadelphia, Pittsburgh, and Scranton) by the Bureau of Municipalities of the Department of Internal Affairs. Thirteenth, it proposed abolishing a number of the State's special funds, transferring their contents to the

149

General Fund. Fourteenth, it proposed reducing the Corporation Bonus Tax. Fifteenth, it recommended revising the method of assessing capital-stock taxes. Sixteenth, it proposed taxing marine insurance companies on underwriting profits (as in other states) rather than gross premiums. Seventeenth, it recommended uniformity in taxation of insurance companies. Eighteenth, it recommended a permanent two-cent tax per gallon on liquid fuels such as gasoline. Nineteenth, it proposed abolishing the annual four-mill Tax on Mortgages, substituting a five-mill one-time Mortgage Registration Tax. And, twentieth, it proposed for second passage the Constitutional amendments on reciprocity and borrowing power, which had been approved by the 1925 Session of the Legislature. These ten are in *Pennsylvania* 1927, pp. 56-58.

In addition, it proposed a resolution (p. 58): "Be it Resolved, That in the judgment of the General Assembly, taxes on transfer of property by inheritance should be reserved to the State Government, and that the Federal Government should now withdraw from this field and leave to the States exclusively this much-needed source of revenue."

And what good came of it at last? The 1925 Session produced five tax-law changes, none of them important (*Pennsylvania Laws* 1925, pp. 51, 685, 695, 702, 806). As we noted, the tax on notary public fees was repealed. The Edmonds Commission had its mandate renewed – important presumably for its purposes, and certainly for ours, but of negligible importance in the history of Pennsylvania taxation. The Liquid Fuels Tax receipts were allocated one half to counties and one half to the General Fund. The tax on gross receipts of utilities and freight and oil transport companies was set at eight mills. And the transfer tax rate was amended to take account of Section 301 of the U.S. Revenue Act of 1924.

150

In the 1927 Session, the allocation of the Liquid Fuels Tax receipts was changed to one fourth to the counties and three fourths to the General Fund, with the permanent tax set a two cents per gallon and a one-cent emergency tax added: this partially embodied the Commission's eighteenth recommendation. Non-profit associations for highway improvement were exempted from the Capital-stock Tax. And transfer taxes were adjusted so as always to be equal to the maximum Federal deduction (*Pennsylvania Laws* 1927, pp. 201, 287, 742, 859).

In the 1929 Session there were three changes (*Pennsylvania Laws* 1929, pp. 677, 1037ff, 1806-07). The four-mill tax on the capital stock of banks and savings institutions was repealed. The Liquid Fuels Tax was set at four cents a gallon (throwing out the Commission's eighteenth recommendation), with one half going to the Liquid Fuels Tax Fund and the other half split between the former recipients. And the Anthracite Tax was phased out, going to 1-percent in Fiscal 1930, 1/2-percent in Fiscal 1931, and then to zero. Then, in the 1931 Session, except for the (very highly modified) Mercur Commission bill, the sum total of tax revision was the institution of a fifty-cent Poll Tax in place of the County Tax on Trades, a redefinition of exemptions from the Capital-stock Tax for corporations owning other corporations, and an eight-mill tax on the gross receipts (intrastate) of motor vehicles transporting for hire (*Pennsylvania Laws* 1931, pp. 117-18, 687-88, 694).

In short, the mountain labored, and labored, and brought forth a quickly-repealed mouse. We will come shortly to the Commission's inability to agree on a long-range policy, which is in some ways the flip-side of the Legislature's neglect of most of the short-range recommendations. The point here is that the repeal of a tax on the fees of notaries public, a temporary setting of a two-cent gasoline tax, and first passage of two minor Constitutional amendments scarcely constitutes success for a four-year high-powered blue-ribbon commission.

On long-range policy, the Edmonds Commission had all the attributes of a hung jury. "In order to remove the inequalities in the existing system of corporation taxes, and to provide for a just distribution of the burden ... two views have been advanced in the Commission. First ... some of the members of the Commission are convinced that the inequalities of the existing capital stock tax ... can all be obviated by the repeal of that tax and the substitution for it of a tax on net profits ... Second, other members of the Commission feel that such a radical change . . . would result in confusion and doubt, leading to litigation, and might seriously jeopardize the revenues of the Commonwealth" (*Pennsylvania* 1927, pp. 48-49). These members recommended patching (and re-tailoring) the existing fabric: interestingly, among the changes they specifically recommended *not* undertaking was repeal of the Anthracite Tax (p. 47).

In short, the Commission split (in its *Final Report*) on the one fundamental and unavoidable question – the question, indeed, at the root of all efforts at tax reform in the years we have studied – the question of the Income Tax. It is worth noting that the Income Tax Amendment, recommended for first passage in the *Interim Report* (passage that it did not, of course, achieve), was omitted from the *Final Report*. Though we are short of relevant Minority Reports, we know that Wood favored the Income Tax and that Wood did not participate in making the *Final Report*. It is not entirely fanciful to assume a 4-3 Commission split in favor of the tax, with Wood as part of the majority.

Because the Commission could not agree on fundamental policy, its twenty recommendation were, in essence, fragmented – twenty separate recommendations rather than one unified bill. The McCamant

152

Commission's majority bill may have been a monstrosity, but it was a unified monstrosity. These fragments were not, on the whole, the sort of thing that legislators readily accept from commissions of any kind: every separate law will require log-rolling, and without a dedicated floor manager for the various bills, it is a virtual certainty they will languish in committee (if they get even that far). But Edmonds was out of the Legislature in 1927, and the only other member of the Legislature on the Commission was Wheeler, whose influence does not seem to have been out of the ordinary. Certainly Wheeler died young in 1935, still a member of the Legislature, and still without major political achievements to his credit. In any event, he did not take a leading role in trying to get the Commission's recommendations passed into law, or even the Mercur Commission recommendation that was passed (Nicholson 1932, pp. 284ff).

Was there a flaw in the Commission that led it to make only these piecemeal proposals? Consider the Commission's membership. Though they do not all strictly fit Digby Baltzell's definition, Edmonds, Wood, and perhaps Connelly were closely akin to Philadelphia gentlemen; Reed, though from Pittsburgh, and Wheeler, though from Warren County, were of that ilk (Baltzell 1958, pp. 31-48, 158-72, 364-83). McKay (at the university level) and Jones (at the local level) were apparently experts in public finance. And Jones, by the way, though self-educated, had at least one strong élite characteristic: he was an Episcopal vestryman (Jordan 1913, s.n. Jones).

Barring the exemption of religious institutions (4-3 vote) and the taxation of forest lands (a significant part of the Commission's rather confused reflections on equity in taxation), it is unlikely there was any significant disagreement among the Commission members on specific issues, and if there was, it should not have been difficult to reach

153

Dodgson solutions (in which, it will be remembered, the solution comes from trading off weak preferences – making the "fewest changes in existing preference orderings"). The members, after all, were all Pinchot men.

But Pinchot was a politician (Pinkett 1970, esp. pp. 67-74). Why were his appointees apparently so a-political in their approach? The answer, I believe, lies in the very nature of a blue-ribbon commission. Tutchings found that commissions composed of corporate/governmental élites ("blue-ribbon" commissions), acting under conditions of high demand, were more likely than other commissions to recommend specific changes in the laws ("regulative" changes), less likely to have them passed, and (apparently) less likely to need to achieve coalitions. The need to achieve coalitions would be inversely proportional to the presence of coalitions on a commission at the very beginning: one does not necessarily need to achieve what one already has. But why would the coalition work to so little purpose? Why would blue-ribbon commissions as a class recommend laws that are rarely enacted?

A proper Philadelphia gentleman does not (in the words of George Wharton Pepper) feel the "itch for public office" – he does his public duty (Pepper was a United States Senator), but out of *bourgeoisie oblige* rather than because he really wants to participate in making things work (Baltzell 1958, p. 131). The Progressive reformers did indeed introduce a cult of efficiency into the American system, but it was by hiring non-élite experts (engineers, city managers), not so much by having the élite become experts (Wiebe 1967, pp. 164-95). In this view, the Wisconsin Idea, at least as John R. Commons defined it, is not fully "Progressive" (which sounds like a very odd statement). Emanuel Philipp argued that La Follette adopted Progressivism, as it was later understood, partly out of expediency (Philipp 1973, pp. 100ff). That may be, but the

Wisconsin Idea was La Follette's greatest legacy to his state (and perhaps the country) – not least because it answered in advance the question Robert Wiebe later asked (Wiebe 1967, pp. 173-76): How could the reformers break into the entrenched power structure? The answer was not by bringing reform to the power structure, but by bringing the power structure into reform – in our case, by bringing the interest groups into the blue-ribbon state commissions, as blue-ribbon members.

This Pinchot quite clearly failed to do in the case of the Edmonds Commission. But Sproul had largely failed to do it with the Mercur Commission, which we have counted a minor success: wherein lies the difference? The answer lies in the way in which commission members act, and specifically in the adoption of those decision premises that constitute their roles. As we shall see, the Edmonds Commission is a magnificent case in point for Simon's argument that if "the goals of an organization cannot be connected operationally with actions . . . then decisions will be judged against subordinate goals that can be so connected" (Simon 1981b, p. 481). In this case, I suggest, because of the member's decision premises, the benchmark for judgment was recommending rather than achieving the desired reforms.

We noted the problem of role decision-premises on the McCamant Commission, arguing that without violation of the House's mandate, it is unlikely the Commission would have functioned at all. It might be thought that, in leaving pure interest-group commissions behind, we would have left this problem behind, but that is not so. The point about looking at role decision-premises here is that the participants did not look at them there. In our concluding chapter, we will draw full comparisons, in this light, between and among all our commissions. Here we need only note that a uniform or nearly-uniform set of role

155

decision-premises can be just as debilitating for a policy-making commission as a set of roles based on interest groups and thus producing clique behavior.

Why? Consider our definitions of success. A commission should, first, propose laws that should solve the problem; then, second, the laws should be passed; and then, third, they should work. The weakness of commissions in general comes from the absence of the necessary linkages and (potential) trade-offs for success of the second kind, and the intelligent commission, or commission agenda-setter (like Kennan) will take that into account. Mercur may not have taken it into account, admittedly, but in the end things worked out as though he had. The weakness of both the pure interest-group commission and the pure blue-ribbon commission must lie in the first area, the proposing of laws that should solve the problem. This "should solve the problem" clause includes a necessity that the laws proposed satisfy the criteria of possible success in the so-called real world of politics. In the case of the blue-ribbon Edmonds Commission, the cult of efficiency (to give it one of its more common names), which was apparently accepted by most of the Commission's members, seems to have gotten in the way.

The key should be suggested by the difference between the form of the Edmonds Commission's output and the form taken by the output of the McCamant Commission, or the Kennan Commission, or the Mercur Commission. The McCamant Commission majority could limit its search space because its role decision-premises dictated a concentration on "getting" the railroads. The Kennan Commission had a self-limited mandate. The Mercur Commission had a narrow mandate, and therefore narrow search space, to begin with. Though both the McCamant Commission and the Mercur Commission proposed long bills, the bills were unified (albeit, in the case of the original McCamant Commission

156

bill, idiotic). But the Edmonds Commission took its grab-bag of bills and, in effect, dumped them on the House floor. It could accomplish its broad mandate, as it understood that mandate, only by limiting search space to what would be efficient, and not considering what could be done. It could, of course, have chosen the opposite tack, had it been a political rather than a blue-ribbon commission. Its members own role decision-premises necessarily (I believe) blinded it to any search but the search for efficiency.

This is not a matter for blame, except perhaps for Governor Pinchot in not setting a more limited agenda (which perhaps reflects a difference between Wisconsin Progressivism and T. Roosevelt Progressivism). The Commission indeed imposed some limitation on itself: it dropped the Wood Plan. But that may have been a wrong decision: the lesson of the Kennan Commission is, in part, that the mobilizing of public opinion, in which the commission itself may be a step, is necessary for tax reform. The revolution must be made in the hearts and minds of men *before* it is made in the Legislature (or, in the original John Adams case, a different kind of battlefield). The Wood Plan could have provided a mechanism for doing just that.

But probably it would not have. Indeed, even if every one of the Edmonds Commission recommendations had been passed into law (barring the Income Tax Amendment), success of the third kind might still have eluded them. When the Legislature created its Joint Committee on Tax Reform in 1937, the Committee noted that it did not expect any of its recommendations to be passed into law (in fact they were not) because the overwhelming reality of the Depression simply would not permit tax reform (*Pennsylvania* 1939, p. 3). Quite likely any Edmonds Commission reforms would have foundered in that same overwhelming reality.

157

But one reform, a minor one, did not founder, as we have seen. We have given the Mercur Commission the eventual, if indirect, credit for the passage of the 1931 Act establishing County Boards of Assessment and Appeal. The Edmonds Commission also recommended that, but there are two reasons for crediting it to the earlier body. First, the pressure from the Chamber of Commerce and the League of Women Voters began with the Marshall-Ludlow bill. Second, the Edmonds Commission was so generally unsuccessful in getting its recommendations passed that its support for this one was unlikely to have had much (if any) effect. It may be the case that Pinchot, in his 1931-35 term as Governor, did apply some pressure to get this measure through, inasmuch as his Commission had also recommended it: it is not clear that even this would justify giving any credit to the Edmonds Commission for its passage.

The importance of the Edmonds Commission, for our purposes, lies in its unimportance for any other. It had virtually no effect on tax reform in Pennsylvania. Wheeler continued in the Legislature until his early death in 1935; Edmonds returned as a Senator in 1938; Jones went on to serve on at least one other commission; Connolly was a well-known tax lawyer; McKay served as an advisor on state taxation; Edmonds headed the National Tax Association (NTA); and McKay served on one of Hoover's commissions. The five members alive after 1927 were all tax experts and successful men. Certainly Reed and Wood were successful men. But the Commission was almost an unmitigated failure, except for any impetus it may have given to the careers of its individual members.

The reason lies in the bounds of those members' bounded rationality. It may also have a subsidiary point of origin in the fact that the informed public opinion which these men presumably represented had not fully made up its mind on the question of the State Income Tax. Tutchings has suggested that commissions are created to isolate an issue from the larger political arena (Tutchings 1979, p. 120). We noted, however, in connection with this, that our commissions might mirror that arena and so not be isolated, as indeed was the case with the McCamant Commission. In the case of the Edmonds Commission, on the other hand, the isolation from the political arena was so complete as to constitute quarantine, even though the Commission still mirrored a confusion in the intellectual arena. After all (though this is an oversimplification), a commission may appeal to theory, or to practice, or to both. In the 1920s, the teachings of tax theory were themselves a trifle confused (Groves 1974, pp. 46-47, 57-62, 73, 97-99, 110, 135, 138-39).

It is probably because of this confusion that the 1923 Commission failed to agree on what tax policy was needed to produce equity, and thus in effect burked the chances of its own success even of the first kind – indeed, particularly of the first kind. But this cannot be taken as a characteristic even of blue-ribbon commissions in general, and certainly not as a characteristic of all commissions. To check this, I briefly investigated an almost exactly contemporaneous commission, the New Hampshire Recess Tax Commission of 1927, to see if it too reflected the same uncertainty: it did (*New Hampshire* 1928, esp. pp. 5-6, 20-33). The earlier commissions we have considered, and the later commission we will consider, did not. We may tentatively conclude, though our sample may not be statistically significant, that this uncertainty was characteristic of the 1920s. It may, however, be the case that a blue-ribbon commission would be more subject to this uncertainty than an interest-group commission, not having so much connection with the political arena. The McCamant Commission majority may have been quite wrong, but it was not uncertain.

The connection with the political arena is important because it ensures that political considerations will be part of the role (that is, the decision premises) of commission members. Franklin Edmonds had links to the political arena, certainly, but his way up the ladder had been through the White Fellowship at Cornell, teaching law at Swarthmore, and the Philadelphia Board of Public Education. Alexander Wheeler's way up had been through Yale, Oxford, the American Field Service, and the AEF. Reed was accustomed to controlling affairs. Connelly was a Reform Republican with only Philadelphia city experience. Wood, McKay, and Jones were more isolated than these four (though Wood perhaps arguably so). By isolation I mean isolation from the politics of the State Legislature: Jones certainly knew first-hand the politics of local finance. It does not appear that any of the seven were thinking much about the practicality of their suggestions as prospective laws.

In the next chapter we will be looking and the ragtag and bobtail of our small self-expert commissions doing their own work, the Matthews Commission of 1947, officially the Tax Study Committee (so called for reasons having to do with its odd institutional status). There was a fundamental shift in the nature of commissions in this period, away from a commission whose members were its own experts toward the modern (and much larger) commission whose purposes are increasingly defined by the techniques of public relations. But before the shift was complete, there was one throwback commission. Some of the reasons for the shift will be suggested in our concluding chapter, but before that, we will consider the 1947 Commission, which presents another interesting lesson on the effect of role decision-premises and the way commissions work.

160

# CHAPTER VI: THE PENNSYLVANIA COMMISSION OF 1947

By 1947 the popularity of the small self-expert tax revision commission was winding down. So far as I can tell, the commission appointed in that year in Pennsylvania was the sole post-World-War-II example of the phenomenon. Anachronistic or not, the 1947 Commission was appointed, not so much because the Governor intentionally went back to the earlier model, as because a complex institutional arrangement produced this unexpected result.

To understand why, we should go back to the Industrial Tax Survey Committee of 1937 and its self-recognized inability to do anything about the problems of taxation. The Committee's Report was issued in 1939: that same year, the Pennsylvania Legislature gave birth to the Joint State Government Commission. This, being a joint committee of members of the two houses of the Legislature, was not a commission in our sense. Even if it had been a commission, moreover, it was clearly not a tax revision commission. But it was the parent body of the Matthews Commission of 1947.

It is not entirely an easy task to follow the history of the tax committees and commissions of the 1940s. The Joint State Government Commission (really a committee) was formed in 1939, with a membership of seventeen, seven of whom sat as a Committee on Finance. This group of seven reported in 1941 (Pennsylvania 1941). Thereafter, the Joint State Government Commission created a separate Committee on the Continuation of the Tax Study (that is, the study begun by the Committee on Finance). The Committee on the Continuation of the Tax Study reported almost interminably (eleven

161

reports between 1943 and 1945), and it also created or accepted its own Tax Advisory Commission, which was however controlled and staffed by the Pennsylvania Economy League and was in some ways a prototype for the large-membership advisory commission of the modern era (*Pennsylvania* 1945, front matter, unnumbered pp.). Finally, the Committee on the Continuation of the Tax Study was supplanted by a newly-created Tax Study Committee, likewise a subcommittee of the Joint State Government Commission, but having two "public" members. It is the presence of these public members and of Secretary Orus Matthews as its Chairman that makes this "committee" actually a commission and a fit subject for our inquiry (*Harrisburg* 1949, *passim*).

Though this Matthews Commission was separated from the Edmonds Commission by more than a quarter-century, there was nonetheless greater continuity between the two than between the much closer Mercur Commission and Edmonds Commission. The original Committee on Finance of the Joint State Government Commission had created a subcommittee of professors to do the work, one of these being our old friend, Professor Marion McKay of the University of Pittsburgh (*Pennsylvania* 1941, p. 3). One member of that Committee on Finance, Edwin Winner, became Chairman of the Committee on the Continuation of the Tax Study: the members of the latter included State Senator Franklin Edmonds and (as Vice-Chairman) State Senator James Geltz (*Harrisburg* 1943, p. iii). The Tax Study Committee (Matthews Commission) of 1947 included Geltz and an Edmonds protegé, Lloyd Wood (*Pennsylvania* 1949, p. [iii]). (In addition, one member of the Industrial Tax Survey Committee of 1937, Frederick Gilder, served on the Committee on Finance, and another, Harry Trout on the Continuation Committee, thus providing some continuity between the 1930s and 1940s, at least.)

162

The Tax Study Committee (1947 Commission) seems to have relied on previous research and on its members' own *expertise* in fulfilling or attempting to fulfill its mandate, which was to investigate systems and methods of taxation in order to provide ways and means "of financing the Commonwealth and its political subdivisions upon a more scientific and equitable basis and to safeguard and enhance the industrial position of the Commonwealth" (*Pennsylvania* 1949, p. 3). The concern with industrial position began to be heard in ever-widening circles in the 1920s (*Pennsylvania* 1927, pp. 18-46, esp. 32ff, Brownlee 1971, Chapter III). The broad mandate of which it was part may be contrasted with the more specific charge of the 1939 Committee on Finance: to investigate pending litigation attacking tax legislation, to calculate expected revenues and expenses for 1939-41, and to make a series of detailed estimates of needs for public assistance, sources of revenue, and probable tax shortfalls (*Pennsylvania* 1941, pp. 1-3). No wonder the Committee on Finance hired a subcommittee of narrow *expertise*: the Matthews Commission, by contrast, had the same kind of mandate as the McCamant Commission or the Kennan Commission or the Edmonds Commission.

The Committee on the Continuation of the Tax Study was, to be sure, limited to the revenue side of the equation, but its mandate was similarly detailed. Even with Franklin Spencer Edmonds on the Committee, who was by that time unquestionably Pennsylvania's leading tax expert, the Committee still went to outside sources, or at least hired outside help, for its reports. We will consider some of the reasons for this in Chapter VII: it is mentioned here for contrast to the Matthews Commission. All this was taking place at a time when the General Assembly had increased taxes (in the word used by the Committee on Finance) "considerably" – though "by leaps and bounds" would have

163

been more accurate (*Pennsylvania* 1941, p. 4). It might thus be thought doubly curious that an old-fashioned commission of this sort (whatever its institutional linkages) should come into being at this point. Postwar optimism might account for it in part (*Pennsylvania* 1945, *passim*). For another part, perhaps we should look at the precise make-up of the Commission.

Like the McCamant Commission, the Matthews Commission had appointments from different sources, in this case two (not counting the Chairman) from the Governor, two by the President Pro Tem of the Senate, and two by the Speaker of the House. The Governor's appointees were the two public members, Philip Sterling and Frank Wilbur Main. The President Pro Tem appointed James Geltz and Lloyd H. Wood. The Speaker appointed Lambert Cadwalader and Warner M. Depuy (*Pennsylvania* 1949, pp. 3-4). The Chairman was the Pennsylvania Secretary of Commerce, Orus J. Matthews.

It is not clear whether Matthews was chosen as Chairman because he was Secretary of Commerce, or whether the Chairman was to be the Secretary of Commerce because that was the position held by Matthews. Orus J. Matthews was born in January 1900, and was thus forty-seven years old: he had graduated from the University of Pennsylvania in 1922 and gone to work for Kidder Peabody, of which he became a partner. He was on the Board of Managers of the Franklin Institute, the Graduate Hospital of the University of Pennsylvania, on the Valley Forge Park Commission, and a member of the Racquet Club, the Merion Cricket Club, the Historical Society of Pennsylvania, the Newcomen Society, and so on, and on (Smull's 1947, p. 640). In short, he was very much the sort of man Pinchot had appointed to the Edmonds Commission.

164

James A. Geltz, the Vice Chairman, was six months the Chairman's junior, a Republican (like every other member of the Commission), from Sewickley – more or less Pittsburgh's equivalent of the Main Line. He had graduated from Penn State, taken his LL.B. from the University of Pittsburgh, been a U. S. Government Attorney 1925-27, Assistant District Attorney for Allegheny County 1929-39, an unsuccessful candidate for the U. S. Congress in 1936, and then elected State Senator in 1938 and re-elected 1942 and 1946, being Majority Leader in 1941-42 (Smull's 1947, p. 305).

The other Senate appointee, Lloyd H. Wood, was coming up on his fiftieth birthday. He had graduated from Ursinus College (Collegeville, Pennsylvania) and Temple University School of Law, after serving in the U. S. Marine Corps in 1918-19. He had been elected to the State House of Representatives from Montgomery County (Norristown) at the same time Franklin Edmonds was elected to the State Senate from Montgomery County, in 1938, and then had succeeded Edmonds in the Senate on the latter's death in 1945. (Smull's 1947, p. 315.) Wood was Lieutenant Governor of Pennsylvania 1951-55, was defeated by Democrat George Leader for Governor in 1954, and died in 1964. He was also Chairman of the Montgomery County Republican Party from 1940 to 1948. (Smull's 1969, pp. 303, 422.)

The two gubernatorial appointees (besides Matthews) were Philip Sterling and Frank W. Main. Of these, Main was distinguished as the first C.P.A. to sit on any Pennsylvania tax commission: he was also the oldest member of the Matthews Commission, being almost sixty-eight at the time of his appointment (*Pittsburgh* 1913, s.n. Main). Main, born in Titusville, had attended Allegheny College, and then had passed his New York C.P.A. exams in 1904. Four years later, he had established, at the University of Pittsburgh, the third course in accountancy in the

165

country, after New York University and the University of Pennsylvania. From 1916 through 1931, he was a member of the Pennsylvania Board of Accountants. He headed his own firm, Main & Co., and he had been active in political fund-raising. (*Pittsburgh Press* 1932.) He died in 1954 (*NY Times* 1954).

The other gubernatorial appointee, Philip Sterling, was sixty years of age, a partner in the law firm of Sterling & Willing in Philadelphia, and a graduate of the University of Pennsylvania College Department (in 1908) and the University of Pennsylvania Law School (in 1911). From 1917 to 1933 he had been a State Representative (Republican), serving on the Joint Legislative Committee on State Finance during Pinchot's Little New Deal. Since then he had been in private practice (Smull's 1933, p. 297).

The two men appointed by the Speaker were Lambert Cadwalader, a scion of one of Baltzell's prototypical Philadelphia families (Baltzell 1958, pp. 72, 82-84, 131, 139, 145, 148, 247, 324), and Warner Depuy. Cadwalader, from Haverford on the Main Line, was rising sixty-five years, a graduate of the Episcopal Academy, St. Paul's School, and Princeton. He had been first elected to the Legislature in 1936 (as a Republican) and regularly re-elected, had served seven years in the Pennsylvania National Guard, and had been on the Pennsylvania World's Fair Commission in 1939-40 (Smull's 1947, p. 366).

Whereas Cadwalader had, so to speak, "arrived" – indeed, had arrived pretty much at the same instant he was born, Warner Depuy was on his way up. He was twenty-nine years of age, from Milford, Pike County (where the States of Pennsylvania, New York, and New Jersey meet), and was a coal, feed, and seed dealer in Port Jervis, New York. But he had graduated from Dartmouth College in 1939, first been elected to the House in 1942 (at twenty-four), and re-elected since

166

(Smull's 1947, p. 371). He served in the Legislature until the 1950 election, was Deputy State Treasurer 1957-61, Deputy Secretary of Revenue 1963-66, Secretary of Revenue 1966-70, Republican candidate for State Auditor 1968, and a member of the State Tax Equalization Board from 1970 (*EPB XXXI*, p. 273, Smull's 1969, pp. 368, 380, Smull's 1971, p. 364, Smull's 1976/77, p. 448). About the middle of his career he stopped his ascent and moved sideways, but in 1947 he was apparently still going up.

Except for Main, this is what Tutchings would call a political commission (Tutchings 1979, pp. 99ff). We would call it mixed, though with a heavy emphasis on the governmental élite – that is, toward the blue-ribbon side. The one thing it clearly was not was an interest-group commission. Main was presumably appointed for his *expertise* in governmental accounting, and the others for their political understanding of the issues. We shall see just how this commission differed from its predecessors in both membership and linkages, what it accomplished, and whether the two are tied together.

First, what did it accomplish? Its mandate was for "scientific and equitable" taxation "to safeguard and enhance" Pennsylvania's industrial position (*Pennsylvania* 1949, p. 5). One might be forgiven for concluding that it made slightly heavy weather of its task. "The sum and substance of scientific endeavor," it pontificated, "is the attainment of certitude. Translated into tax language, this means the enactment of tax statutes which facilitate the determination of the liability with a minimum of discretion on the part of taxpayers and taxgatherers" (pp. 6-7). I am not at all convinced that this was the normal meaning of "scientific" in 1949 – it would be quite inaccurate now – nor am I convinced it was what the Legislature meant, if indeed it meant anything whatever by the word. But the definition is on a par with the

167

Commission's view of the problem raised by the word "equitable" (which was merely a staple of tax-reform discussions throughout our period).

"On the other hand" – that is, unlike the word "scientific" with its very definite meaning – "the legislative directive that the Committee recommend 'ways and means of financing the Commonwealth and its political subdivisions upon a more . . . equitable basis' presented the members . . . with some interpretive difficulties. In a period of rapid economic change such as the present, concepts of equity do not pass unchallenged" (p. 7). Bravely, the Commission strove to overcome this problem (though it is not entirely sure they had the problem itself defined correctly): "Nevertheless, men must somehow manage to agree upon some few basic concepts of equity" – and the Commission, with great travail, managed eventually to do just that (p. 7). "The Committee's recommendations are based upon two simple precepts. First, a worthy public general-purpose expenditure should be financed by means of broad-based general taxes. Second, the tax base or bases should be selected to facilitate the determination of the tax liability with a minimum of discretion on the part of the taxpayers and taxgatherers." Having thus proceeded to conflate equity and science, the Commission finally cut the cackle and came to the recommendations. We will try to determine later why it took them so long.

The Commission recommended abolishing the taxes on capital-stock and corporate franchises, the Corporate Loans Tax, and the Corporate Net Income Tax. It recommended establishing a tax on employed capital and retaining the raft of "temporary" taxes created during the Depression, except the one on soft drinks. A tax on investment income should be substituted for the County Personal Property Tax (which was "avoided and evaded"), and there should be a 1

168

1/2-percent tax on unincorporated-business and professional revenues (*Pennsylvania* 1949, pp. 3-6).

On the question of local taxes, the Commission made two sets of recommendations. The first was that all school districts be restricted, by statute, to the imposition of real-estate and per-capita taxes, and that permissive taxation be imposed at only one level of local government (the city/town level), with these taxes restricted to wages, salaries, unincorporated-business and professional income, and per-capita levies. The second dealt with the financing of state-mandated local functions, to be carried out preferably (the Commission's preference) by returning to the subdivisions part or all of a State Income Tax, preferably a graduated one, which would of course require an amendment to the State Constitution (*Pennsylvania* 1949, II, pp. 2-4).

Finally, the Commission recommended the imposition of a retail sales and use tax on tangible personal property – except food for off-premises consumption and goods already subject to a state excise tax – with three quarters of the proceeds being distributed among the local school districts and the remainder to the municipalities (*Pennsylvania* 1949, II, pp. 11-12). The principal subjects of State excise taxation were gasoline, cigarettes, beer, and liquor. It should be noted that the Commission was proposing to take away the "temporary" soft-drink tax with one hand and then tax soft drinks with the other.

Were these recommendations passed into law? In 1949, as in previous years, the Legislature's first step was extension of the "temporary" taxes (note the words "extension" and "temporary"), almost all extended *en bloc* and at the very beginning of the Session. Specifically, there were extensions of the Liquid Fuels Tax (up two cents to 1951), cigarette tax, Corporate Net Income Tax, the manufacturing non-exemption from franchise taxes, the Gross Receipts

Tax, and the Liquor Control Board Sales Tax (*Pennsylvania Laws* 1949, pp. 315ff, 336, 345, 358, 363, 366, 631, 824). A tax was imposed on marine insurance underwriting profits (p. 899) – where have we heard about that before? Carbonated water was included in the tax on soft drinks, which was clearly not eliminated (p. 1015). The municipalities were restricted from taxing manufacturing, farming, or natural resources (p. 1459). School districts of the first class (Philadelphia and Pittsburgh) were granted the right to impose a Mercantile License Tax and additional business, real-estate, and personal-property taxes (pp. 1661, 1676). And the "temporary" tax on malt beverages was extended to 1951 (p. 1669).

In 1951, the first step was to make the First-Class School-District Property Tax permanent (*Pennsylvania Laws* 1951, p. 237). The Corporate Net Income Tax went up (p. 449). The manufacturing exemption was again postponed (p. 462). The Gross Receipts Tax was extended (pp. 468, 1761). The tax on cigarettes was made permanent, as recommended by the Commission, and so were the "emergency" tax on liquor and the tax on malt beverages (pp. 471, 479, 481). The Liquid Fuels Tax was extended for two years, and a fuel-use tax imposed on dealers exempt from the Liquid Fuels Tax (pp. 485, 1969). A Corporation Income Tax was imposed on those corporations exempt from the existing law for reasons having to do with the prohibition on taxing interstate commerce (pp. 1417ff). A realty transfer tax was imposed, the Inheritance Tax raised, the mutual-company exemption from the Premiums Tax eliminated, and the State given the power to issue tax anticipation notes (pp. 1742, 1713, 1710, 1646). It was a busy session, and it did enact one of the Commission's recommendations, but only one, and that cosmetic.

The 1953 Session saw extensions of the Fuel Use Tax, the Liquid Fuels Tax, and the Realty Transfer Tax (*Pennsylvania Laws* 1953, pp. 250, 252, 257). The Poll Tax in cities of the third class was changed to a Residence Tax, a 1-percent Use and Storage Tax was imposed on tangible personal property, a Franchise Tax exemption established for personal property, the Bank and Trust Company Property Tax was insignificantly amended, and first-class cities were required – which is to say, Philadelphia was required – to submit Real Estate Tax increases to the electors (*Pennsylvania Laws* 1953, pp. 267, 377, 495, 1301, 1200). The Corporation Income Tax, Corporate Net Income Tax, and Gross Receipts Tax were continued (pp. 482, 534, 646). And a 1-percent Sales Tax was imposed "for public school purposes" (p. 403).

In short, in the three sessions following the Matthews Commission's Report, three of the Commission's recommendations were adopted: in 1949 (and perhaps 1953), restriction of the taxing power of the municipalities; in 1951, the making of some of the temporary taxes permanent (and some others became permanent *de facto* if not *de jure*); in 1953, the beginning of the State Sales Tax (though at 1-percent rather than 2-percent, and all for education rather than three quarters for education and the other one quarter for the municipalities). By comparison with the Edmonds Commission this looks good. In a way, it looks good even beside the Kennan and Mercur Commissions. So, it may be asked, why am I not calling the Matthews Commission a success?

Perhaps we should rehearse our definitions of success. First, the commission should propose laws that will solve the problem it is charged to solve: that is, it should define the policy needs and set the relevant policy. (In most cases, the needs will be set out in the mandate.) Second, the relevant laws should then be passed. Third, they

171

should bring about the desired result. One problem with calling the Matthews Commission a success is not merely that only some of its proposals were enacted but that its proposals were in fact set up to alter tax policy, and their selective enactment, far from altering tax policy, merely confused it.

Despite its philosophic maunderings, the Commission did in fact propose a sweeping set of changes. Corporate taxation would be rationalized. The permanent need for *all* the "temporary" taxes would be recognized (*inter alia*, so they could play their part in future budgeting). Municipalities would be limited in their taxing power, but they would receive funds from the State Sales Tax (and from the Income Tax for State-mandated projects). There would be a general broad-based progressive Income Tax, and at the same time a shift from property taxation generally toward income taxes.

The limitations were indeed placed on the municipalities, but they got nothing in return. The state still refused to pay for State-mandated municipal expenses. No steps were taken toward a progressive Income Tax. The permanent need for some, but not all, temporary taxes was grudgingly recognized. Corporate taxation remained an unrationalized quagmire. There was no shift from property taxes toward income taxes. The one undeniable achievement was the State Sales Tax: everything else was fiddling. But should the Commission not at least be given credit for bringing the Sales Tax into being?

It did propose the tax, and the tax was enacted, changing the shape of the Pennsylvania tax system, at least in part. Certainly part of the credit is due the Matthews Commission. It may be profitable here to examine the entire relation of the Joint State Government Commission and the idea of the Sales Tax – briefly, if not in detail. Though flawed, this was the Joint State Government Commission's chief success. We

172

must, of course, remember that this Commission is really a committee, and the only part of its success that interests us is the part due to its Tax Study Committee, which we are calling the Matthews Commission. In any case, having noted why the success was flawed, we should look for the reasons the Matthews Commission was successful at all, and see what they can tell us about the nature of the Commission. The place to begin is with the eleventh and final volume of the Committee on the Continuation of the Tax Study (of the Joint State Government Commission).

This is the volume prepared by the Tax Advisory Committee for the Committee on the Continuation. To be exact, it is the volume prepared by the Pennsylvania Economy League under the aegis of the Tax Advisory Committee for the Committee on the Continuation. It was apparently prepared at the suggestion of the Pennsylvania Economy League, which is a businessman's group. And among the recommendations it made was this: "That for the purpose of bringing about a reduction in local taxes on real estate, state taxes, dedicated for public school purposes, be levied in the form of a state sales and compensating use tax at the rate of two and one half percent, to supplement the proposed shift of the utilities gross receipts tax and the insurance premiums tax (state collected) to the use of school districts for the same purpose" (*Pennsylvania* 1945, p. [unn.]).

Some of the Pennsylvania Economy League's (or Citizen's Tax Advisory Committee's) other recommendations also found their way into the Matthews Commission's Report, and every one of these was passed. The other carry-over proposals, by the way, were for making the cigarette, gasoline, malt beverage, and liquor taxes permanent: how much these constituted an interest-group issue is not clear. The point to be made here is that we might consider the Sales Tax an interest-group

173

proposal, and it is arguable that it was successful because it had an interest group behind it. In other words, even the Matthews Commission may have been taking interest-group politics as well as ordinary legislative politics into account. Because of the Commission's institutional connection to the Tax Advisory Committee, there may have been an invisible interest-group presence in its meetings.

This may sound fanciful, but I think it accurately describes what was going on. It cannot be accidental that the two sets of recommendations taken over by the Matthews Commission from the Pennsylvania Economy League (two sets out of a considerable number of proposals) were both passed, and that they comprised two of the three Matthews Commission proposals passed, out of six major sets of proposals made. The successful proposal not taken over from the Pennsylvania Economy League was the limitation of municipal taxing power: but even here the League had recommended reduction of municipal taxes, albeit in amount (of property tax) rather than in number of taxes.

We might speak of this invisible interest-group presence as a concealed portion of the agenda set by the Matthews Commission and presumably by Matthews (the most likely to have had strong ties with the Pennsylvania Economy League) if not by Geltz (who had served on the Committee on the Continuation, to which the League's Report was directed). Interest groups, it seems, can be represented in more ways than one – and this on what we have already noted was not an interest-group commission.

Given its place in a continuing series of similar bodies (though none of the others was sufficiently similar to satisfy our definition of a small self-expert commission), we can say the Commission was created in conditions of high demand. We can also clearly define its

174

composition, in Tutchings terms, as corporate/governmental élite. Its recommendations were for specific legislative ("regulative") actions. What was the outcome of those actions?

In general, it was to move from regressive toward proportional taxation, if not fully progressive taxation. Pennsylvania had, even as I was originally carrying out this study, one of the most regressive of all property taxes (Phares 1980, p. 144). It still pretty much has it. It is true that a general sales tax is regressive, and it is true that cigarette, gasoline, and beer and liquor taxes are fairly steeply regressive (Phares 1980, pp. 90-91). But the net effect of the package of proposals recommended by the Matthews Commission – if they had been passed as a package – would have been to alter the incidence of taxation so that the burden was less concentrated on the lower income groups, and also to have centralized collection. The effect of the proposals actually passed, however, was to shift the burden more onto the shoulders of the lower income groups. Municipalities were restricted to the particularly regressive property tax, the most regressive of the temporary taxes were made permanent, and a regressive Sales Tax was established (Phares 1980, pp. 29-36, 90-91, 144). That is why I say, despite the passage of several of their recommendations, that the Matthews Commission really cannot be considered a success.

We must be careful not to make it appear that a successful commission is one that establishes an income tax, an inaccurate simplification that might be suggested by the presence of the Kennan Commission for comparative purposes. But the Income Tax was in fact, if not in the Matthews Commission's philosophizing, the key to the envisioned tax reform. Equalization – or tax "equity" – had more and more come to mean not equalization as between city and country, or between manufacturing or transportation and agriculture, but between or

175

among different income classes (Maxwell 1977, pp. 106-110). To some extent, perhaps, the Commission's self-developed problems with the idea of equity may not have been entirely chimerical: there were changes in what the word meant from 1889 to 1923 to 1947. But the members still made remarkably heavy weather of their mandate. However that may be, the simplest way toward equalizing the burden among income classes was and is a progressive Income Tax.

Such a tax, as it did in Wisconsin, would require a revolution in attitudes in Pennsylvania. The successful or partly successful commissions we have looked at thus far were steps in the education of the public – education to convince the public of the need for change. The whole series of tax bodies convened and convoked in Pennsylvania from 1937 to 1947 may have been engaged in an educational endeavor (certainly that was how the Committee on the Continuation of the Tax Study defined its mandate), but in that series the Matthews Commission at best represents a minor step.

Once again, I think, a commission was partially blinded by its unconsidered role decision-premises. Main's role, we will assume, was to penetrate the secrets of government accounting, and we will assume he did a good job. All the others members were or had been in positions of power in the State government. The agenda included some interesting propositions; the aura around the Commission was recognizably that of blue ribbons; but the perception of roles here was unlike that of any of our other commissions.

This can be seen in the relief with which the Commissioners turned from their philosophizing about science and equity to the plain – and obviously much more familiar – business of proposing legislation. We may contrast John A. Wright on the 1889 Commission or Kossuth Kennan on the 1897 Commission. To them the primary problem was to convert those principles of political economy dealing with taxation into proposals for tax revision. The same could be said for John Penman Wood, whose absence from the Edmonds Commission at the end of its deliberations seems to have led to a *Final Report* less coherent in its philosophy than the *Interim Report*. Even the Mercur Commission, with its different and much narrower mandate, still seems to have been less interested in drawing up proposed laws than in establishing basic policy: John H. Fertig of the Legislative Reference Bureau drew up the detailed proposal.

It is true that the members of the Matthews Commission began with some confused philosophical efforts. But they were nevertheless oriented toward legislation, and they acted as legislators on the Commission. They knew, in one sense, that this was not their mandate, or rather that it was only half their mandate. But, like Herbert Simon's two men in Milwaukee, they were simply incapable of seeing the whole: they accepted the sub-goal (in this case, to get legislation proposed) because their vision could not encompass the tax reform and the understanding of tax philosophy to which they were called.

This may seem to be overstating the case. After all, the proposed legislation, had it all been passed, would have brought Pennsylvania closer to tax equity as tax equity was generally defined in 1949. That is true – but then the Marshall-Ludlow Bill, had it been passed, would have brought Pennsylvania closer to tax equity as tax equity was defined by the Mercur Commission's mandate in 1919. The difficulty is that the Marshall-Ludlow Bill was not passed, and neither was the package of legislation the Matthews Commission proposed. Eventually public opinion swung to the side of the Mercur Commission proposals, but so far as a graduated Income Tax is concerned, it has not, as of 2006, swung to the side of the Matthews Commission package. The Matthews

Commission seems to have succumbed to a perfectly understandable impulse to propose legislation some of which (at least) would be passable.

To put it another way, the Commission, up to a point, acted as we would expect a mixed or corporate/governmental elite commission to operate (a "3-1-4" commission in the Tutchings classification): then it broke the usual mode by having a number of its specific recommendations passed. If we look at the Commission as an arm of the Legislature – which it was, institutionally – rather than as an ad-hoc arm of the Executive, we can see why. That it was a legislative rather than an executive commission might be thought to remove it from the legitimate bounds of this study, but in fact it does not. The McCamant Commission was partly chosen by the Legislature, and the Matthews Commission was partly chosen by the Governor, and both were under cabinet officials. Both belong. What the institutional background of the Matthews Commission shows is, in part, what self-perceived roles made the members act the way they did.

Note that the members' preferences were very likely to be both single-peaked and coincident: all were Republicans, all but Main were or had been in the Legislature, all but Main had either rich suburbs or Ivy League schools in their background, or both. First appearances, at least, should suggest a Condorcet solution to their problem. And the institutional linkages suggest that this solution would be more likely to find its way into law than the solutions of any of the other commissions to the problems in their mandate.

But only part of the package was passed, and certainly the problems were not solved. And why did the Commission propose a tax that could not be passed – a tax that has indeed not yet been passed? If, as I have said, it was too prone to recommend passable legislation, why

178

on earth did it propose as the keystone of its legislative structure a law that clearly could not be passed? The answer, I suggest, is that there was a confusion of roles. The members of the Commission, though clearly uncomfortable with tax theory, even perhaps inarticulate (though burbling) on the subject of tax theory, tried to force themselves into their unaccustomed role. They came up with a package embodying their findings within that role. Then they (or four of them) worked to pass whatever pieces of that package could be passed, even though the effect was to reduce rather than increase tax equity. They would have been better off, and the State would certainly have been better off, if they had stayed within the bounds of their unaccustomed role, avoided their accustomed roles, and seen none of their proposals passed into law. Note that both Depuy and Cadwalader left the Legislature after the 1950 Session, as did Wood (to be Lieutenant-Governor). Depuy took up a new career as a tax expert within State government.

Lying behind all of this, and broadly differentiating this commission from the others, is the almost incredible (and almost catastrophic) growth in the State government, and therefore of the needs of the state government, from the days of the Edmonds Commission to the time after World War II, and indeed to the present day. The lament of the Industrial Tax Survey Committee in 1939 could serve as the keynote: the members knew that their recommended reforms would be swallowed up in the government's need for more and more and more revenues regardless of source or incidence or equity. The Sales Tax, once in place, was raised, and raised, and raised again (*Pennsylvania Laws* 1955, p. 1707, *Pennsylvania Laws* 1959, p. 729, *Pennsylvania Laws* 1963, pp. 49ff, *Pennsylvania Laws* 1967, p. 918, and so on). Even the taxes that remained "temporary" were re-enacted each session (*Pennsylvania Laws* 1955, pp. 58, 59, 128, *Pennsylvania Laws* 1957, pp.

38, 31, 55, 57, 181, *Pennsylvania Laws* 1959, pp. 284, 322, 729, 911, and so on). And there was a procession of larger commissions trying vainly to solve the problem of squeezing blood from a turnip equitably. These last included the Emergency Tax and Revenue Fact-Finding Committee (1951), the Tax Study Committee (1952-55), the Tax Policy Advisory Committee (1956), the Tax Study and Revision Commission (1967-68), the Governor's Tax Reform Committee (1972), and the Cyert Commission (1979-82), for which the first draft of this study was initially drawn up.

The Matthews Commission's mandate was impossibly large: perhaps that fact lies at the root of the conflation of science with equity. Perhaps the members were limiting their mandate, by their own interpretation, to the establishment of some kind of certainty in taxation. Of course, taxation is widely acknowledged to be one of the two certain things in this world, but the amounts are not certain, and it was to this that the Commission really directed its attention. Unfortunately, its proposed tax revisions had little or nothing to do with certainty, except insofar as centralized levy and collection is more certain than decentralized levy and collection. The surest of all taxes is the Income Tax: that is precisely the one that got away.

In any event, the net effect of the bills passed was negligible, except for the simple addition of the Sales Tax to all other taxes. The changes were supposed to protect "the effectiveness of productive processes" and to end "reliance upon real property taxation as the principal source of local revenue" (*Pennsylvania* 1949, II, pp. 1ff). Such reliance (in the Commission's view) was "no longer practical and equitable" because (1) "there has been a wide variation of assessment practices resulting in inequitable assessment of many classes of property," because (2) "there is considerable evidence to indicate that

180

assessed valuations have tended to lag behind market values," and because (3) "there has been a gradual increase in the proportion of tax exempt real property." All this suggests that the effect of the Mercur reform had rather worn off or been overtaken by events, and that it would have been greater if the 1943 Act had not been a compromise. On the other hand, every taxation commission whose report I have read has made roughly the same comment, regardless of the relative honesty and efficiency of the assessors. As to what credence is given – you pay your money and you take your choice.

Note that, although equitable considerations were involved, the reasons for the Commission's recommendations here are largely practical: to maintain the effectiveness of productive processes, to keep assessments up to date, and to reduce problems resulting from tax-exempt property. Moreover, the chief equitable concern was the fairness of property taxation from jurisdiction to jurisdiction, though of course the fairness of a property tax as against a broad-based State tax was tied in with this. The answer to any inequities was perceived to lie in reducing the reliance on property taxes rather than increasing their fairness. The introduction of the Sales Tax clearly reduced the relative burden of property taxes: if any new tax is added, the percentage of the burden made up by each old tax is reduced. But it does not seem to have reduced the absolute burden, and it does not seem to have enhanced the effectiveness of productive processes. Philadelphia industry continued to do about as well as it had been doing (*PEL* 1956, *passim*).

The Pennsylvania Economy League conducted five studies of the tax burden on business and industry in Pennsylvania, between 1956 and 1969 (*PEL* 1956, 1957, 1962, 1967, 1969). In 1956, it was found that, seven years after the Matthews Commission Report, the State was in an exceptionally unfavorable industrial tax position. The next study, in

181

1957, found the situation to be substantially improved, principally from the restoration of Pennsylvania's historic exemption of manufacturing investment from the basis for the Capital-stock Tax and the Franchise Tax. The restoration of this exemption had been recommended in the Tax Advisory Commission's report to the Committee on the Continuation of the Tax Study in 1945. It was not picked up by the Matthews Commission, and indeed, as we have noted, the suspension of the exemption was re-enacted in the 1949 Session of the Legislature (*Pennsylvania Laws* 1949, p. 366).

In both these Economy League studies (1956 and 1957), combined State and local tax liabilities of Pennsylvania's manufacturing corporations were found to weigh relatively less on them than the State tax burden alone: that is, to put it more clearly, it was found that manufacturers were not paying as big a share of local taxes as they did of State taxes. The 1962 study, made at a time when Pennsylvania's broad-based tax on consumer sales had become the State's major revenue producer, showed an improved (and approximately mid-level) position for Pennsylvania manufacturers in the relative burden of state taxation. Things did not change very much – and if at all, not for the better – between 1962 and the next study in 1967, or its update in 1969. Beyond that point we need not go. The fact is that the Tax Study Committee of 1947 – the Matthews Commission – simply did not make the one recommendation it should have made above all others (certainly in view of the particular interest group involved) if it wanted "the effectiveness of productive processes" not to be impaired. And it does not much matter if we are involved in a case of self-fulfilling prophecy. Whether we are or not, the Commission overlooked an easy bet.

It was said above that the effect of the Matthews Commission recommendations was negligible, barring the addition of the Sales Tax

182

to the tax-gatherer's arsenal. But surely the Sales tax was a very large addition – so large that by 1962 it brought in more money than any other tax. Yet I am reluctant to count its passage a success for the Matthews Commission, on the grounds that it was proposed as part of a package, to fulfill a particular mandate, and when it was passed separately, it produced quite the opposite effect from the one desired. Put it this way. If the Commission had recommended the Sales Tax to make taxation less regressive, we should have thought that a failure of the first kind. It would have recommended a law that would do the opposite of what was desired. The recommendation of the proper course of action is the *sine qua non* for the other kinds of success. Passage of an inapposite law would not be success of the second kind. What we have here, with the failure of the Legislature to enact the entire package, Progressive Income Tax and all, is precisely the enactment of a law inapposite to the Commission's mandate. It would be tendentious in the extreme to call this success.

However, it should be pointed out that just before the time the Matthews Commission was sitting, there was passed the most significant tax revision law in Pennsylvania within our period, and arguably the most significant passed from the adoption of the 1873 Constitution to the present day. This is the act "empowering cities of the second class, cities of the second class A, cities of the third class, school districts of the second class, school districts of the third class and school districts of the fourth class to levy, assess, and collect . . . certain additional taxes subject to maximum limitations for general revenue purposes" – otherwise the Municipal Tax Enabling Act of 1947 *(Pennsylvania Laws 1947, II, p. 1145)*. This occupies a position in the history of Pennsylvania taxation analogous to (if not quite the same as) the position of the 1911 Income Tax Law in the history of Wisconsin taxes. Unlike the Wisconsin law, it has a largely hidden history.

Before we go over that history, it may be useful to set out the provisions of the Municipal Tax Enabling Act. The first section gives the cities and school districts of the relevant classes the power to levy and assess such taxes as they shall determine – but not on "a privilege, transaction, subject, occupation or personal property which is now or does hereafter become subject to a State tax or license fee" and not "on the gross receipts from utility service or any person or company whose rates and services are fixed and regulated by the Pennsylvania Public Utility Commission" and not (except for ticket taxes for amusements or taxes on title transfers) "on the privilege of employing such tangible property as is now or does hereafter become subject to a State tax" (*Pennsylvania Laws* 1947, II, pp. 1145-46). This and the fourth section may be considered the heart of the bill. But the fifth section is also important.

The second and third sections, by contrast, deal with notice of intention to levy or assess taxes and with matters of appeal – both essentially questions of mechanics (pp. 1146-47). The fourth section, though dealing with what might be considered a question of mechanics, nonetheless fills out the power conferred by the first section, and tells exactly where the buck stops. It permits the cities and school districts "to provide by ordinance or resolution for the creation of such bureaus or the appointment and compensation of such officers, clerks, collectors . . . as may be deemed necessary for the assessment and collection of taxes imposed under authority of this act" (pp. 1147-48).

Section Five (though the marginal note reads "Payment prior to effective date credited") deals with the fact that payments of taxes adopted under this act, as well as of certain taxes adopted prior to the

184

act, "shall be credited to and allowed as a deduction from the liability . . from any other like tax" – with some exceptions (p. 1148). The remaining three sections remove limitations on tax amounts "under existing laws" (but not future laws), give municipalities the power to prescribe and enforce penalties for nonpayment, and provide that if some part of the law is declared unconstitutional, the remainder of the law will still be in effect (p. 1149). This count of the sections omits Section Nine, making the law effective immediately upon enactment, which was June 25, 1947. The 1947 Act was subsequently amended, but so far as major revision is concerned, and also of course so far as our period is concerned, this was much the most important step taken in the history of Pennsylvania tax revision. The question before us in whether it can be traced to any of our tax revision commissions.

As we have already noted, the Matthews Commission specifically recommended that school districts of all classes be restricted to real-estate and per-capita taxes, that permissive taxes be restricted to one level of government (cities and towns), and that they be further restricted to income and per-capita levies (*Pennsylvania* 1949, II, pp. 9-10). Now the Matthews Commission met after the 1947 Act had been passed, and it reported quite a time after that passage: moreover, it recommended *restrictions* on municipal taxing power, by kind of tax. Quite clearly the Municipal Tax Enabling Act of 1947 not only did not come from the Matthews Commission but was inimical to its conclusions. In addition, it did not come from the 1943-45 Pennsylvania Economy League Report. That report likewise suggested reductions in municipal taxes – though in amount, not in the kinds of taxes.

Was the germ of this change perhaps implanted instead by one of the earlier commissions – not Mercur's to be sure, but perhaps McCamant's or, more likely, the Edmonds commission? After all, the

185

Mercur Commission reported in 1921 and achieved its final mixed success in the passage of a part of its recommended law in 1943: a lapse from 1927 to 1947, though improbable, ought to be checked for. We should note, however, that outside sources tell of the continuing effort to achieve the Mercur recommendations, which means we are not restricted to internal or statistical evidence linking presumed cause and effect. Even if we find apparent continuity of ideas in the Edmonds Commission and the 1947 Act, it may be no more than coincidence. And even if we have real continuity of ideas, we might have had it without the need for a report: both *Report* and Commission might be irrelevant to the continuity.

It turns out that we have no problem in tracing connections between the Edmonds Commission reports and the 1947 Act: quite simply, there seem to be none. The Edmonds Commission, as will be remembered from Chapter V, took over the Mercur Commission's *Report* on the assessment and collection of (existing) local taxes. The only other local tax recommendation it made, either in the *Interim Report* (1925) or the *Final Report* (1927), was a "Subjects of Local Taxation Bill" adding to those subjects "privately-owned improvements erected on public lands" (*Pennsylvania* 1927, p. 43). The origins of the 1947 Act, wherever they may lie, clearly do not lie here.

Nor, of course, do they lie in the McCamant Commission's *Report*. It is far far too long a time from 1889 to 1947 – almost the whole period of our study – to expect a discovery that the State Senators and Representatives who passed the 1947 Act had been reading John Armstrong Wright on the sly (or on anything else). But it is interesting, if no more, that the expansion of the municipal taxing power in the 1947 Act brought the tax system of the Commonwealth of Pennsylvania closer to the ideal that Wright had set out: local governments should be

186

allowed to levy taxes appropriate to local purposes, on vehicles in order to maintain roads, on merchants' real property (as embedded or embodied profits from local business), on liquor sold locally, on local amusements, on householders (as embedded or embodied local income), all for municipal and school purposes (Wright 1889, p. 48). True, Wright suggested State revenue sharing (specifically the return of excess State Income Tax to the municipalities whence it came) and he assumed purely local businesses and purely local roads: time has changed that. Nonetheless, though quite clearly the 1947 Municipal Tax Enabling Act had nothing to do with Wright's *Minority Report* or *Memorandum*, it did represent a turning toward his principles, which no Commission and no tax revision had previously accepted or embodied, at least in Pennsylvania – as this study should by now have made clear. To which point it may be responded, *so what*? Is this purely a matter of (at best) interesting coincidence or (at worst) sheer and uninteresting irrelevance?

I think not. I would find in the passage of this law, uninfluenced – even unencumbered – by any commission report, a salutary indication of the precise weakness of the tax revision commission of the sort we have been studying. Perhaps the weakness most glaringly highlighted would belong to the Matthews Commission, meeting at this time and making contrary recommendations, but the glare and light are (I suspect) unjust. If we assume the approximate accuracy of Wright's analysis (and I do), then none of our small, self-expert, law-recommending commissions made the necessary recommendations for across-the-board tax equity, and it is reasonable to conclude that such commissions in and of themselves are not the best machine for tax revision.

By my assuming the approximate accuracy of Wright's analysis, I mean that I accept as one of the cardinal points in equity of taxation the principle of suitability (as it used to be called in the finance textbooks) –

187

the fitting of the source of revenues to the use of revenues. To be sure, one may search largely in vain for the making of this point in the works of those summarized and categorized in Professor Groves's *Tax Philosophers*, and there is no doubt that suitability is only a subgoal within the general area and purpose of tax equity (Groves 1974, pp. 30ff). But as Herbert Simon has taught us, it is part of our bounded rationality to seek subgoals we can identify and understand, rather than over-all and over-arching general goals we cannot (in both senses of the word) comprehend.

Perhaps this suitability may be considered a part of the qualitative analysis of taxation that Professor Groves identified in the work of John R. Commons (Groves 1974, pp. 131-35). I am not meaning to suggest here any linkage, direct or indirect, between Wright's model and the work of any later commission. I am meaning to say that the failure of the 1947 Commission to agree with the principles of Wright's model, at the same time the 1947 Act was embodying them (albeit with some changes in circumstances), is an indication of a flaw in the Commission's structure or procedure. The idea was clearly in the air, but it was not in the Commission Report.

Indeed, the divergence between the Act and the *Report* is so great that it suggests quite an extraordinary degree of role-boundedness – blindness, one might say, self-induced by decision-premises – on the part of the Matthews Commission members. Whether that is a fair statement or no, let us consider, for an illuminating contrast, the relationship between the 1897 Kennan Commission in Wisconsin and the Wisconsin Income Tax, briefly summarizing some of the material in Chapter IV in light of the Pennsylvania experience.

It will be remembered that the Kennan Commission was the odd-man-out among tax revision commissions, having in effect been not so much a commission as an extension of the person of Kossuth Kent Kennan. It will also be remembered that, at Kennan's instigation, the Commission altered its own mandate in the process of preparing its Report, which was in any case really his Report (Philipp 1973, p. 100). It will also be remembered that the 1911 Act we have traced to the 1897 Commission (by way of intervening commission and a process of education), was not in the minds of the Kennan Commission as the be-all, end-all, or cure-all in the tax revision process.

In fact, so far as we can tell, nothing was in the minds of the Kennan Commission as a be-all, end-all, or cure-all: "There has seemed to be a popular impression that the present tax commission would furnish the legislature with an elaborate and complete system of taxation ... embodying all needed reforms. But the . .necessary reforms are not likely to be brought about by the work of any one commission" (Kennan 1898, p. 8).

In short, the role of the Commission was, despite its mandate, not the creation of immediate reform but the creation of the means and climate for reform. About the means eventually adopted, the imposition of the 1911 State Income Tax, we have already seen that Kossuth Kennan was neither particularly enthusiastic nor particularly skeptical. The idea – though Seligman held back and Ely had changed his views – was in the air, and Kennan had played a part in putting it there. It should be noted particularly that the climate of opinion was preeminently formed not by the academicians but by the men at the other end of State Street – precisely the sort of men that made up Pennsylvania's Matthews Commission a half-century later. Indeed, it may be worthwhile to remind ourselves that the Matthews Commission included four members of the same Pennsylvania House of Representatives that voted for the 1947 Act – and that they themselves were among those voting for it, in their roles as members of Governor Duff's Republican majority, in the Session *before* the Commission met.

All of this makes the contrasting outcomes an important subject for inquiry. If there had not been a 1947 Commission, or if we had not seen how a commission could (as with the Kennan Commission) eventually produce a fundamental revision of the tax structure, the divergence between the 1947 Act and the 1947 Commission might not seem so much in need of explanation. But there was, we have, and it is. And the explanation would seem to lie in the role-boundedness of the members of the Matthews Commission, and particularly of the legislative members. They saw themselves, in effect, as wearing "intellectual" hats in one context and "practical" hats in the other, or others (I would argue), rather than embodying altogether the particular amalgam of interest-group, *expertise*, and practicality that characterized the Wisconsin Idea and, not incidentally, the Kennan Commission.

Of course, no commission's effects, for good or ill, last forever, or anything like it. The Wisconsin Income Tax is still with us, to be sure, but the "permanent" Wisconsin Tax Commission that was Kennan's way of bringing about reform ended in 1939 (Groves n.d., p. 2). We can only ask for success over a period. Even that was not provided by the Matthews Commission.

As the effects of the Commission worked themselves out in partial legislation and the continued regressivity of the Pennsylvania tax system, the parade of committees and commissions went on. First, there was the Pennsylvania Emergency Tax and Revenue Fact-Finding Committee, only tangentially involved with tax revision, consisting of the presidents of Penn State, Temple, the University of Pennsylvania, and the University of Pittsburgh, with three faculty members from each – including, once again, Marion McKay (*Pennsylvania* 1951, p. iv). The

190

Committee, appointed in Fall 1951, reported in December 1951. It was followed by the Tax Study Committee appointed on April 18, 1952, by Governor John Fine.

The Tax Study Committee was "to make a reappraisal of the State tax system in relation to growing revenue requirements for public school subsidies and other purposes" (*Pennsylvania* 1953, p. vi). It had ten members (including Albert Coons, once a student under Franklin Edmonds at Central High), which puts it on the borderline of being a small commission, but even though it may have been self-expert, it was not a tax revision commission in our sense. It did recommend a lot of fiddling with individual taxes, both in its initial report in 1953 and a subsequent report in 1955, and even proposed a flat-rate 1-percent State Income Tax, but its concern was increasing revenues rather than bringing about tax equity (*Pennsylvania* 1953, pp. xxv-xxxvi, *Pennsylvania* 1955, pp. 1-27).

Similarly, the 1956 Tax Policy Advisory Committee, in a report prepared by its paid staff (to be exact, by David Kurtzman and Pennsylvania Economy League Director John Ingram), decided it would be an idle endeavor "to develop a tax program for the distant future, necessarily dependent upon constitutional changes or sweeping realignments in the responsibilities of government" while the State went on needing immediate revenues (*Pennsylvania* 1956, p. 2) – in other words, no Progressive Income Tax. Admittedly, the Committee also discussed the flat-rate Income Tax, going on to show a shift in the burden of taxation to lower-income families (pp. 7-9). But by this time we have reached a point where the membership of the committees or commissions is less important than the staff in the decision as to what is recommended, while continuing to be important for what legislation is

191

passed. In other words, both the nature of a commission and the purposes of its members have been changed.

We will consider how the change ties in with what we have observed and the model of commission behavior we have constructed, when we come to our summing up in Chapter VII. Here, however, we should note that this continuing procession of committees and commissions, each with much the same mandate, and with no hint that anyone is even thinking of full-scale tax revision any more, is perhaps the best qualitative evidence we could have that none of our broad-gauge Pennsylvania commissions was successful. Indeed, even the Mercur Commission, with its narrower mandate and apparent eventual (though partial) success, seems not to have made a lasting contribution. The record of Pennsylvania tax revision commissions over the sixty years from 1889 to 1949 – both in what they did not achieve and in what was achieved without them or despite them – makes us wonder why anyone thought they would work.

In our final chapter we will sum up why they did not, and we will suggest that an historiographical failure to understand the Wisconsin Idea and its inherent instability is related to this series of failures. Not that the Pennsylvania commissions were created with the Wisconsin Idea in mind – though some of them might have been: the point is rather that commissions of this sort may be successful only where there exists that unusual combination and balance of forces to which the name "Wisconsin Idea" has been given.

# CHAPTER VII: CONCLUSIONS

A commission, as we noted in Chapter I, may "work" in one of three ways: it can be charged to address a particular problem and propose laws that will (or should) solve that problem; the laws it proposes can be passed; and the laws it proposes, when passed, can solve the problem. Parts of this process may occur indirectly, as when the Mercur Commission proposed laws that were passed only after the proposals had aroused other organizations to educate the public, so that very similar laws were eventually passed. Or they may occur indirectly in another way, as when the Kennan Commission proposed laws that were passed, which produced another commission, which educated the public and finally recommended laws that were passed – after the education – and may have solved the problem.

The problem, for all our tax revision commissions, was essentially the problem of tax equity, and in this concluding chapter we will be considering the differing definitions of that term. Two of our commissions had limited but nonetheless real success in all three ways. One was successful in the first respect only. The other two were unsuccessful. In neither case in which the commissions "worked" was it as a *policy-making* commission.

That puts the matter in a nutshell. What we are trying to do here is see what kinds of meat we can extract from the nutshell – or, to vary the metaphor, how we can look inside the black box of commission processes to reconstruct what in fact has gone on. We have adopted a model of over-all human behavior based on the Theory of Bounded Rationality proposed by Herbert Simon, and we have tied that behavior in with the commission models and typology of Terence Tutchings. In doing all this, we have more or less fulfilled the accepted six-fold definition of what is involved in the field of "applied history" – specifically (1) analogy, (2) trend assessment, (3) the provision of perspective, (4) historical induction, (5) the use of history in evaluating national myths, and (6) the use of history to prove (test) the policy rule by looking for the exception. This is a pioneering study, in at least two ways: in making a case study of commissions at all, and in this particular application of theory to history.

Case studies of commissions are roughly as rare as hen's teeth. Ronald C. Moe, in *his The Hoover Commissions Revisited*, noted that, of "detailed case studies of major individual commissions, there are none." He was referring to Presidential commissions, and his book was an attempt to remedy the situation for the two Hoover Commissions. The most detailed study I have found of a gubernatorial commission, by Arthur Waskow, covers the 1919 Chicago Riot Commission in less than forty pages (Platt 1971, pp. 20-58). Case studies of Presidential commissions by Thomas Wolanin (Wolanin 1975) are very brief. And as for the application of theory to history on this level, I know of none.

But what does our study show? What can we learn from it? We begin with the 1889 Revenue Commission appointed largely by the Legislature of Pennsylvania, which we have called the McCamant Commission. Like the Tax Conference of Pennsylvania Interests that followed it, this was conceived as a meeting ground for representatives of railroads, merchants, financiers, men of industry, farmers, labor, and (possibly) local government. The qualification in that last sentence arises from the question in my mind whether Giles Price represented local government or local agricultural interests. The presence of a

194

representative of County Commissioners on the 1919 Mercur Commission (Addie Gumbert) suggests the former.

The McCamant Commission's mandate was for tax equity, here defined as the proper balance between the farmers and the railroads, or perhaps between the countryside and the city. The mandate distinguished between financial and mercantile interests, on the one hand, and manufacturing interests, on the other. The two groups overlapped and could be taken together as constituting "city" interests, but it should be remembered that Bolles, representing the manufacturing interests, proposed what was virtually a "single tax" on railroads.

The Commission's agenda-setter was, as it turned out, the Governor, but he appointed only three of the eight Commission members. Because the members were chosen to play roles, we could reasonably expect them to do just that: they did. Had the mandate in the original enabling act been followed, it is unlikely there would have been any achieved coalition. In the absence of any achieved coalition, it is unlikely there would have been any relevant recommendations forthcoming.

It may be well here to review the possible forms a "solution" (or achieved coalition) can take. A commission may have a majority favoring a single outcome, without any necessity for trading off favored and less-favored provisions among the members. In other words, we may have a Condorcet solution. This will happen for interest-group commissions (where almost all decision premises are "role" decision premises) only when there exists a majority clique. In the absence of such a clique, there will be no determinate solution, because the property of the "median optimum" will not hold.

A commission might also reach a de Borda solution, but only if the distance separating the preference orderings was the same throughout:

195

that is, since the de Borda procedure is to assign "to each alternative for each committee member one point for each alternative to which it is preferred by that member" (as in voting for the Most Valuable Player in baseball), a de Borda solution will be politically feasible only in cases where there are no heavily preferred (or heavily opposed) alternatives. Since the 1889 Commission had no mandate to follow this procedure, and since no interest-group representatives are likely to be without heavy preferences and heavy oppositions, no de Borda solution could be expected.

Finally, if there were heavy preferences and (as a corollary) outcomes about which commission members did not especially care, then bargaining might produce a Dodgson solution. In this outcome, it will be recalled, the solution is "the element that would become maximal with the fewest changes to existing preference orderings" – changes that would take place only amongst weakly preferred alternatives, in the absence of the opportunity for log-rolling. That is, commission members might give up weakly-held preferences even if the only thing received in exchange was the establishing of a consensus within the commission: they would give up strongly-held preferences only if they received something much more significant in exchange – which would, by definition, require log-rolling. Since the 1889 Commission, like all the others except the 1947 Matthews Commission, had almost no opportunities for log-rolling, we should not have expected a Dodgson outcome any more than we would have expected one of the other two. (I recognize the fact that this statement casts doubt on whether the Matthews Commission is properly a commission at all. Since it fulfills all the definitional requirements except the absence of significant formal legislative linkages, we have treated it as one: but the matter of linkages must be kept in mind.)

We would not have expected a Condorcet or a de Borda or a Dodgson solution from the 1889 Commission, but the Commission did in fact come up with a Majority Report, signed by William Martin, Giles Price, Leonard Rhone, Austin Taggart, and Samuel Wherry. It came up with that Majority Report because there was a majority clique, made up of these five men. There was a majority clique because the selection process designed to produce a balanced interest-group commission had been short-circuited so as to produce an unbalanced interest-group commission. Without that short-circuiting it is highly unlikely, as we noted before, that there would have been any majority report with any significant content.

Because there was a majority clique, the agenda-setting within the 1889 Commission was wrested from the Governor's hands: that is, the majority decided that the agenda would consist of hitting the railroads (which in the majority's eyes was clearly the better part of tax equity), while Governor Beaver had apparently decided on a slightly different agenda. The fact that he had decided on a different agenda is revealed by McCamant's Minority Report, and by the fact that it was McCamant's Minority Report that the Legislature adopted. One can scarcely believe the Auditor-General would have done it entirely on his own.

Note that on this reading the two most interesting reports from the point of view of tax philosophy – by John Armstrong Wright and Albert S. Bolles – are flatly irrelevant to the outcome. Yet Wright and Bolles were, in essence, the "blue ribbon" members of this essentially interest-group Commission: the irrelevance of their views in the political process following the issuance of the Commission's Report does not augur well for the success of blue-ribbon commissions generally. Indeed, Wright's *Report* (at least) reads as though he expected argument to carry the day (Wright 1890, p. 37, Wright 1889, pp. 100-36). A very

197

strange idea, one might conclude – and an idea endemic in at least one later commission, in the 1920s.

Whether the 1889 Commission is close enough to us in time and circumstances for any argument by analogy to be relevant in using it to find out whether we should appoint tax revision commissions in 2003 – that is a question we should put aside until we have looked at the progress from 1889 to 1897 to 1919 to 1923 to 1947, and thence to the present. If the progress seems to be through a period of largely similar concerns and largely similar circumstances, then the argument from analogy might hold not merely for 1889 and the present, but for all our past commissions (taken together) and the present. We will evaluate the argument from analogy when we have looked at all five.

We will also, having looked at all five, be able then to consider the meaning of certain "buzzwords" in our history relevant to tax revision commissions. The most obvious of these is "tax equity" – here defined as the incidence of taxation on the farmer by the majority clique or the comparative incidence on agriculture and industry by McCamant and Governor Beaver (Pennsylvania 1890, pp. 32-36). But the most interesting buzzword turns out to be the word "commission" itself, as it relates to the Wisconsin Idea and to the idea of Progressivism.

This in turn will tie in with the question of periodization, or at least with the "spirit" of the Progressive Era, or Era of the Search for Order. We may even be on the track of a difference between the Progressivism of a Gifford Pinchot or a Theodore Roosevelt, on the one hand, and that of a Robert La Follette or John R. Commons, on the other. By no means do we have sufficient data for a conclusion here, but the discrepancy between the Wisconsin exemplar and the Edmonds Commission of 1923 seems too great for mere accident. Of this, more later.

198

To be sure, even our five examples are not statistically significant. But what Alexander George has called the mode of historical introduction, or controlled comparison, will be seen to yield a coherent theoretical picture, after we have recapitulated the histories of our five commissions. It is, moreover, a theoretical picture borne out by the course of events (so far as tax revision commissions are concerned) since the Matthews Commission *Report* in 1949. Both this theoretical picture and the matter of how the Progressives really dealt with commissions, or really thought they would work, or thought they would really work, will help us in evaluating a persistent national myth – what I called in the first chapter the Foundation Myth of the Era of the Search for Order. As we might quite reasonably suspect, not only is the myth untrue factually, but the men who created it seem to have known it was untrue, at least in the form others understood it.

All this, of course, leads up to the final question, which is whether we can draw policy rules from this particular past experience. It turns out, I will argue, that we can: the exceptions to the general inutility of tax revision commissions of the sort studied here are so exceptional as to leave the rule unscathed. And it turns out also that the characteristic post-World-War-II variety of tax revision commission – indeed the characteristic post-World-War-II commission of any sort – can be read as an attempt to solve the problems that made the old form of commission suspect. We chose our particular set of commissions in an attempt to hold some difficult variables constant for our case studies, and it may turn out that the later commissions are more intractable. What is certain is that they are very different, in ways that are at first blush relevant to their predecessors' problems. The field of applied history has introduced the idea of the retrospective technology assessment: we may have been engaged in a retrospective procedure assessment.

With this for prologue (or possibly interruption), we may go on to the "successful" Wisconsin State Tax Commission of 1897, the Kennan Commission. Though interest groups were represented on the Commission, it was different from the McCamant Commission in two significant ways at the time of its creation, and in two significant ways at the time it issued its Report. At its creation, it was a "mixed" rather than an "interest-group" (or in the Tutchings terminology, a "public interest") commission, and it had only three members rather than eight. At the time of its Report, it opted for a principal recommendation that was easy rather than difficult for the Legislature and the Governor to accept, and the agenda-setting that it (or Kossuth Kennan) had wrested from the Governor was not wrested back.

Here perhaps we should pause to review the Tutchings findings, and those of Daniel Bell, on the manipulability of commissions – actors, actions, and ends – and on the success of commissions by type. It has been noted that the least successful commissions are those proposing specific legislative action for redistributive ends. It has been noted that such recommendations are more likely to be tied to achieved commission coalitions for "low-demand" rather than "high-demand" commissions, with all of ours being high-demand. It has been noted that blue-ribbon or mixed commissions are both more likely than interest-group commissions to make such recommendations, and more likely to get them passed into law – with mixed commissions having a better success ratio. We have controlled for the low-demand/high-demand variable by considering only high-demand commissions. The greater success for mixed commissions turns out to fit quite well into our *schema*. The fact that the recommendation of specific laws for

200

redistributive ends rarely works is highly significant in appraising the achievement of Kossuth Kent Kennan in particular and the degree of "success" for all our commissions in general.

What Kennan did, in Bell's terms, was to convert a policy-making commission into a fact-finding or evaluative commission -- or, in the Tutchings terminology, recommend a "knowledge/plan" outcome rather than a regulative/redistributive outcome (Tutchings 1979, pp. 53ff). He did this in the face of a contrary mandate. He may have been able to do it "legitimately" through some kind of bargaining with Burr Jones and George Curtis to reach a Dodgson solution, or he may simply have pulled the wool over one of both pair of eyes, In any event, he was clearly aided in his endeavor by the small size of the Kennan Commission. It is even possible that we have here a case of the median optimum solution, which, as we know, is much more likely in small bodies than in large.

In the public mind, in Wisconsin at least, the Kennan Commission merged with the successor body recommended in its Report. If recent historical work is taken as evidence, it merged so thoroughly as to make it a body in the Progressive mold, and thereby to confuse the subject of Progressive tax philosophy quite thoroughly. This I take to be symptomatic of the indirection by which the goal of tax equity was achieved. This indirection, as I have already noted, I consider symptomatic of "successful" tax revision commissions. The "mixed" characteristic of the commission – which is also a keynote of the Wisconsin Idea as Commons expressed it – is likewise symptomatic.

All State commissions seem to have a Governor's man on them – McCamant on the 1889 Commission, Curtis (more likely than Jones) in 1897, Myers in 1919, Edmonds on the 1923 Commission, Matthews in 1947. That is as we should expect it: the curious thing is that the two

201

"successful" commissions were those where the Governor's man was not in control. They were also the two whose outcomes were indirectly achieved, a point to which we shall return.

Now we may consider the Governor an interest, though not an interest group. And we may say that the interests represented on the Kennan Commission were the railroads (Kennan), the lumbermen including the Governor (Curtis), and the conservative money men or old-line Gold Democrats (Jones). Thus far the Kennan Commission sounds rather like a smaller variant of the McCamant Commission, and we can point to additional similarities – as, for example, the "star" quality of the two railroad men, Wright and Kennan. But notice here the fact that Kennan could seize control of the three-man Commission, and especially the fact that he was both a blue-ribbon expert and an active political force. In that respect, at least, he was an avatar of the Wisconsin Idea, and the Progressive historiography that linked his work to that of La Follette's permanent Tax Commission was true in essence if apparently false in fact. Kennan is, indeed, a prime example of a significant figure in need of scholarly attention, not only for his own career, but for what light that career sheds on the question of Progressivism in Wisconsin. And not only his career, but that of his brother George Kennan and his son George Frost Kennan.

There has never been another three-person tax revision commission appointed in any State by any Governor. The original Mercur Commission (appointed in 1920 under the 1919 mandate) was the next smallest in the long history of State tax revision commissions. It had a mandate even more limited than the one Kossuth Kennan chose to fulfill – tax equity, to be sure, but not in the farmers-against-the-railroads or lumbermen-against-the-railroads sense of our two previous commissions. It was charged to achieve tax equity in the assessment and

202

collection of the property tax in the Commonwealth of Pennsylvania (*Pennsylvania* 1921, p. 3). This limited mandate is important in two respects, one of which will also serve to illuminate the importance of Kennan's limiting the mandate of his own Commission.

As we noted before, following Herbert Simon, no human organism has more than limited computing capacity, and we necessarily apply our own limits to any task that faces us. We limit our examination of decision premises and our search space, both. But if we can switch our available resources from maintaining a relatively wide search space to examining the relevance of our decision-premises (that is, to looking beyond our role-determined premises), we will be less bound by our roles. The narrower the search space implied by a commission's mandate, the less role-bound the commissioners should be. Thus the restriction of the Mercur Commission's mandate to matters of property tax equity, and specifically equity in assessment and collection, made it less likely that the Commissioners would simply play their roles, and more likely that they would reach agreement.

The likelihood was further increased by the fact that Governor Sproul, for all his own Progressivism (Klein 1980, p. 442), chose the Commissioners for geographical balance, though geography was largely an irrelevant matter. In a sense, he treated as interest groups the various regions of the State – thereby limiting the availability of role decision-premises, even if the Commissioners had a tendency to take refuge in them. For our purposes it does not matter if the Governor's technique was planned or accidental: the lesson is that it worked.

The other respect in which the limited mandate here is important lies in the fact that it identified equity with efficiency: that is, it assumed that everyone agreed on what was equitable – reassessment to reflect fair value (or ability to pay) and even-handed assessment everywhere ("no favorites") – and asked the Commission to find a way to bring that about. Our other commissions were charged with figuring out what was equitable, but this one only with figuring out how to get there. And it is one of the characteristics of this Era of the Search for Order that this particular kind of ordering – efficiency rather than equity – was much the easier to achieve. The Mercur Commission was allowed to sidestep the question *whether* the Property Tax was equitable, in order to concentrate on making it as equitable as possible (*Pennsylvania* 1921, p. 3).

This the Kennan Commission could not do, but Kennan nevertheless concentrated his own arguments on efficiency rather than equity – as with his remarks on the Income Tax. Moreover, by his limiting his Commission's effective mandate to fact-finding, he not only disarmed argument (based on role decision-premises) within the Commission; he also demonstrated the Commission's own efficiency, or his own efficiency, in the chosen field. In short, the Kennan Commission was charged with finding the highest measure of economy and equality in taxation, but "the highest measure of economy and equality in taxation cannot be reached at a single bound" (Kennan 1898, p. 8) – and Kennan chose instead to demonstrate that a commission could find facts, to suggest that the fact-finding continue, and to begin a process of education.

Whether he snookered or persuaded his co-Commissioners into agreeing with him we do not know. In Mercur's case, where the mandate was limited by the enabling act rather than by the Commission's own agenda-setting, we can be fairly sure that the agreement was genuine. First, there is no Minority Report. Second, Myers (as the Governor's man) wrote the *Report* and John Fertig (appointed by Governor Sproul to the Legislative Reference Bureau) wrote the bill. Mercur had the bill introduced into the Senate and Representative Marshall himself introduced it into the House. No scrap of evidence suggests any opposition by Gumbert (who set up the appearance before the County Commissioners) or by Zimmerman. There was no reason for the Commissioners to disagree (no roles that required them to do so), and there is no reason for us to assume that they did.

It is true that Governor Sproul showed no enthusiasm for pushing the Commission's recommendations. Partly that may have been because intra-party political conflicts were putting Sproul on the regular Republican rather than the Progressive side of things in 1921-22, but much more important was the fact that the recommendations simply could not be passed into law without a campaign to put public pressure behind them (Klein 1980, p. 442). Even the peculiar mix of interest-group politics and blue-ribbon *expertise* that has characterized the Wisconsin Idea (as Commons understood it) has suffered electoral and legislative failures when it has lost touch with political reality, or, to put it another way, with the concerns of the people (Margulies 1968, pp. 284-86). The fact that an idea is valid and that powerful interests support it is not is not in itself a combination sufficient to guarantee that the idea will be embodied in a law.

Perhaps we should not need to be reminded of this, but the Kennan Commission provides a reminder, and the Mercur Commission strengthens it. If Sproul turned his back on the Commission's bill, it was not because he opposed it but because the time had not yet come for its passage – assuming, of course, that he had acted in good faith in appointing the Commission in the first place. Given the evident tax problems in the State – Sproul's predecessor had gone so far as to lament Pennsylvania's fiscal plight within the text of a bill (*Pennsylvania Laws*

1917, pp. 839-40) – and Sproul's own experience on the do-nothing 1909 Committee, as well as his generally Progressive views, this seems a fair assumption. In the end, of course, in part, and after a long and tortuous trail had been followed, it turned out that the time had come, and the bill was passed. But the Mercur Commission's Report, like the Kennan Commission's Report in Wisconsin in 1898, was primarily the beginning of an educational campaign, not of legislative action.

The lesson, if lesson there was, seems not to have been realized by Gifford Pinchot and Franklin Edmonds. Perhaps success of various kinds had gone to their heads: Pinchot had wrested the governorship from the regulars and Edmonds, in his very first term in the Legislature, had given his name to the bill substantially reforming the State's educational system (Klein 1980, p. 442). Whatever the reasons, which are beyond the scope of this study, the Edmonds Commission was relatively large – seven members against the Mercur Commission's original five and the Kennan Commission's three – and was made up virtually entirely of blue-ribbon members without functional constituencies, and it was given an extremely broad mandate.

Too broad, in the event: the Commission made more than twenty final recommendations, with some additional recommendations in the *Interim Report* (*Pennsylvania* 1925) that did not make it into the *Final Report* (*Pennsylvania* 1927). Only one of its members, the industrialist John Penman Wood, tried to devise a long-range plan for equitable taxation. Several, including in particular John Patrick Connelly, disagreed with the eventual Majority Report on the question of taxing church property, and there were some other disagreements in detail that suggest contrasting views of equity. But these views were never debated or even spelled out as they were with the McCamant Commission (*Pennsylvania* 1927, pp. 49-53). The blue-ribbon experts of the

206

Edmonds Commission seemed to be able to decide, by and large, *how* things should be done but not *what* things should be done. At least the functional constituencies (or interest groups) of the McCamant Commission had views of equity that their representatives made quite explicit. Indeed, they had such strong and divergent views that agreement would have been impossible if the House had not packed the Commission.

So far as the effectiveness of the Commission was concerned, that was an error in one direction. The Edmonds Commission suffered from an equal error in the other direction. With the possible exception of Archibald Jones, the members were all divorced from interest-group politics, unless one wishes to consider "Philadelphia gentlemen" to be an interest group. However one wishes to consider the matter, the important point here is that the blue-ribbon Commissioners were just as bound by their blue-ribbon role and the decision-premises based on it as the McCamant Commission members had been bound by their interest-group roles and their decision-premises.

There were a few instances in which the Edmonds Commission members represented interest groups (as with Connelly and the Roman Catholic Church, perhaps), but those were not what prevented the Commission's being a success. Its mandate was simply too broad to allow the abandonment of role decision-premises, and the role decision-premises were too far removed either from political finagling or the philosophy of taxation to permit success.

It may seem odd that I include the philosophy of taxation as an area in which commissions might be considered successful, since this is no part of our original definition of success. There are two reasons for doing so. First, an era in taxation theory was coming to an end: the "faculty" to pay (in Seligman's formulation) had finally been identified with income (Seligman 1911, pp. 3-18, Groves 1974, pp. 44-47). And at the same time, the search for new sources of revenue (Clifton Yearley's subject) had laid the groundwork for our present State tax systems (Yearley 1970, pp. 225-50). All times are transitional, of course, but the Edmonds Commission was meeting at a time when both tax theory and tax practice were in even more than a usual state of flux. A strong examination of first principles was called for – the kind of examination a philosopher of taxation might have made, and which indeed John Penman Wood started to make. But this is not the only reason for suggesting that an interest in the philosophy of taxation, and indeed the presence of a Commissioner who defined his role as that of tax philosopher, would be an ingredient of success.

The other reason, not restricted to the particular characteristics of the 1920s, has to do, once again, with what we have called the Wisconsin Idea. John R. Commons (who, after all, wrote *The Legal Foundations of Capitalism*) has been defined as the exemplar: of his interest in philosophical first principles there can be little doubt. But Harold Groves, whom we have quoted a number of times, would do as well: he was both a distinguished Professor of Economics and a member of the State Legislature and of various gubernatorial commissions. The Wisconsin Idea did not die with the elder La Follette in 1925: more to our point, perhaps, the blue ribbon to be pinned on Wisconsin-Idea commissioners was an intellectual blue ribbon. The Kennan Commission fitted the Wisconsin mold partly because of Kennan's intellectual – one might even say academic – *expertise* in the field of taxation. Of course, on the McCamant Commission, Bolles and Wright had that, but the majority clique was too strong for them and too role-bound for success. It is significant, I believe, that Edmonds and

McKay developed their *expertise* in taxation after they were on the Edmonds Commission, or at the very least not before.

In one way it would appear that commission success, as we have defined it, depends on the commission's being in the middle-ground betwixt interest groups and blue ribbons. That is, however, not quite the right way to put it. Two of our commissions were given, and they accepted, broad mandates: in both cases they failed, and in both cases the failure had to do with the inevitability of fixed role decision-premises, given the broad search space implied by the mandate. It made no effective difference whether the decision-premises came from roles as interest-group representatives or as blue-ribbon members of an elite. The two more successful commissions overcame the problem of role decision-premises (1) by limitation – in one case, self-limitation – of the mandate, and (2) by mixing political constituency, interest-group constituency, and a blue-ribbon quality, with each member having more than one role. In addition, (3) the successful commissions were small – in one case very small – and (4) made up mostly of lawyers (Gumbert, with almost thirty years of work in legal surroundings, being the only apparent exception).

We have one more commission still to summarize, and perhaps we ought to pause here to recall the peculiarities a commission possesses that an ordinary legislative committee does not. These are two. First, it has no linkages with any subject or organization outside its mandate and therefore, in effect, no logs to roll: thus the "exchange" theory of committee behavior finds commissions outside its bounds of concern or competence (but see Koford 1981, pp. 11-12). Second, its mandate is fixed by its enabling act, which means the agenda will be largely fixed (though it can be subverted either in the appointment process, as with the McCamant Commission, or by one member of a small commission, as with Kossuth Kennan – and even the McCamant Commission eventually came back to its original agenda when McCamant's Minority Report was presented to the Legislature (*Pennsylvania* 1890, pp. 32-36, *Pennsylvania Laws* 1891, pp. 229-43). The second of these holds true for our final commission, the Tax Study Committee (Matthews Commission) of 1947-49. The first does not, and once again we have an exception to prove (test) a rule.

The Matthews Commission had logs to roll, and in the rolling succeeded in getting three of its recommendations passed, though (as we have noted) the net effect of passing only these three was to reduce rather than increase tax equity as generally now (and then) understood. The effects of our other "successful" commissions were much slower, perhaps smaller (in the near run), but, like the mills of God, they were much surer too. We might also say that they were purer. One of the virtues of a commission (though in some cases a singularly useless virtue) has been thought to be its standing aside from the ordinary political process. The Matthews Commission, because of its institutional peculiarities, did not stand aside.

Like our other unsuccessful commissions, this had a broad mandate, and like them, it was not notably smaller than the average for the small self-expert commissions we have been studying. On the other hand, like our successful commissions, it was "mixed" – interest-group, blue-ribbon, and with political constituencies. It had fewer lawyers than the successful commissions, by percentage, but it also had fewer lawyers than were on the Edmonds Commission. Wherry, Bolles, and McCamant were the lawyers on their Commission; Kennan, Jones, and Curtis were all lawyers (admittedly the same as on the McCamant Commission and Matthews Commission, but three out of three rather than three out of seven); Mercur, Myers, Zimmerman, and Marshall

210

were the lawyers on the 1919 Commission;  Edmonds, Reed, Jones, and Connelly were the lawyers on the 1923 Commission;  Geltz, Wood, and Sterling were the lawyers in 1947.  The data here are inconclusive.

Indeed, in all of this there is, I think, nothing especially revealing – except the metaphorical red flag being waved by the immediate passage of a mixed bag of laws rather than the slow educational progress initiated by our successful commissions.   This policy-making commission turned out to be making laws rather than policy, laws that in fact contravened the policy it recommended.

The joker was that the recommended policy required the graduated Income Tax, to shift the incidence of taxation toward the upper-income groups.  Without that still unconstitutional tax, the new Sales Tax simply shifted the incidence of taxation down the income scale.  The *Report* of the Matthews Commission shows no significant minority dissent, which is what we might reasonably expect from a body five of whose seven members were or had been Republican members of the State Legislature.  The apparent unanimity suggests an achieved consensus, likely (our Tutchings model tells us) to be associated with regulative recommendations rather for low-demand than for high-demand commissions (Tutchings 1979, pp. 95, 99).  Since all ours are high-demand commissions, this suggestion of an achieved consensus may not be accurate:   perhaps the consensus already existed when the Commission members were named.

In that case we might expect the outcome to be similar to that of a one-role body like the Edmonds Commission – whose one role was of course that of blue-ribbon "Philadelphia gentleman" member of the elite. That is, the fault with a blue-ribbon commission may be not that it is blue-ribbon but that its members are all playing a single role, with a single set of unexamined decision-premises.  Our evidence is not sufficient to support this view, but it seems to point in this direction. To be sure, the Matthews Commission itself was well-stocked with Philadelphia gentlemen or their equivalents: as I say, we cannot determine the relative importance of the blue-ribbon quality in leading to failure for small self-expert commissions, and the Kennan Commission is a case to the contrary. We can only say that the Edmonds Commission and the Matthews Commission failed, and that both had the characteristics of "blue-ribbon-ness" and "one-role-ness" (but note that the McCamant Commission majority clique also suffered from "one-role-ness").

The Matthews Commission will thus have reached a Condorcet solution, possibly also a "median-optimum" solution: it will have been able to do this either because the members were already in substantial agreement or because a consensus was formed through paiwise voting on alternatives. Given the Tutchings findings on the nature of achieved commission coalitions, the second seems less likely.

If indeed the Matthews Commission had a pre-determined outcome, it forms a link between the pre-World-War-II small self-expert commissions and the larger and much different commissions in vogue after 1950. After 1950 increasing attention is paid to staff and to the "representative-ness" of commission members. The staff does the work. The members present the results of that work to the public with their prestige behind it (Wolanin 1975, pp. 3-10, 96-128): I know from my own experience that this was the model for the 1979 Pennsylvania Tax Revision Commission. This, in a way, is an answer to the problem posed by the general inutility of commissions of the sort we have been studying here.

When the first Commission on Organization of the Executive Branch of the Government (First Hoover Commission) was established

212

in 1947, both "Hoover and his associates realized that the first most pressing job would be to build a staff. They realized that the political attitudes of the staff could be the most important factor in shaping the eventual proposals of the Commission" (Arnold 1976, p. 51). And one historian of the Hoover Commission notes that the "extent to which 'politics' played a role in the staff selection process should not be surprising . . . for it is endemic to the commission concept" (Moe 1982, p. 63 n. 21). One supposes that is true now: it was not true for the commissions we have been studying.

The point is that the staff, not the members, now come up with the recommendations. The words of a recent historian of post-World-War-II Presidential commissions would ring rather oddly in our context, but they are true for his: commission members, he writes, "have an unusual capacity to persude other political actors to adopt their recommendations and agree with their findings" (Wolanin 1975, p. 32). The bifurcation of the commission idea has produced members who are both representative of interest groups (as George Meany, for example, was representative of Labor) and of "blue-ribbon" quality. And it has produced staff members who "are most often lawyers and middle-level substantive experts. . . . Their training and professional experience incline them toward a method of problem solving that proceeds by collecting the available data and analyzing it in terms of making pragmatic adjustments and modifications in the existing programs and approaches" (Wolanin 1975, p. 101). In short, the staff fulfills the requirements for our first kind of success (or else fails to fulfill them), and the members fulfill our requirements for the second kind of success. The Matthews Commission showed hints of that development when it took over much of the work of the Committee on Continuation of the Tax Study.

Perhaps this does not seem an unreasonable arrangement. Perhaps, if other commissions were as unsuccessful as those we have been looking at, this bifurcation of responsibilities seemed a way out. But it presents two problems. First, it makes analysis of the black box's insides very much more difficult: commission members are generally well-enough known to permit some form of collective biography (and analysis based on that), but commission staff are not. Tutchings notes (Tutchings 1979, p. 47) that "only fourteen of the staff directors were listed in the biographical references, and a search for information on the hundreds of other staff members proved to be fruitless" – and this for Presidential commissions. (But see Wolanin 1975, pp. 107-10). Second, and more to the point of our conclusions, the problems of bounded procedural rationality, the resultant unexamined role decision-premises, and the whole complex preference-ordering decision problems are still with us. It is true that log-rolling has become more likely, and we may therefore have laws both recommended and passed. But there is a greater weakness institutionalized in the present system, as well as a greater strength.

The words quoted above on the make-up of commission staffs should provide a clue. We have already noted the possibility that the weakness we have found with blue-ribbon commissions is really a weakness of one-role commissions. We have noted the somewhat unfocussed mature of the Edmonds Commission's recommendations. We have noted the Progressive concern for "engineering" efficiency, and we might also note here that Presidential commissions are increasingly seen as part of our Progressive heritage (Moe 1982, pp. 5-12). Curiously, gubernatorial commissions have been studied almost not at all, though it might be argued they form the historic link between the Progressive Era and the modern Presidential commission (this seems to

214

me a fruitful field for study). Finally, we should recall the surprising conclusion that the "Wisconsin-Idea" commissions prospered (if that is the word) partly because the members each filled more than one role and partly because they limited their mandate or it was limited for them.

These points suggest that the bifurcated commission is a wrong response to the problem, quite apart from its increasingly unworkable size. On the matter of size, it may be observed that the First Hoover Commission had seventy-nine staff members, the 1979 Pennsylvania Tax Revision Commission very nearly the same (Moe 1982, p. 28, personal observation). If "successful" commissions in fact combined both blue-ribbon and interest-group attributes (with some political connections) in their membership, it should make sense to try to achieve that mixture in modern commissions – but not at the expense of putting the real decision-making in the hands of a one-role staff, and particularly in the hands of a staff whose own agenda is "making pragmatic adjustments and modifications in the existing programs and approaches" (Wolanin 1975, p. 101). What would be the point of establishing a commission that mixed blue-ribbon attributes and interest-group attributes (with political "clout"), if the roles assigned to its members were simply to agree upon and publicize the work of its staff? Granted the staff work might be good. Quite certainly it would be sufficiently limited in its novelty to be passed by the Legislature if it had already passed the commission through a "median-optimum" solution. But equally certainly the virtues of this new sort of commissioner have little to do with what goes on inside the black box of commission procedures. And if we are expected to think that the commissioners really did the analytical work themselves – why, that is blue smoke and mirrors, not blue ribbons.

This is a wrong response. The old kind of commission achieved, in our two "successful" cases, a good beginning in the education of the public toward courses of action that were originally politically inexpedient (if not impossible), but were apparently necessary to achieve the desired equitable outcome. The "unsuccessful" commissions were those which were more attuned to the passage of specific "regulative" laws. In short, they were short-sighted, more concerned with the trees – or, in the case of the McCamant Commission, a particular tree – than with the forest. We have now made it easier for "regulative" commission reports to be passed into law (though, as Tutchings tells us, not very easy even so). This seems an odd way of going about educating the public, or achieving any other kind of success.

Perhaps the small self-expert commission died out because commissioners of the appropriate sort died out. Perhaps there was a brief period, prolonged for a while in Wisconsin, when the kind of person needed to make the Wisconsin Idea work could be found in sufficient numbers to make commissions of this sort work. Perhaps the increasing specialization which seems to be the hallmark of present engineering efficiency has deprived us of the Kossuth Kennans, or even the Rodney Mercurs of today. This last may give Mercur too much credit, but it is worth noting that his background was not narrow or specialized, that he was at least a second-generation public servant, and (perhaps not incidentally) that he was precisely of Kossuth Kennan's generation. In any case, we do not know that the twenty-person commission with the eighty-person staff cannot ignite the train of the same educational process where the old self-expert commission succeeded – if it tries.

These are matters for a different study or series of studies. I should like to see them made, though the problem of gathering data on staff

216

may prove insuperable. I should also like to see more state tax revision commissions of the old sort covered as I have covered these. As a guide, perhaps, for those studies, and a conclusion for this, let us try to sum up our approach and our findings here.

Our model proposes a connection between breadth of accepted mandate and rigidity of role decision-premises: the broader the mandate, the broader therefore the search space to be covered, and the more rigidly the role decision-premises will come into play in commission procedure. All other things being equal, a narrower mandate will lead to greater examination of decision-premises and thus less role-bound decision-making. But, of course, if roles are otherwise reinforced, the all-other-things-being-equal proviso does not hold.

Our model also proposes no essential difference between the kinds of one-role commissions so far as bringing about eventual tax equity is concerned. There are differences in the precise mechanics of failure, to be sure. The McCamant Commission failed, as we have noted, by substituting clique activity for Commission activity, with the result that the legislation eventually proposed to the Legislature (McCamant's own Minority Report) had nothing much to do with the Commission's deliberations: it neither reflected the agenda of the majority clique nor the *expertise* of Wright and Bolles – except insofar as McCamant may have accepted Wright's view that the majority clique was making unreasonable demands on the railroads' ability to supply information.

The Edmonds Commission failed at least arguably because it conceived its mission as the passing of detailed legislation – of a "package" of tax bills – in the mode of outside experts telling the Legislature just what it ought to do: this may well be the common failing of commissions whose members are all playing "blue-ribbon" roles. I realize there may be a value judgment on popular democracy concealed somewhere at the base of my view on this, but the evidence presented here is certainly consistent with the view.

The Matthews Commission, institutionally much different from the Edmonds Commission, nevertheless seems to have failed from similar causes: it too was a blue-ribbon commission proposing specific legislation, and though its institutional linkages provided it with half a loaf of legislation passed, rather than none, the half-loaf turned out to be sufficiently tainted, and the old adage reversed. I have been unable to determine whether the legislative members of the Matthews Commission really sought to ensure an all-or-nothing passage of the recommendations.

Despite the differences in the mechanics of failure, the fundamental connection between role-bounded rationality, broad mandate, and specific "regulative" recommendations, on the one hand, and failure on the other, seems to hold. We held certain variables constant by choosing our small self-expert commissions – specifically, degree of demand and level of information costs. Of the other variables considered important in the Tutchings typology, decision costs were not controlled for, and were in fact the only "organizational" variable left to vary; personnel was, of course, categorized into blue-ribbon, interest-group, and mixed in type. The "demand" variables – circumstances of creation, issue areas, and temporal variations – showed no substantial divergence from commission to commission. We used the Salisbury-Heinz typology for actors/action/ends -- "regulative" actions, "redistributive" ends, and so on – as modified by Tutchings.

The measurement of decision costs being impossible to carry out directly, Tutchings adopted as a proxy variable the degree of dissent within the commission, which was in turn closely related to the size of the commission (Tutchings 1979, pp. 31-32, 92). Since we know that

218

the difficulty in reaching a median-optimum solution is tied directly to the number of persons involved, the Tutchings finding should not surprise us. Our smaller commissions were far more successful, but whether the differences can be successfully quantified, and if so whether they are statistically significant, we have not determined here: our sample, though useful for controlled comparison (historical induction), is in any case statistically significant.

The decision-cost variable is inconclusive for Tutchings: it does not seem to be much more conclusive for us. In any event, decision costs are not inside the black box: the proxy variable used to represent them is a behavioral variable relating to the commission, but the reality it reflects is a reality in the outside political world. The amount of political disagreement should be used as a proxy variable only if the commission mirrors the larger political arena, a mirror which Tutchings (p. 120) finds problematic. If what the proxy variable reflects is indeed reality, I am not convinced the reflection is seen other than very darkly in a very bad glass, but it is apparently the best available.

The Tutchings typology seems to be applicable to our commissions, even though it is based on a study of Presidential commissions in the post-World-War-II period. Our findings are sufficiently consistent with those in *Rhetoric and Reality* to suggest the continued use of the Tutchings model in this sort of inquiry. Moreover, it appears that the model of bounded rationality and sub-goal identification (recommending laws rather than policy, for example, or killing railroads for fun and profit) helps explain our findings, with the key being role-bounded rationality. Roles, it will be remembered, are defined (in Simon's model) as subsets of decision-premises largely immune from examination.

219

All of this, of course, is predicated on the assumption that our commissions are sufficiently similar to form a class (self-expert small tax revision commissions) suitable for examination as a class. To assume this permits us to argue from analogy, to apply the techniques of history to a particular policy problem (provide historical "perspective"), and to make a structured and focussed comparison within the class. By establishing the class, we are forgoing the opportunity (if any) of tracing detailed historical developments from one commission to another: we are not, however, forgoing the opportunity of tracing historical trends in the idea of a commission or in the idea of tax equity.

Because our commissions have a root connection with the central "good-government" (or "goo-goo") myth of the Progressives, the idea that a blue-ribbon group both can and should set policy, we have been engaged in a study of that foundation myth. It is true we have set as a condition of "success" the passage of commission recommendations into law, but that could occur either because the recommendations really did reflect the public will, or because the elite members of the commission could triumph over the public will: in other words, calling this success is not a value judgment on popular democracy or elite policy-making. If, however, we find commissions (with only far-out exceptions) to be uniformly dysfunctional, that would constitute an attack on the goo-goo myth. We do, and it does. Moreover, the attack is strengthened by the fact that the Wisconsin Idea lying at the heart of La Follette Progressivism can itself be seen to disagree with this mythic view.

The idea of a commission passed from a meeting-place of interest-group representatives to an assemblage of the blue-ribbon elite: in doing so, it passed through an intermediate stage which was roughly historically contemporaneous with the heyday of the Wisconsin Idea.

Chronologically, the commissions we have considered followed in their nature the "ideal" commission as it moved from one pole to the other.

The idea of tax equity also changed through time. It began by being a matter of the incidence of the property tax in the 1889 McCamant Commission, even though tax philosophers, including John Armstrong Wright, were already moving beyond that definition. It wound up being a matter of the incidence of all taxes. In between it split into two questions, that of practical (or "engineering") efficiency, and that of theoretical "faculty" to pay. The question of "faculty" was already in the air in 1889: by 1919 an income tax was generally regarded as the fairest, but the old idea of a single tax for all purposes had died, and the task set for the Mercur Commission was making one of the other taxes fairer by improving the efficiency of its assessment and collection. Nevertheless, the germ of the 1919 view was in John A. Wright's "Memorandum" in 1889, and neither differed significantly from what Kossuth Kennan thought or what John Penman Wood thought or what the Matthews Commission decided. Efficiency of collection, equity of incidence, and the question of a graduated income tax – those were the bells on which the various commissions rang their changes.

Because there were variations we have applied different sets of tests for equity. Because the McCamant Commission was looking at one specific issue – at least the majority clique and McCamant himself were looking at one specific issue – we have looked at the results of McCamant's bill in accordance with what was generally understood as representing tax equity *at that time*. It would not be equitable in us to require of them in 1889 an understanding of taxation reached only in the twentieth century. Because the net result of the Kennan Commission was (eventually) the Wisconsin State Income Tax, we have looked at the

221

incidence of that tax in determining the Commission's success – at least, we have looked at it for a reasonable period after the law was passed.

Because the Mercur Commission was charged with making property taxes more requitable, by improving the efficiency of assessment and collection, and because the partial passage of legislation in 1931 provided something like a laboratory setting for testing equity (of one kind), we have applied a different test from the ones applied for the earlier commissions. Because the Edmonds Commission was unsuccessful in getting its recommended laws passed, we have not needed to make any test for success of the third kind. And we have been able to use the estimates of others in our analysis of the Matthews Commission's effectiveness, these representing yet another test for the equity of tax incidence. Note, however, that in all cases but that of the McCamant Commission, we have abided by the definitions of equity that are acceptable at present – essentially those of E. R. A. Seligman.

Have we proved anything? As the word "prove" is ordinarily used, we have not. But we have tested the proposition that state tax revision commissions of the sort considered here will fail. We have looked at two partial apparent exceptions to the rule and found that, in essence, they were not commissions of the policy-making or rule-recommending sort at all. In the course of our inquiries, we have cast doubt on one of the foundation myths of the Progressive Era (Era of the Search for Order), called attention to haziness surrounding the definition of the Wisconsin Idea, and engaged in some "retrospective procedure assessment" that suggests commissions of the modern (post-World-War-II) variety may not have been a proper response to the failures of the old commissions.

We have also, by looking at gubernatorial commissions, filled in a blank in commission history, which has more or less leapt from a few

222

dubious Nineteenth-Century examples of Federal commissions (and one even more dubious Eighteenth-Century example) to the full-blown Twentieth-Century phenomenon. In so doing, we have dragged from obscurity a number of men who had at the very least some impact on events, some significance in the history of their time – and whose utter obscurity in the present day raises a highly significant question. How much do we really know about the way changes come about? Or, to put it another way, does either quantitative analysis or elective political history really constitute a view of things as they were?

An economic historian who has been engaged in minor crunching of numbers may not seem the best person to be criticizing number-crunching, and an advocate of the inutility of commissions plays an odd role himself when arguing that it is necessary to look at commissions as well as at the politicians who appointed them. But, as we noted at the outset, there have been 110 state tax revision commissions as of the time this was written: by sheer numbers as well as by the importance of their mandate, they constitute an important subset of all gubernatorial commissions. And gubernatorial commissions constitute an important subset of all commissions. Commissions are an important, if out-of-the-way, part of U. S. political history and of our present political system.

Tutchings (1979, p. xv) uses the word "nonroutine" to describe the presence of a commission, and neither he, nor Wolanin (1975, p. 248), nor Moe (1982, p. x), could find any full-scale analyses of the phenomenon before their work. Of the three books, only Tutchings provided a model and only Moe a full case study. Wolanin has a great deal of useful information on Presidential commissions generally, but is too case-specific to provide a model usable here, and too brief in his case studies to provide the kind of information we have developed on our commissions. It is only fair to say his is the best historical account

223

of the Presidential commissions of the post-World-War-II period and the post-World-War-II sort, but its limitations and its focus have obviously reduced its usefulness for our purposes.

The men who made up our commissions, and others, were not negligible, and an idea does not grow up unconnected with the men who exemplify it in action. The best example of that, from our five commissions, is probably Kossuth Kennan, but I would venture than John Wright and Albert Bolles, Rodney Mercur and Benjamin Ludlow, Franklin Edmonds and many of his Commissioners, Lloyd Wood and Lambert Cadwalader, all helped fix in the minds (at least) of Pennsylvanians an idea of what a commission is all about – an idea that is still with us. Moreover, because the interplay of the commission members was what largely determined commission success, the characteristics of those members are historically important if the commissions are historically important – which they are.

Granted, to do what I have done here on the scale necessary for full and definite conclusions even about tax revision commissions would be a Herculean task. Doubtless there are much more important tasks which political scientists, economists, historians, public policy experts, can all undertake. But when we say this, we must be aware that we are, with all our research, only scratching the surface.

I suspect there are significant implications for the fact that commission decision-making is flawed, given that a commission is the purest form of a committee, having neither exterior log-rolling nor "cross-committee" bargaining. I suspect that our most immediately important finding, however, is that blue-ribbon commissions may be just as role-bound as interest-group commissions. Academically, it is significant that this kind of "applied historical" approach can be used in a policy setting, going beyond the kind of legislative history often used in determining the circumstances and purpose of a particular law. But for myself I would come back, in the final analysis, to a different point.

This study had its origins in a simple idea: the 1979 Pennsylvania tax revision commission could profit from looking at its predecessor commissions' mistakes (Strauss 1980). The problem was that the mistakes were made by people, not by abstractions, though in the end we were able to abstract somewhat from the personal characteristics of those who peopled the commissions. My guess is that we have had just enough straw to make the personal bricks to build an image of the commissions in action. In some cases theory has helped us do that, but we have had to turn for our data (in the absence of relevant personal papers) to such despised sources as "pay-for-inclusion" county biographical histories, potted legislative biographies, and even an occasional press release. My point is that this is a history "not of the princes and prelates" and not particularly by number-crunching, but in some middle ground and making a middling sort of conclusion – and that it is not at all as straightforward as it seemed it would be when I first undertook it back in late 1979.

And, having made that point, with its implicit plea for more of this middling (and interdisciplinary) sort of endeavor, I should go on to say that I am convinced tax revision commissions of this sort were doomed to inutility and failure, barring exceptional circumstances and the exceptional man to take advantage of them. Moreover, I am convinced that the large post-World-War-II commissions were not likely to have been the right answer to the inutility of the old self-expert small commissions. And I would not be in the least surprised if what holds true for gubernatorial tax revision commissions holds true for policy-making or policy-recommending commissions of all sorts. Commissions with role-bound members will fail, and most certainly fail

225

if the members are bound by a single role. In the normal course of events all members will be bound by their roles, and usually their single roles. The only way out is to convert the commission into a fact-finding body whose purpose it is to begin a chain of educations. But even this is possible only when the members have multiple (or irrelevant) roles, the commission has a narrow mandate, and the problem involved is capable of solution.

It can happen here. But the odds are it will not.

# BIBLIOGRAPHY

We begin with a note on manuscript collections. In fact, of all the members of our five commissions, only William H. Martin of the McCamant Commission, Kossuth Kennan and Burr Jones of the Kennan Commission, and John Penman Wood of the Edmonds Commission seem to have left any collection of papers that has survived and is available at the present time. Martin's (in the Darlington Library at the University of Pittsburgh) and Wood's (at the Pennsylvania State Library at Harrisburg) have virtually nothing relevant to our purposes, and Kennan's (in private hands) and Jones's (at the State Historical Society of Wisconsin) nothing at all that I have been able to discover.

Similarly, the Governor James Beaver Papers at Pennsylvania State University are silent where they might have been expected to give help. On the other hand, the Ely Papers at the State Historical Society of Wisconsin are useful in documenting Ely's shifts in opinion, his apparent lack of correspondence with John Armstrong Wright (though he did later correspond with members of the Tax Conference of Pennsylvania Interests), and his disengagement from the Kennan Commission, though not from Delos Kinsman and the Wisconsin income tax.

In addition, the Groves Papers at the Society contain his short history of the Wisconsin tax system, his memoirs, and data on his own participation in commissions fulfilling the Wisconsin Idea. Another collection found useful for the work presented here is the Olmsted Collection at the Pennsylvania State Library: the use is not from manuscripts but from a scrapbook of newspaper clippings, compiled by M. E. Olmstead, dealing with tax revision in Pennsylvania, 1889-97.

Correspondence with the Bradford County Historical Society, which houses the papers of Ulysses Mercur (1818-87) but not of his son Rodney, did reveal the fact that Rodney Mercur stuttered so badly as virtually to preclude a public political career.

The sources cited are listed below alphabetically according to their parenthetical designation in the text.

## SOURCES CITED

Arrow 1951
Kenneth Arrow, *Social Choice and Individual Values* (New Haven: Yale University Press for the Cowles Foundation, 1951).

Auditor-General 1898
[Pennsylvania] *Report of the Auditor-General* (Harrisburg: State Printer, 1898).

Auditor-General 1932-44
[Pennsylvania] *Report of the Auditor-General* (Harrisburg: State Printer, v.d., 1932-44).

Axelrod 1976
Robert Axelrod, ed., *Structure of Decision: The Cognitive Maps of Political Elites* (Princeton: Princeton University Press, 1976).

Baltzell 1958
E. Digby Baltzell, *Philadelphia Gentlemen: The Making of a National Upper Class* (Glencoe: Free Press, 1958).

Beers 1898
J. H. Beers and Co., *Commemorative Biographical Record of Central Pennsylvania* (Chicago: the compiler, 1898).

Bell 1966
Daniel Bell, "Comment: Government by Commission" in *The Public Interest*, 3 (Spr 1966), pp. 3-9.

*Bench and Bar* 1903
American Historical Society, *Twentieth Century Bench and Bar of Pennsylvania* (Chicago: the compiler, 1903).

Bernholz 1981
Peter Bernholz, "Cyclical Group Preferences, Log-Rolling, Pareto-Optimality, and the Paradox of Liberalism" in Tullock (noted below), pp. 59-78.

Bolles 1890
Albert Bolles, "Report" in *Report of the Revenue Commission Appointed by the Legislature of the Commonwealth of Pennsylvania March 25 1889* (Philadelphia: State Printers, 1890).

Bradford Letter n. d.
Letter to the author from the Bradford Historical Society, undated (1981), regarding Rodney Mercur. See discussion of MS sources above.

Bradsby 1903
H. C. Bradsby, *History of Bradford County* (reprint ed., Bradford: Tioga County Historical Society, 1976).

Brownlee 1971
W. Elliot Brownlee, jr., *Progressivism and Economic Growth* (Port Washington: Kennikat Press, 1971).

California 1910
[California] *Report of the Commission on Revenue and Taxation* (Sacramento: State Printer, 1910).

Casey 1981
Marion Casey, *Charles McCarthy: Librarianship and Reform* (Chicago: American Library Association, 1976).

Checkland 1980
S. G. Checkland, "The Historian and Public Policy in the 1980s" being the Presidential Address to the Economic History Conference 1980.

Cheyney and Oberholtzer 1902
E. P. Cheyney and E. P. Oberholtzer, *University of Pennsylvania: Its History, Influence...Characteristics* (Boston: Houghton Mifflin, 1902).

Condorcet 1785
M. J. A. Nicolas Caritat de Condorcet, *Essai sur l'application de l'analyse de la probabilitie des decisions rendres a la pluralité des voiz* (Paris: the author, 1785).

*Congress* 1971
[U. S. Congress] *Biographical Directory of the U. S. Congress 1774-1971* (Washington DC: Government Printing Office, 1971).

*DAB* XV
*Dictionary of American Biography*, vol. XV (New York: Scribner's, v.d.)

Dodgson 1876
Charles Lutwidge Dodgson, *A Method of Taking Votes on More Than Two Issues* (Oxford: the author, 1876).

Dye 1976
Thomas R. Dye, *Who's Running America: Institutional Leadership in the U.S.* (Englewood Cliffs: Prentice-Hall, 1976).

Ely 1888
Richard T. Ely, "Minority Report" in *Report of the Maryland Tax Commission to the General Assembly, January 1888* (Baltimore: State Printers, 1888).

Ely 1888b
Richard T. Ely, *Taxation in American States and Cities* (New York: Harper Brothers, 1888).

Ely 1896
Richard T. Ely, "Seminary Minutes" in Ely Papers, State Historical Society of Wisconsin (Madison).

Ely 1924
Richard T. Ely, *The Outlines of Economics* (4th ed., New York: Harper Brothers, 1924).

*EPB XXXI*
A. D. Keator, ed., *Encyclopedia of Pennsylvania Biography*, v. 31 (New York: Lewis Publishing Co., 1948).

Fiorina and Plott 1978
M. P. Fiorina and Charles Plott, "Committee Decisions Under Majority Rule: An Experimental Study" in *American Political Science Review*, v. 72 (1978), pp. 575-598.

Fiske 1981
Edward B. Fiske, "Lessons of History Applied to the Present" in *New York Times*, March 10, 1981, pp. c1, c4, about the Carnegie-Mellon Applied History Program (including a brief interview with the author).

George 1979
Alexander George, "Case Study and Theory Development: The Method of Structured Focused Comparison" in P. C. Laurden, ed., *Diplomacy: New Approaches in Theory and Policy* (New York: Random House, 1979).

Grofman 1981
Bernard Grofman, "The Theory of Committees and Elections: The Legacy of Duncan Black" in Tullock (noted below), pp. 11-46.

Groves n.d.
Harold M. Groves, "History of the Tax System" and "Reminiscences" in Groves Papers, State Historical Society of Wisconsin.

Groves 1967
Harold M. Groves, "Property Taxation of Intangibles" in Richard W. Lindholm, ed., *Property Taxation USA* (Madison: University of Wisconsin Press, 1967).

Groves 1974
Harold M. Groves, *Tax Philosophers* (Madison: University of Wisconsin Press, 1974).

Hansen 1983
Susan B. Hansen, *The Politics of Taxation: Revenue without Representation* (New York: Praeger, 1983).

*Harrisburg* 1943
[Pennsylvania, Joint State Government Commission, Committee on the Continuation of the Tax Study] *Report*, 11 v. (Harrisburg: State Printer 1943-45).

Jordan 1913
John W. Jordan, *Genealogical and Personal History of Northern Pennsylvania* (New York: Lewis Publishing Co., 1913).

Keator 1948
A. D. Keator, ed., *Encyclopedia of Pennsylvania Biography*, v. 31 (New York: Lewis Publishing Co., 1948).

Kennan 1898
Kossuth Kent Kennan, Introduction to *Report of the Wisconsin State Tax Commission* (Madison: State Printer, 1899).

Kennan 1899
Kossuth Kent Kennan, *Report of the Wisconsin State Tax Commission* (Madison: State Printer, 1899).

Kennan 1910
Kossuth Kent Kennan, *Income Taxation: Methods and Results* (Milwaukee: the author, 1910).

Kennan 1912
Kossuth Kent Kennan, "The Wisconsin Income Tax" in *Quarterly Journal of Economics*, v. 26 (November 1912).

Klein 1980
Philip S. Klein and Ari Hoogenboom, *A History of Pennsylvania* (2d ed., University Park: Pennsylvania State University Press, 1980).

Koford 1982
Kenneth Koford, "An Optimistic View of the Possibility of Rational Legislative Decision-Making" in *Public Choice*, v. 38 (1982).

Margulies 1968
Herbert F. Margulies, *Decline of the Progressive Movement in Wisconsin* (Madison: State Historical Society of Wisconsin, 1968).

McCamant 1890
Thomas McCamant [Auditor-General], "Report" in *Report of the Revenue Commission Appointed by the Legislature of the*

*Commonwealth of Pennsylvania March 25 1889* (Philadelphia: State Printers, 1890).

Moe 1982
Ronald C. Moe, *The Hoover Commission Revisited* (Boulder: Westview Press, 1982).

Montgomery 1923
T. L. Montgomery and A. D. Keator, eds., *Encyclopedia of Pennsylvania Biography*, v. 14 (New York: Lewis Publishing Co., 1923).

Mueller 1979
Dennis C. Mueller, *Public Choice* (Cambridge UK: Cambridge University Press, 1979).

*National Cyclopedia*
*National Cyclopedia of American Biography* (New York: Appleton, v.d.)

*NICB* 1924
National Industrial Conference Board, *The Tax Problem in Wisconsin* (New York: the Board, 1924).

Nicholson 1932
Blake Edwin Nicholson, *The Collection of Local Taxes in Pennsylvania* (Philadelphia: the author, 1932).

*NY Times* 1954
*New York Times*, Obituary page, November 19, 1954.

*NY Times* 1957
*New York Times*, Obituary page, March 16, 1957.

*NY Times* 1958
*New York Times*, Obituary page, July 6, 1958.

Olmsted 1892-6
M. E. Olmsted, Scrapbook in Olmsted Papers, Pennsylvania State Library, Harrisburg.

Parkinson 1957
C[yril] Northcote Parkinson, *Parkinson's Law* (Boston: Houghton Mifflin, 1957).

PEL 1956, 1957, 1962, 1967, 1969
Pennsylvania Economy League, *Taxes Paid by Industry* (Harrisburg and Pittsburgh: the League, 1956, 1957, 1962, 1967, 1969).

*Pennsylvania* 1890
*Report of the Revenue Commission Appointed by the Legislature of the Commonwealth of Pennsylvania March 25 1889* (Philadelphia: State Printers, 1890). Parts (Bolles, McCamant, Wright) here listed seriatim.

*Pennsylvania* 1909
*Report of the Joint Committee of the Senate and House of Representatives of the Commonwealth of Pennsylvania to Consider and Report upon a Revision of the Corporation and Revenue Laws of the Commonwealth* (Harrisburg: State Printer, 1909).

236

*Pennsylvania* 1921
*Report of the Tax Law Revision Commission* (Harrisburg: State Printer, 1921).

*Pennsylvania* 1925
Pennsylvania Tax Commission, *Report* (Harrisburg: State Printer 1925).

*Pennsylvania* 1927
Pennsylvania Tax Commission, *Final Report* (Harrisburg: State Printer, 1927).

*Pennsylvania* 1929
*Report of the Commission to Study the Distribution of State Subsidies to School Districts* (Harrisburg: State Printer, 1929).

*Pennsylvania* 1939
*Report to the General Assembly of the Industrial Tax Survey Committee* (Harrisburg: State Printer, 1939).

*Pennsylvania* 1941
[Joint State Government Commission] *First Report on the Tax and Financial Problems of the Commonwealth of Pennsylvania* (Harrisburg: State Printer, 1941).

*Pennsylvania* 1945
(Joint State Government Commission [Pennsylvania Economy League]) Committee on the Continuation of the Tax Study, *Report*, v. 11 (Harrisburg: State Printer, 1945).

*Pennsylvania* 1949
*Report of Findings and Recommendations on the Pennsylvania Tax System*, 2 v. (Harrisburg: State Printer, 1949).

*Pennsylvania Laws* 1891, 1917, 1919, 1921, 1927, 1947, 1949, 1951, 1955, 1959, 1963, 1967
*Laws of Pennsylvania* (Harrisburg: State Printer, v.d.).

*Pennsylvania Legislature* 1919, 1921, 1943, 1947, 1965
*Acts of the Legislature* (Harrisburg: State Printer, v.d.), esp. *1919, 1921*.

Phares 1980
Donald Phares, *Who Pays State and Local Taxes?* (Cambridge MA; Oelgeschlager, Gunn, 1980).

Phelan 1908
Raymond V. Phelan, *The Financial History of Wisconsin* (Madison: University of Wisconsin, 1908).

Philipp 1973
Emanuel L. Philipp, "Taxation Reform in Wisconsin" in his *Political Reform in Wisconsin*, ed. S. P. Caine and R. E. Wyman (Madison: State Historical Society of Wisconsin, 1973).

Pinkett 1970
H. T. Pinkett, *Gifford Pinchot: Private and Public Forester* (Urbana: Univ. of Illinois Press, 1970).

*Pittsburgh* 1913
Pittsburgh Press Club, *Prominent Men of Pittsburgh and Vicinity* (Pittsburgh; the Club, 1913).

Pittsburgh 1932
*Pittsburgh Press*, December 18, 1932.

Platt 1971
Anthony M. Platt, *The Politics of Riot Commissions 1917-1970: A Collection of Official Reports and Critical Essays* (New York: Collier-Macmillan, 1971).

Plott 1967
Charles R. Plott, "The Notion of Equilibrium and Its Possibility under Majority Rule" in *American Economic Review*, v. 57 (1967), pp. 787-806.

Price and Rhone 1892
Giles Price, Leonard Rhone, "Report" in *Report of the Tax Conference of Pennsylvania Interests 1892* (Philadelphia: Conference, 1892).

Reichler 1982
Joseph L. Reichler, ed., *Baseball Encyclopedia* (5th ed., New York: Macmillan, 1982).

Salisbury and Heinz 1970
Robert Salisbury and John Heinz, "A Theory of Political Analysis and Some Applications" in Ira Sharkansky, ed., *Policy Analysis in Political Science* (Chicago: Markham, 1970).

Seligman 1892
Edwin R. A. Seligman, *On the Shifting and Incidence of Taxation* (Baltimore: Johns Hopkins University Press, 1892).

Seligman 1911
Edwin R. A. Seligman, *The Income Tax* (New York: Macmillan, 1911)

*Senate* 1921
*Journal of the Senate of the Commonwealth of Pennsylvania for the Session of 1921* (Harrisburg: State Printer, 1921).

Smull's 1887, 1921, 1931, 1933, 1947, 1969, 1971, 1976/77
*Smull's Legislative Handbook of the Commonwealth of Pennsylvania* [later simply *Legislative Handbook of the Commonwealth of Pennsylvania*] (Harrisburg: Smull's, then State Printer, v.d.).

Simon 1957
Herbert Simon, *Models of Man* (New York: Macmillan, 1957).

Simon 1976
Herbert Simon, *Administrative Behavior* (New York: Macmillan, 1976).

Simon 1981
Herbert Simon, *Sciences of the Artificial* (2d ed., Cambridge MA: MIT Press, 1981).

Simon 1981b
Herbert Simon, *Models of Bounded Rationality*, 2 v. (Cambridge MA: MIT Press, 1981).

Stearns 1981
Peter N. Stearns, "Applied History and Social History" in *Journal of Social History*, v. 14 (Summer 1981), pp. 533-537.

*Tax Conference* 1892-6
*Report* including *Report of the Committee Appointed . . . To Examine the Tax Laws of Other States* (Harrisburg: the Conference, 1892), also (Fourth Meeting) *Minutes* (Harrisburg: the Conference, 1894).

Texas 1899
*Report of the Tax Commission of Texas* (Austin: State Printer, 1899).

Thelen 1978
David P. Thelen, *Robert La Follette and the Insurgent Spirit* (Boston: Little Brown, 1976).

Tucker 1887
Robert Tucker, "The Evils of Indirect Taxation" in *Forum* 2 (1887), quoted in Yearley (see below).

Tullock 1981
Gordon Tullock, ed., *Toward a Science of Politics* (Blacksburg: Public Choice Society, 1981).

Tutchings 1979

Terence Tutchings, *Rhetoric and Reality: Presidential Commissions and the Making of Public Policy* (Boulder: Westview Press, 1979).

Ward 1980

James A. Ward, *J. Edgar Thomson: Master of the Pennsylvania* (Westport: Greenwood Press, 1980).

Weeks 1892

Joseph Weeks, *Valuation, Taxation and Exemptions in the Commonwealth of Pennsylvania: A Report to the Tax Conference of Pennsylvania Interests* (Harrisburg: the Conference, 1892).

*Who Was Who* 1942

*Who Was Who in America 1931-1940* (Chicago: Marquis Co., 1942).

Wiebe 1967

Robert H. Wiebe, *The Search for Order 1877-1920* (New York: Hill and Wang, 1967).

Wike 1960

J. Roffe Wike, *The Pennsylvania Manufacturers' Association* (Philadelphia: University of Pennsylvania Press, 1960).

*Wisconsin* 1897

*Report of the Wisconsin Tax Commission* (Madison: State Printer, 1899), for material in report not written by K. K. Kennan.

*Wisconsin* 1901
*Report of the Wisconsin Tax Commission* (Madison: State Printer, 1901).
Not the same as the Kennan Commission.

*Wisconsin* 1929
Wisconsin Tax Commission, *The Taxes of the State and Its Political Subdivisions 1901-1928* (Madison: the Commission, 1929).

*Wisconsin Bar* 1924
*Proceedings of the Wisconsin Bar Association for 1924* (Madison: the Association, 1924).

Wolanin 1975
Thomas R. Wolanin, *Presidential Advisory Commissions: Truman to Nixon* (Madison: University of Wisconsin Press, 1975).

Wood Papers
Papers of John Penman Wood in Pennsylvania State Library, Harrisburg. See comments on MS Collections, above.

Wright 1889
John A. Wright, "Memorandum on a System of Taxation Submitted to the Commission" in *Report of the Revenue Commission . . . 1889*, pp. 100-36.

Wright 1890
John A. Wright, "Report" in *Report of the Revenue Commission . . . 1889*, pp. 37-99.

*WW PA* 1939
*Who's Who in Pennsylvania 1939* (Chicago: Marquis Co., 1942).

Yearley 1970
Clifton K. Yearley, *The Money Machines: The Breakdown and Reform of Governmental and Party Finance in the North 1860-1920* (Albany: State University of New York Press, 1970).

www.ingramcontent.com/pod-product-compliance
Lightning Source LLC
Chambersburg PA
CBHW071336280526
45787CB00001B/119